Studies in Economic Ethics and Philosophy

Springer
Berlin
Heidelberg
New York
Barcelona
Budapest
Hong Kong
London
Milan
Paris
Santa Clara
Singapore
Tokyo

Studies in Economic Ethics and Philosophy

P. Koslowski (Ed.)
Ethics in Economics, Business, and Economic Policy
(out of print)
192 pages. 1992

P. Koslowski · Y. Shionoya (Eds.)
The Good and the Economical
Ethical Choices in Economics and Management
212 pages. 1993

H. De Geer (Ed.)
Business Ethics in Progress?
124 pages. 1994

P. Koslowski (Ed.)
The Theory of Ethical Economy
in the Historical School
345 pages. 1995

A. Argandoña (Ed.)
The Ethical Dimension of Financial Institutions and Markets
264 pages. 1995

Gerhold K. Becker (Ed.)

Ethics in Business and Society

Chinese and Western Perspectives

With 1 Figure
and 9 Tables

Springer

Professor Dr. Gerhold K. Becker
Hong Kong Baptist University
Centre for Applied Ethics
Kowloon Tong
Hong Kong
E-mail: CAE@HKBU.EDU.HK

Cataloguing-in-Publication Data applied for

Die Deutsche Bibliothek - CIP-Einheitsaufnahme

Ethics in business and society : Chinese and western
perspectives ; with 9 tables / Gerhold K. Becker (ed.). - Berlin
; Heidelberg ; New York ; Barcelona ; Budapest ; Hong Kong ;
London ; Milan ; Paris ; Tokyo : Springer, 1996
  (Studies in economic ethics and philosophy)
  ISBN 3-540-60773-0
NE: Becker, Gerhold K. [Hrsg.]

ISBN 3-540-60773-0 Springer-Verlag Berlin Heidelberg New York

© Springer-Verlag Berlin · Heidelberg 1996
Printed in Germany

SPIN 10517130   42/2202-5 4 3 2 1 0 - Printed on acid-free paper

Acknowledgment

The essays in this volume represent investigations into contemporary ethical issues in the cross-cultural setting of Hong Kong; most of them grew out of papers delivered in a lecture series organised by the Centre for Applied Ethics in Hong Kong. The strong support of all colleagues who contributed to this collection of essays and the financial assistance of the Centre towards its publication is gratefully acknowledged.

I am also indebted to the editors of the Series *Studies in Economic Ethics and Philosophy*, particularly to Professor Peter Koslowski, as well as to Springer Verlag, Heidelberg, for their acceptance of this volume for inclusion in the series.

Hong Kong, September 1995   Gerhold K. Becker

Contents

CONTENTS

Part Two
Ethical Issues in Society

Ethics Between East and West:
The Example of Hong Kong

Introduction

GERHOLD K. BECKER

I. Asian vs. Western Values

Modern society is characterised by a growing tension between the aware-ness of ethical responsibility and the continued erosion of universally acknowl-edged values and moral standards. It is widely felt that ethical problems of a new dimension have arisen everywhere "for which there is no precedent in the standards and canons of traditional ethics" (Hans Jonas).

The general disorientation in matters of ethics is particularly significant in the rapidly developing societies of East Asia and their booming economies. Their astonishing achievements, to be sure, are based on a variety of factors and unique socio-political constellations. The proverbial industriousness of their people, however, and their rigid work ethics combined with their passion-ate embrace of Western technologies and technological innovations may ac-count for much of this success.

Recently, the causal analysis of the growing prosperity and heightened self-esteem of East Asian societies has focused on their ethical frame of reference. It has been argued that a distinctive set of Asian values is to be attributed a decisive role in the social and economic development in Asia. There is a new sense of pride and achievement in this emphasis which appears no longer confined to intellectuals seeking inspiration from their cultural heritage, nor to political leaders turning to the past for the justification of their present rule. Cover stories on Asian values and the "The Asian Way" in magazines such as *Asiaweek* (March 1994), *The Economist* (May 1994), *Asian Business* (June 1994), and the *South China Morning Post* (1995) indicate that the search for a specific Asian identity based on their own traditional moral values has firmly taken root in various Asian societies and is about to replace the mesmerised look to the West.

Since these values are believed to be superior to their Western counterparts, they need to be carefully safeguarded against influences from the West which otherwise would undermine the solid foundation upon which the Asian boom is established. In particular, many Asian governments seem "resentful of what they call Western attempts to dictate their culture and view of human and religious rights".[1]

By focusing on the uniqueness of Asian values, some Asian leaders emphasise the differences which, in their view, do not permit the application of the moral value standards of the West to their cultures. Countries such as Malaysia were instrumental in enshrining in the so-called Bangkok Declaration (1993) the notion of incompatible Western values.

The disenchantment with the West and the disillusionment with its achievements is usually blamed on the social woes which seem to suggest the bankruptcy of the whole underlying value system. The advocacy of Asian values serves, at least to a large extent, the strategic and understandable purpose of protecting aspiring Asian societies from the host of socio-political problems rampant in the West. Yet, in view of history as well as the continuous and welcome import of Western technologies, it might be doubtful whether such a defensive strategy can indeed succeed.

Hong Kong provides an interesting focus not just for the debate about distinct Asian values and their presumed superiority to those of "the" West, it also presents most of the ethical scenarios which inform the current ethics debate in the Western democracies. Yet, more importantly and due to its unique political and geographic situation, it presents many contemporary ethical problems as if through a looking glass. One of East Asia's most productive economies and a vibrant city at the crossroads of value systems, it is here that traditional Chinese beliefs and Asian customs merge with Western technologies, economic theories and liberal ideas about political participation. Gateway to China and China's "window to the West", Hong Kong has achieved a rather unusual blend of traditional Chinese and so-called Western values and beliefs whose viability will be put to test in an unprecedented social "experiment" when the flourishing and virtually paradigmatically capitalist British colony is handed back to communist China in 1997. As Laurence Goldstein put it: "For many scholars, Hong Kong is, right now, the right place to be. The historian is a privileged witness to the unfolding of an unprecedented drama in which sovereignty over a free-wheeling capitalist colony is returned to an authoritarian communist state. The political scientist can observe the design for a new system of government actually in the process of being hatched (...) The economist faces the urgent problem of determining what political and social conditions must be preserved in order to ensure a continuing thriving economy."[2] And the ethicist, we may add, can draw on all of those problems and quite a few more characteristic of situations when traditional communities struggle with the impact of sudden and unprecedented wealth as well as with a technological transformation of their society of singular proportions.

Hong Kong is truly a society in transition, a society whose time is running short and which therefore cannot afford to wait long before it has to make decisive choices, choices also in ethics. The time factor which is so infamous in various ethical dilemmas applies here to the society as a whole; it may also account for some of its not just morally significant shortcomings.

II. Ethics in a Cross-cultural Perspective

The authors of this volume are scholars and researchers based in Hong Kong who have been living and working in the territory for many years.[3] They are not only representative of the increased research interest in ethical issues across the academic spectrum of Hong Kong universities, but also of the inter-disciplinary approach which has become the hallmark of work in applied ethics. As is well documented, ethics research, at long last, has left behind its disciplinary confines and, even more so, the philosophical ivory tower and begun to permeate the full scope of the academic and scientific agenda. The present volume reflects this situation in that its authors take up a variety of ethical issues in the contexts of their respective disciplines ranging from health care, sociology, education, and philosophy to business, management, law, politics and public administration. Due to their educational background, they are familiar with Western as well as Asian, particularly Chinese, ethical traditions which almost inevitably provide their research with a fascinating cross-cultural perspective.

Gael McDonald's paper in collaboration with *Raymond Zepp* and *Pak Cho-kan*, however, is explicitly comparative in that it investigates the *Ethical Perceptions of Australian and Hong Kong Managers*. Noting an imbalance between the economic importance of Asia and the limited number of general ethics studies conducted so far in the Asia-Pacific region, their empirical investigation focused on a particularly neglected field of cross-cultural research: the ethical perceptions of managers of certain behavioural situations. The results of *Ma Hing-keung*'s empirical study of the *Moral Orientations and Moral*

Judgment of Chinese Adolescents suggest that altruistic behaviour, in Hong Kong as in the West, is embedded in what he calls a hierarchy of human relationships.

The investigation into the distinct ethical tradition of China and its relevance for modern rights-based ethics theories prevalent in the West takes centre-stage in the papers by *Chad Hansen* and *Julia Tao*. Both explore the conceptual implications of the perspicuous absence of the notion of rights in classical Chinese ethical discourse. Both concede, of course, that there are deep differences in Chinese and Western moral attitudes. Yet, their papers add much-needed scholarly rigour and intellectual refinement to the current debate about the socio-political implications of a distinct Asian approach to ethics and values.

Tao concludes in her paper, *The Moral Foundation of Welfare in Chinese Society: Between Virtues and Rights*, that Confucian ethical ideals and the liberal tradition of the West are not mutually exclusive but can and should complement each other: "The moral foundation of welfare in Hong Kong society should be based upon a dignified practice of rights, an excellence of character and a vision of good life. The Confucian tradition and the liberal tradition, through continuous mutual engagement and mutual criticism of the relations between virtues and rights, can provide the philosophical anchorage for the creation of the institution of welfare and for the development of virtuous citizens held together by a shared vision of the good life and welfare society."

In his article *Chinese Philosophy and Human Rights: An Application of Comparative Ethics*, Hansen goes beyond Confucianism and draws on the various streams in the rich intellectual heritage of China. He points out that "we should not identify Confucianism with the 'pure and unsullied' Chinese tradition any more than we should identify orthodox Roman Catholic attitudes with Western morality". Emphasising the complexity of the Chinese tradition as well the variety in Confucianism itself, Hansen argues that arguments for human rights can find their proper place within the framework of Chinese thought and "within a Chinese community of moral reasoners". Even if those arguments might not have convinced Confucius himself, Hansen believes there are conceptual means from within the Confucian tradition to show that Confucius's "conception was wrong and that it should include elements of human rights".

The conceptual and even more so the practical challenge of the coexistence of Asian (Chinese) and Western value systems in Hong Kong is implicit in a number of other papers. *Frances Wong and Rance Lee*, while tackling the ethical implications of health-care services and health-care reform in Hong Kong, take note of specific attitudinal differences in Chinese patients which exacerbate the usual ethical problems in the field. Western and Chinese medicine with their "distinct systems of concepts, skills and organisation of services" exist in the form of a "hierarchical pluralism": whereas traditional Chinese medical practices are widely used by the Chinese residents, "Western medicine has been superior to Chinese medicine in terms of all the major dimensions of hierarchy, i.e. power, prestige, and wealth." They conclude that health-care policies and services should not merely be congruent with economic development and technological progress, "but also with the prevailing cultural values and moral standards in society."

Lo Ping-cheung examines the ethical implications of reproductive technologies in the context of current policy initiatives in Hong Kong. *Joel Zimbelman* offers a comprehensive assessment of the ethical significance of *Testing for HIV in Hong Kong*. While the focus of both papers is on Hong Kong, their considerations and recommendations are also of great significance to similar issues elsewhere.

Terry Lui relates the concept of administrative ethics as it has developed in the West to the particular situation in Hong Kong. She argues that "the assumptions that have guided the 'Western' approach to public service ethics may not be entirely applicable", and opts instead for a "selective adoption of Western standards of administrative ethics in the local context".

Finally, the volume also includes reflections on issues which, although hotly debated in Hong Kong, are neither restricted to nor explicitly discussed in the context of Asian and Hong Kong society. *Ip Po-keung* in his paper *Profit and Morality* tackles some of the most notorious problems in business ethics and offers a number of recommendations which will facilitate the recognition of social responsibilities in business. *Li Hon-lam* offers a novel approach to "the most intractable of all moral problems" (Thomas Nagel), abortion. Assuming that currently no certainty is available of whether or not the foetus is a person, he argues for a new "strategy of reasoning under uncertainty" which might help to solve the problem. In adopting Pascal's Wager, he concludes that except for "cases of rape, gross deformation of foetus, and foetus endangering the life of the mother, abortion should not be allowed".

Lastly, *Laurence Goldstein*'s paper addresses the question *Is the Dissemination of Pornography Harmful to Women?* Starting from the assumption that pornography indeed does harm to women, he inquires "just how we can assess the *degree* of harm" as well as whether or not there is "a privileged moral perspective [i.e. that of the women concerned] which is simply unavailable to a large proportion of the population". Relating the harm done by pornography to the implications of censorship for liberty and for what Dworkin has called the "right to pornography", Goldstein concludes that "men are generally in a weak position, and women are generally in a strong one in confronting certain aspects of the question of whether pornography ought to be censored".

Notes

1. Marshall, Paul, 1994, "Bad Company: Western Values Criticized in Asia", *Areopagus*, Vol. 7, 4, p. 11

2. Goldstein, Laurence, 1990, "Philosophy in Hong Kong", *Cogito*, Vol. 4, No. 3, pp. 192–7, p. 192

3. The only exception is Joel Zimbelman who came to Hong Kong on a one-year research appointment as a Senior Fulbright Scholar in 1993.

Part One

Ethical Issues in Business and Administration

Chapter 1

The Moral Foundation of Welfare in Chinese Society: Between Virtues and Rights

JULIA TAO

I. Introduction

Ideas of welfare and the institutions which give them expression are the intimate reflections of a society's or a culture's philosophic beliefs about the nature of the self and about moral agency. They are a society's or a culture's shared understanding of what it means to be a moral agent: the fundamental characteristics of being human.

In Western liberal democracies, the concept of individual rights is fundamental to the self-understanding and self-identification of the people of these societies. It is, in the words of Charles Taylor (1992), one of the *shared social imaginaries* which provide for a special mode of connectedness in those societies, based on which a particular form of collective life can be forged. Shared social imaginaries are the shared images people have of themselves. They are fundamental to the self-understanding and self-identification of the people of these societies. Thus it is not surprising that in Western liberal democratic societies, a theory of individual rights, such as that developed within the framework of deontological liberalism, occupies a prominent place in contemporary debates on the normative basis of welfare provision in these societies.

In China, by contrast, mainstream social and political thought has developed without a notion of individual rights, at least until the beginning of the 20th century. The notion of rights did not seem to feature in the self-understanding and self-identification of the ancient Chinese. Even in modern Chinese society such as in Hong Kong today, the concept of individual rights is far less important a notion than in the West in structuring our social life and in shaping our political discourse.

The present paper examines the major underlying moral principles and beliefs, and their attendant notions of selfhood and moral agency, in the two main philosophical traditions of Chinese Confucianism and Western liberalism under which Hong Kong society has developed. Its initial starting point is that Western liberalism and Chinese Confucianism represent two very different philosophical traditions. Liberalism as a moral and political thesis emphasises individual rights, free choice and moral autonomy. Chinese Confucianism is a virtue-centred morality which seems to have no notion of rights, which emphasises personal virtues, the common good and role-fulfilment. As David Wong (1986) argued:

> The dominant morality of ancient Chinese culture is virtue-centred... A virtue-centred morality gives a central place to the concept of a good common to all members of a community. The common good is made possible and is at least partially defined by a way of life in which all members cooperate to achieve it... A rights-centred morality does not give a central place to the common good and a shared life.

Thus the received opinion is that Confucianism, mainstream Chinese philosophical tradition, has developed without any concept of rights. It has further been argued that the Confucian moral tradition has difficulty in embracing any objective universal moral standards such as human rights because of the lack of emphasis on moral autonomy and the absence of any notion of equal human worth in this philosophical tradition. Is the notion of individual rights compatible with the concept of human virtue emphasised in the Confucian tradition? Are there indeed no notions of individual autonomy and moral equality in the Confucian moral scheme? To what extent is the rights-based morality in liberalism commensurate with the role-based morality in Confucianism? What contribution do they make to the construction of a moral foundation of welfare in Chinese society which is compatible with the moral self-understanding and beliefs of the Chinese?

II. Examination of the Thesis that There is no Concept of Individual Rights in Confucianism

In his essay on "Power, Rights and Duties in Chinese History" (1979), presented at the 40th George Ernest Morrison Lecture in Ethnology, Professor Wang Gunwu, currently Vice Chancellor of the University of Hong Kong, wrote: "The ancient Chinese only knew of duties but had no notion of rights." He cited classics such as the *Book of History*, the *Tso Commentary on the Spring and Autumn Annals* and *Mencius*, which describe how the key relationships in society were expressed in terms of specific duties:

> The father is righteous and protective;
> the mother is loving and caring;
> the elder brother is fraternal;
> the younger brother is respectful;
> and the son is filial.

And

> Affection between father and son; righteous conduct between ruler and subjects; distinction between husband and wife; proper order between the old and the young; and trust between friends.

The renowned contemporary Chinese philosopher Liang Sou-ming (1974) has also written that "the greatest shortcoming of Chinese culture is that *the individual* can never be discovered". He went on to say: "In the Chinese thinking, individuals are never recognised as separate entities; they are always regarded as part of a network, each with a specific role in relation to others. And the Chinese have only known the concept of duty, but not the concept of rights, as in a social relationship one should respect and value the other party rather than just oneself."

Thus as a society, it seems that traditional China is characterised by a lack of rights for the people. The notion of rights did not feature in the self-understanding and self-identification of the ancient Chinese, since according to Professor Wang, modern ideas of political, legal, civil and human rights were introduced into China only at the beginning of this century. Henry Rosemont, in his article "Why Take Rights Seriously?", made the same observation that there was no concept of rights in Confucianism. He also based his claim on the linguistic fact that there was no word for the English term "a right" in ancient Chinese writing. That there was "no lexical item for rights" in ancient Chinese language was taken as evidence that there was "no concept of rights in ancient Chinese thought". This led him to further conclude that the Confucian conception of the self was so closely tied to such concepts as roles and relationships that it was incompatible with the concept of rights.

11

It may be true that there is no linguistic evidence which shows that there has ever been any such expression which is equivalent to the English term "a right" in Confucian writings. But the fact that there is no single expression in Chinese which can be translated by the English term "a right" does not necessarily imply that there was no concept of rights in Confucianism (Lee, 1991). The counter-argument is that the concept of rights can be expressed in a complex phrase without the requirement of using the single word "right". Gewirth made the point that:

> Persons might have and use the concept of a right without explicitly having a single word for it; a more complex phrase might signify or imply the concept of a right, even if no single word for it is used.

It has been further argued by Lee that Confucianism is a role-based morality does not prevent it from having a notion of rights. Role-based morality also requires the concept of rights to make the role performance possible. Even if the term "a right" was not used, moral positions and corresponding normative relations of each party, normally described by the terms "rights, duties" in Western ethical language, were clearly defined, explained and implied in the foregoing passages from the classics. Thus, even if the ancient Chinese language, until the modern adoption of the term "a right (*chuan-li*)" from the Japanese, did not have a single expression literally translatable by the English term "a right", the ancient Chinese have had a working understanding of the concept expressed in more complex phrases.

It is, however, also clear that the Confucian understanding of rights is quite different from a modern Western liberal view of individual rights. In Confucianism, there is no concept of rights that are held equally by all individuals apart from their social roles and relations as exemplified in the natural rights tradition and human rights theories of Western liberalism. The Confucian conception of rights can be characterised as role-attached, institutional (or conventional), unequal, in contrast with the liberal conception of natural rights which can be characterised as role-detached, non-institutional (or pre-social) and equal (Lee, 1991). In modern Western liberal thought, individual rights or human rights are role-detached rights which are held equally by every human being regardless of social role and position. Confucian understanding of rights is role-attached and relationship-based. This is explained in terms of the Confucian vision of social order, which comprises three interrelated elements: (1) roles and positions; (2) hierarchical relationships between these roles and positions; and (3) a formalised code of conduct prescribed by these roles and positions. Situated in a role-differentiated social nexus, with the hierarchical difference of social relationship, each individual is thought to hold different rights and obligations in accordance with his role and positions. With the change of one's social role, correspondingly not only one's social position, but one's rights and responsibilities will also vary. Excellent conformity to the role expectation constitutes the excellent working of the system. The Confucian conception of the self is so firmly tied to one's role and status in a hierarchical social nexus that a universal claim of equal rights of man has difficulty finding its home in Confucianism.

The duty-based morality of Confucianism is not incompatible with the notion of "rights". But there is no concept of universal rights in the traditional moral thinking of Chinese Confucianism. Confucianism tends to recognise only implicit, role-attached, duty-based, particularistic rights. The concept of rights is also not considered to be fundamental or primary in the Confucian ethical scheme. In contrast, liberalism emphasises the notion of abstract, universal equal rights. J.L. Mackie (1984) even made the claim that we cannot have moral philosophy without rights – that "there cannot be an acceptable moral theory that is not rights-based". For liberals, rights function to protect the individual autonomy necessary for the rational planning and pursuing of individual projects. Rights also function to protect fundamental interests of individuals. The primacy of rights is due to the sanctity of the individual and the value of liberty emphasised in liberal thought. Ronald Dworkin (1977) stated:

> Individual rights are political trumps held by individuals. Individuals have rights when, for some reason, a collective goal is not a sufficient justification for denying them what they wish, as individuals, to have or to do, or not a sufficient justification for imposing some loss or injury upon them.

Thomas Scanlon (1978) further explained:

> [C]oncern with rights is based largely on the warranted supposition that we have significantly differing ideas of the good and that we are interested in the freedom to put our own conceptions [of the good] into practice.

The notion of the human subject being prior to, and independent of, experience is a necessary requirement of moral agency in Western liberalism. This is predicated on a theory of the subject which is resistant to a "constitutive" conception where self-identity depends on social location and relations with others. It holds that a human being is fully autonomous only if he is free to discover what is distinctive about himself as an individual. Man understands himself best when he sees himself as separate from other men. Privacy is valued because it permits every person to discover what is unique about himself – to discover his own "true" and "unique" personality. The human subject in liberal moral and political thought is thus conceived as a sovereign agent of choice who has rights which are inviolable and which cannot be compromised.

13

To liberals, the central concern of morality is finding terms of peaceful coexistence among persons with different conceptions of the good. Justice and the sanctity of individual rights are emphasised in deontological liberalism in particular because of the belief that what is most essential to our personhood is not the ends we choose but our capacity to choose them. The underlying belief is that people are capable of self-direction because of the faculty of reason, which can function independently of desires and other physical influence. Man's most desirable condition is one in which the formation of his beliefs and the direction of his choice-making stems from himself rather than from outside agencies. Hence the emphasis on separateness of persons and the distinctness of individuals in liberalism.

Individual rights characteristically function to protect a sphere of autonomy and fundamental interests of individuals by providing a normative category that is mandatory, definite and binding. According to liberals, having rights is good since it enables us to "stand up like men". As Joel Feinberg explained, to have a right is to have a claim because:

> [H]aving a claim consists in being in a position to claim in the performative sense, that is, to make a claim to.

By identifying "having a claim" with "being in a position to make a claim to", liberals emphasise that having a right is not having a thing in a nominative form, but a kind of normative capacity-placing of a person in such a position that he can demand things as his own due, not as a matter of the giver's generosity. Moreover, what is important in the activity of making a claim is that "making claim to can itself make things happen". Thus, according to Feinberg's performative conception of a right, to have a right is to have a capacity, or to have a power, or to be in a position to make things happen at the discretion of the claimant. The normative power of rights lies in the fact that rights represent those minimum conditions under which human beings can flourish and which ought to be secured for them, if necessary by force (John Kleinig, 1978). Joel Feinberg (1970) further indicated that "not to claim in the appropriate circumstances that one has a right is to be spiritless or foolish".

Does the lack of a concept of individual rights in Chinese Confucianism imply the lack of notions of individual autonomy and equal human worth in the Confucian morality?

III. Examination of the Thesis that There is no Place for Individual Autonomy in Chinese Confucianism

In Western liberalism, moral agency and individual selfhood is constituted by the claiming of rights. Modern liberal rights theorists seek to offer a conception of the individual as capable of defining his own good, making his own choice, and having inviolable rights of liberty. Within the rights theories, one may further identify two different approaches. For a negative rights theorist such as Nozick, who emphasises autonomy as the basis of rights, a strictly limited set of near-absolute individual rights constitutes the foundation of morality. The central means of protecting human inviolability is through a set of rights which impose constraints upon the possible range of interference by others. "They form a protective bastion enabling an individual to achieve his own ends in a life he shapes himself, and that... is the individual's way of giving meaning to life" (Hart, 1979).

For positive rights theorists, such as Alan Gewirth (1982), a meaningful life requires not only the protection of freedom from deliberate restriction, but opportunities and resources for its exercise. Identifying human rights with claim rights, Gewirth regards them as protective of the conditions of human action and justifies those conditions as necessary "to fulfil the general needs of human agency". Because human beings are prospective purposive agents that can claim rights, Gewirth believes that "all the human rights, those of wellbeing as well as those of freedom, have as their aim that each person have rational autonomy in the sense of being a self-controlling, self-developing agent who can relate to other persons on a basis of mutual respect and cooperation". The view they have eventually come to take is to regard rational agency as a universal and necessary condition for morality and therefore a possible foundation for a theory of rights. The "agency-autonomy approach" put forth by Gewirth is of great significance to the development of welfare states in contemporary Western liberal democracies. In similar vein, Raymond Plant contends that welfare rights are to be ascribed to rational agents who have a capacity for agency.

The notion of human subjects as equal distinct entities being prior to, and independent of, experience is a necessary requirement of moral agency in the liberal project. The initial starting point of this deontological liberalism is the Kantian formulation that individual persons have a fundamental dignity as rational beings. Hence they are capable of prescribing to themselves, ascertaining and conforming to the moral law because of the faculty of reason. Individual persons have worth and dignity because of their capacity for "purposive agency" and "moral autonomy". For Kant, individuals deserve respect because they have a special ability to know moral principles through reason. Our worth as individuals stems from our ability to act as law-givers unto ourselves. Such self-understanding among deontological liberals as freely choosing, autonomous beings, unconditioned by the contingencies of circumstances, is predicated on the Kantian view that only such a subject could be that "something which elevates man above himself as a part of the world of sense" (Lukes, 1985) and enables him to participate in an ideal, unconditioned realm wholly independent of our social and psychological inclinations. Only this thoroughgoing independence can afford us the detachment we need if we are ever freely to choose for ourselves, unconditioned by the contingencies of circumstances. Thus dignity and autonomy are linked in the liberal project. Within the liberal self-conception, individual persons are free and equal agents.

In contrast, moral agency and the self of the individual in the Chinese Confucian tradition is established through the performance of roles. The individuality of the self is constituted by the web of unique role relations which one possesses and by the way concrete responsibilities are performed by the self in each particular set of role relationships. As observed by Professor Tu Wei-ming in his essay "Selfhood and Otherness in Confucianism" (1985), the self develops its contours, unfolds its characteristics, takes shape, becomes actual and individuated through engaging and interacting in a network of relations with others. It is believed that without the structure offered by these role relations and the possibility of interacting with another self within the role structure, the self will remain forever an abstract potentiality for lack of a vehicle for its realisation and actualisation in the objective world. In other words, self-individuation is possible only through a process of engagement with others within the context of one's social roles and relationships.

To the Confucian Chinese, therefore, the self is always a relational self, a relational being – a point well captured by John C.H. Wu (1967), who wrote:

> Traditionally, a Chinese seldom thought of himself as an isolated entity. He was a concrete individual person who moved, lived and *had his being* in the natural milieu of the family...

It is in the midst of one's social relations that one learns to be human and realises one's humanity. In a truly reciprocal role relationship where there is mutuality of role performance, "self" and "other" are both constituted as well as constitutive of each other in the relationship and in the interaction which takes place within it. On the Confucian conception, neither "self" nor "other" is a means to the other's end, yet at the same time, each is absolutely necessary to the other for its realisation and fulfilment as truly human. It is in one's role relationships and role performance that the self finds the source of one's sanctity as a human being, and the basis of one's self-esteem, worth and fulfilment. Thus the Confucian moral tradition stresses human relatedness, rather than separateness of persons, as the essence of man's existence. The self of the human subject is explained relationally, as the occupant of social roles, not as a equal discrete entity. There can be no fulfilment for the individual in isolation from his fellow man. In the Confucian ethical system, being a person is something one does, not something one is. Humanity is an achieved status. Personhood is an achievement, rather than a given, or a right of birth. The *Analects* says: "The realisation of oneself is called '*jen*'." It refers to an achieved state of humanity which can only be cultivated and developed in inter-human relationships, i.e. in the social context.

The family is valued as the place where one first learns about one's roles and duties as a human being and also where one learns to practise fulfilling those roles and duties. These roles and relationships constitute, in the words of MacIntyre, our individual moral starting points in life. In fact, the insistence that we begin our task of self-realisation in the context of the immediate dyadic relationships in which we are inevitably circumscribed is a basic principle underlying the father-son relationship in Confucianism. According to the *Analects*: "Filial piety and fraternal deference – these are the roots of becoming a person." Filial piety, the keynote construct in the Confucian ethical system, is the source of the capacity of the self to transcend its individual interests and concerns in the immediate present and to develop regard and compassion for others beyond oneself. A key idea expressed in the *Book of Mencius*, one of the Chinese classics, is: "Honour the aged in your own family, so that the aged in other families shall be similarly treated; Nurture the young in your own family, so that the young in other families shall be similarly treated." Confucians believe that respect and reverence for the past, the aged and one's ancestors have a unifying effect on the living who are thus able to see themselves as part of a tradition, part of the flow of life, reaching back through the past and forward into the future (Wong, 1986). Generations are therefore linked together by a sense of duty, and the fulfilment of duty. Confucian ethics is a humanistic ethics in a man-centred world. It is a practical humanism which teaches that the moral and spiritual achievement of man "do not depend on tricks or luck or esoteric spells or any purely external agency" (Fingarette, 1972). It emphasises self-cultivation, self-development and self-transformation. This is consistent with the basic conception of man in the *Analects* as a being born into the world with the potential to be shaped into a truly human form. However, it is man's own strength, rather than the mediation of some supernatural agent, which is the source of actualising his potential. Hence the emphasis on self-reliance and self-responsibility in Confucian ethics. Thus conceived, the Confucian self is both bounded and empirically based on the one hand, constituted by circumstances and experience; but on the other hand, it is open and unbounded in its capacity to reflect on and to participate in the cultural tradition of filial piety.

Thus Rosemont was only partially accurate in his observation that:

> [In the Confucian alternative to the rights-based morality,] there are no disembodied minds, nor autonomous individuals... Where we invoke abstract principles, they invoke concrete roles... For the early Confucians there can be no *me* in isolation, to be considered abstractly; I am the totality of roles I live in relation to specific others. I do not play or perform these roles; I am these roles. Where is there room for freedom and creativity within this concept cluster?... The Confucian moral language has no terms... corresponding to freedom, liberty, autonomy... or rights.

The fact is that Confucian role-based morality also emphasises individuality and moral autonomy. The view held by the Confucians is that through role relationships, one experiences one's relatedness to others; through role performance, actualised in the fulfilment of duties, one experiences one's individuality. Fulfilling filial duties by caring for one's parents, being always aware of one's attachment and relatedness to what has gone before oneself, and therefore to what is wider and beyond oneself, is of paramount importance to the Chinese in their understanding of themselves as humans. The self is morally autonomous, engaging in an open-ended process of self-cultivation and self-realisation through the performance of duties. Generations are linked together by the fulfilment of duties, creating a kind of bonding between self and others in human society. On this relational understanding of the self, the individual is not the "modern disengaged consciousness", to whom life appears as nothing but a series of unconnected episodes, such as the slave described in *Slave and Social Death* (Orlando Patterson, 1982):

> Everything has a past, including sticks and stones. Slaves differed from other human beings in that they were not allowed freely to integrate the experience of their ancestors into their lives, to inform their understanding of social reality with the inherited meaning of their natural forebears, or to anchor the living present in any conscious community of memory.

As Arthur Danto (1985) observed to the Confucian thinker: "When one strips the relationships off, nothing recognisably human remains to tread the paths of nothingness." And, "although the temptation to shed these relations may very well have been, in the abstract, as tempting to the Chinese thinker, as the stunning of reason through intoxication and frenzy has been to the West... these are furloughs from our essence, transitory abandonments of the heart of being, to which we are inevitably returned".

IV. Examination of the Thesis that Confucianism Lacks a Notion of Equal Human Worth

The priority of liberty in liberal thinking in the West has led to an emphasis on the values of individuality, autonomy and dignity as the main values of the liberal tradition. Its initial starting point, as discussed earlier, is the Kantian formulation that individual persons have a fundamental dignity as rational beings. Kant (1797) made the observation that "the dignity of humanity in us" provides us with a duty that we not "suffer [our] rights to be trampled underfoot by others with impunity". Similarly, the Declaration of Human Rights stated that "All human beings are born *free and equal in dignity and rights*". Ronald Dworkin (1977) also argued that government must treat people with equal concern and respect:

> Government must not only treat people with concern and respect, but with equal concern and respect. It must not distribute goods or opportunities unequally on the ground that some citizens are entitled to more because they are worthy of more concern. It must not constrain liberty on the ground that one citizen's conception of the good life of one group is nobler or superior to another's.

Feinberg similarly noted that: "In attributing human worth to everyone we may be ascribing no property or set of qualities, but rather expressing an attitude – the attitude of respect – toward humanity in each man's person." It is an "attitude" to choose a side, to take a "human point of view".

Does Confucianism have an "attitude" of equal human worth and dignity? Scholars such as Donald Munro (1985) and Tu Wei-ming argued that Confucian ethics offer an alternative notion of moral autonomy, and of individual worth and dignity. As pointed out by Munro, in the Confucian system, there is also a doctrine of "natural" equality based principally on Mencius's argument that all men have a "*moral hsin*" and hence all men have the capacity to become Yao or Shun (Sage Emperors in the ancient times). "*Moral hsin*" is "*jen*" in Chinese and is translated as "benevolence", "perfect virtue", "moral mind/heart", or "authoritative personhood". To prove that the "*moral hsin*" is possessed equally by all men, Mencius illustrates his argument thus:

> When I say that all men have a mind/heart which cannot bear to see the sufferings of others, my meaning may be illustrated thus: even nowadays, if men suddenly see a child about to fall into a well, they will without exception experience a feeling of alarm and distress. They will feel so, not as a ground on which they may gain favour of the child's parents, nor as a ground on which they may seek the praise of their neighbours and friends, nor from a dislike for the reputation of having been unmoved by such a thing". (*The Book of Mencius*, IIA.6).

19

The conviction that human beings in general can be counted on to feel impelled to save children from falling into wells as evidence of our likemindedness enables Mencius to sustain and affirm that ordinary human beings are not only capable of becoming sages but are fundamentally like sages. He reinforces this idea by stating that the Sage Emperors Yao and Shun "were just the same as other men", and that any man, no matter what his background, might by diligence achieve their status or stature. And as Mencius says, because it is a moral mind/heart possessed equally by all, "the sage only apprehended before me that of which my mind approves along with other men".

The emphasis on the natural equality of man is based on a belief that man's nature is decreed by Heaven. (The word Heaven or "*T'ien*" in Chinese is just another name for the natural order, it has no anthropomorphic character.) Inherent in human nature is the potential for excellence, the source of our human worth and dignity. The Master said: "Heaven is the author of the virtue that is in me." On this view, man's nature is a "given" that exists from birth. There is also a strong emphasis in the Confucian system of thought that all things are in a constant state of growth, change and transformation. This is related, on the one hand, to the Confucian image of the "*moral hsin*" of man as being like a seed of grain capable of going through a process of growth and development akin to that of a plant. Mencius said:

> The heart of compassion is the seed of benevolence; the heart of shame, of dutifulness; the heart of courtesy and modesty, of propriety; the heart of right and wrong, of wisdom. Man has these four seeds just as he has four limbs. For a man possessing these four seeds to deny his own potentialities is for him to cripple himself...

Whereas liberalism conceives of human worth in terms of rational autonomy – human beings are worthy because "all men have a point of view of their own" (Feinberg) – Confucianism conceives of human worth in terms of moral perfectibility or personhood. For Confucianism, human beings are worthy because they can become morally perfect through self-cultivation – to become a sage or an exemplary person. On the other hand, the Confucian view of role relations and role structure is dynamic rather than static (King, 1985). Despite a hierarchical conception of the social order in terms of functional divisions, there is no implication that one cannot move from one social position to another under the Confucian conception. Neither does its dynamic conception of the self as a continually growing and transforming entity admit of an interpretation of human behaviour as being completely determined by the role structures. As stated in the *Analects*: "By nature, men are nearly alike; By practice they become very different". The view of the Confucians is that life and the circumstances in which men find themselves are their possibilities. It is therefore men's responsibility to make these possibilities a reality or actuality through living – to render the reality not only just a personal reality, but a human reality as well. The life to which man is given is not given to him ready-made: man has to keep filling it for himself, occupying it through choosing a way of being man, that man seeks to realise in man's living. Hence, despite the division of positions and role relations, Confucianism attaches great autonomy to the individual self because of its belief that the individual is an active self capable of reaching a state of moral autonomy and achieving "*jen*".

V. Between Virtues and Rights: The Moral Foundation of Welfare

As pointed out by Norman Barry (1990), there is increasing concern in the recent development of welfare theories that the "welfare" problem is not exhausted by a rational consideration of the question of efficiency – of merely solving the problem of deprivation or maximising utilities. He drew attention to the fact that: "Throughout the history of the welfare debate issue is a theme of communitarianism and citizenship that recommends a form of welfare society: a vision of a social order that is not merely characterised by rational deprivation-alleviating institutions and policies but by the fostering of intimate communal bonds." And: "In this conception of welfare society, equality, for example, would be valued as much for its communitarian-enhancing effects as for its specific deprivation-reducing role."

Furthermore as pointed out by Drover and Kerans, until the late 1980s, theories of welfare in Western liberal democracies have developed under the presupposition that the question of welfare is primarily about the distribution of resources. But Dover and Kerans argued that "welfare or wellbeing entails three stakes: identify, resources and relationships, especially caring relationships". They further explained that: "Welfare claims emerge out of dissatisfactions experienced in the private sphere, but are articulated by groups who care, and who, by achieving solidarity, are able to name their needs, hence to translate their private dissatisfactions into public issues." Therefore, the purpose of claims-making to enhance welfare is "the unlearning of unfreedom" and the establishment of new institutional and symbolic patterns, the making of one's identity and oneself anew. Claimants of welfare are not merely consumers of public services and public policies. An emphasis on rights gives moral weight to the process of claims-making because: "Having rights enables us to 'stand up like men', to look others in the eye and to feel in some fundamental way the equal of anyone" (Feinberg). The ultimate goal of claims-making is the shifting of public discourse such that the social identity of these groups is at least partially recognised. This discourse of recognition and identity is central to the question of welfare because, as argued by Charles Taylor (1992), non-recognition or misrecognition, shows a lack of due respect. In addition, it can inflict a grievous wound by causing self-depreciation, imprisoning someone in a false, distorted, and reduced mode of being.

In similar vein, Richard Rorty argued that violations of human rights are often not recognised as such by the violators, because they do not regard their victims as human in the relevant sense: often the victims are seen as less than human. A genuine ability to show recognition and equal respect and concern for others, according to Rorty, depends upon a progress of our moral sentiment. This consists in an increasing ability to see the similarities between ourselves and people very unlike us as outweighing the differences, in sufficiently acquainting people of different kinds with one another so that they are less tempted to think of those different from themselves as only quasi-human. Such a progress of sentiments echoes the words of Hume who held that "corrected (sometimes rule-corrected) sympathy, not law-discerning reason, is the fundamental moral capacity".

In support of the ideal of equal human worth, liberalism emphasises respecting others' rights as one's own; Confucianism on the other hand emphasises having concern for others' wellbeing as one's own (Lee, 1991). Confucius said:

> A benevolent man helps others to take their stand in so far as he himself wishes to get his stand, and get others there in so far as he himself wishes to get there.

The Confucian ideal community is not composed of mutually disinterested, independent, rational individuals; the Confucian communitarian society is one composed of virtuous individuals who are benevolently disposed to recognise and who sympathetically care for others' wellbeing as if it were their own. The concept of rights is useful for the creation and establishment of institutions; the concept of virtue is important for the building of character and for moral development. The moral foundation of welfare in Hong Kong society should be based upon a dignified practice of rights, an excellence of character and a vision of good life. The Confucian tradition and the liberal tradition, through continuous mutual engagement and mutual criticism of the relations between virtues and rights, can provide the philosophical anchorage for the creation of the institution of welfare and for the development of virtuous citizens held together by a shared vision of the good life and welfare society.

References

Barry, Norman, 1990, *Welfare*, Minneapolis, University of Minnesota Press

Confucius, *The Analects* (Lun Yu), trans. D.C. Lau, Hong Kong, The Chinese University Press, 1983

Danto, Arthur, 1985, "Postscript: Philosophical Individualism in Chinese and Western Thought", in Donald Munro (ed.) *Individualism and Holism: Studies in Confucian and Taoist Values*, Ann Arbor Centre for Chinese Studies, University of Michigan

Drover, Glenn, & Patrick Kerans, 1993, *New Approaches to Welfare Theory*, Edward Elgar, Aldershot

Dworkin, Ronald, 1977, *Taking Rights Seriously*, Cambridge, Harvard University Press

Feinberg, Joel, 1970, "The Nature and Value of Rights", *Journal of Value Inquiry*, 4 (1970), 243

Fingarette, Herbert, 1972, *Confucius: The Secular as the Sacred*, New York, Harber Torch Books

Gewirth, Alan, 1982, *Human Rights Essay on Justification and Application*, Chicago University Press

— 1973, *Social Philosophy*, Prentice Hall

Hart, H.L.A., 1979, *Law, Liberty and Morality*, Oxford, Oxford University Press

King, Ambrose, 1985, "The Individual and Group in Confucianism: A Relational Perspective", in Donald Munro (ed.), *Individualism and Holism: Studies in Confucian and Taoist Values*, Ann Arbor Centre for Chinese Studies, University of Michigan

Kleinig, John, 1978, "Human Rights, Legal Rights and Social Change", in E. Kamanda and Alice Erh-Soon Tay (eds.), *Human Rights*, Edward Arnold, London

Lee, S.H., 1991, *Virtues and Rights: Reconstruction of Confucianism as a Rational Communitarianism*, Unpublished PhD Thesis, University of Hawaii

Liang Sou-ming, 1974, *Chung-Kuo-wen-hua Yao-i* [The Essential Features of Chinese Culture], Hong Kong, Chi-chen T'u-shu Kung-ssu

Lukes, Steven, 1985, *Individualism*, Oxford, Basil Blackwell

Mackie, J.L., 1984, "Can There be a Right-Based Moral Theory?" in Jeremy Waldron (ed.) *Theories of Rights*, Oxford, Oxford University Press

Mencius, *The Works of Mencius*, Harvard-Yenching Institute Sinological Index Series, Peking, 1941

Munro, Donald, (ed.), 1985, *Individualism and Holism: Studies in Confucian and Taoist Values*, Ann Arbor Centre for Chinese Studies, University of Michigan

Rosemont, Henry Jr., 1989, "Why Take Rights Seriously? A Confucian Critique", in Leroy S. Rouner (ed.), *Human Rights and the World's Religions*, Notre Dame, Ind., University of Notre Dame Press

Scanlon, Thomas, 1978, "Rights Goals, and Fairness", in Stuart Hampshire (ed.) *Public and Private Morality*, Cambridge University Press

Taylor, Charles, 1992, *Multiculturalism and "The Politics of Recognition"*, Princeton, New Jersey, Princeton University Press

Tu Wei Ming, 1985, "Selfhood and Otherness: the Father-Son Relationship in Confucian Thought", in *Confucian Thought: Selfhood as a Creative Transformation*, New York University Press

Wang Gunwu, 1979, "Power, Rights and Duties in Chinese History", *The Fortieth George Ernest Morrison Lecture in Ethnology*, Canberra, The Australian National University

Wong, David, 1986, *Moral Relativity*, Berkeley, University of California Press

Wu, John C.H., 1967, "The Status of the Individual in the Political and Legal Tradition of Old and New China", in *The Chinese Mind*, Charles Moore (ed.), Honolulu, University of Hawaii Press

Chapter 2

Profit and Morality:
Problems in Business Ethics

Ip Po-keung

I. Introduction

Ask the man on the street his views about how ethical he thinks Hong Kong businesses are. It seems that not many will give you a very favourable answer. An extreme cynic may probably tell you that there are absolutely no business ethics here, while a moderate cynic may inform you that ethical concerns of businessmen here are very primitive, if they exist at all. Such cynical views about business ethics here should cause no surprise. Despite its spectacular and enviable economic success, Hong Kong business is not famous for ethical concerns.[1] What makes Hong Kong tick is the amazing resilience, adaptability, resourcefulness and self-reliance of its people, including its highly versatile and shrewd business community. But success in business has not been accompanied by good performance in ethics. For most people, success means productive adaptability and ultimately, profitability in the increasingly competitive marketplace. Whether morality should be counted toward success is a

highly contentious issue from which businessmen often intentionally or unintentionally try to shy away. For many in the business community and beyond,
ethics and morality just do not mix with business. They belong to different
categories, like water and oil, which don't mix. For the sophisticated, the notion of business ethics is in effect a contradiction in terms, very much like the
concept of a rounded triangle.

Those who share Milton Friedman's view of business ethics will even go so
far as to assert that morality and business should not mix with each other
(Friedman, 1962). Indeed, in the early 1960s, Friedman succeeded in generating a well-publicised debate on the social responsibility of corporations. Let us
begin our discussion with this debate.

II. The Moral Neutrality View

As an ardent defender of the moral neutrality of corporations, Friedman
argues vehemently that the legitimate goal of business is to make a profit
within the bounds of law. The claim that a corporation should take up social
responsibilities that go beyond profit-making is a misguided one based on
muddled thinking. He criticises the view that corporate personnel should have
moral responsibilities. Such a view, he claims,

> "shows a fundamental misconception of the character and nature of a
> free economy. In such an economy, there is one and only one social
> responsibility of business – to use its resources and engage in activities
> designed to increase its profits so long as it stays within the rules of the
> game, which is to say, engages in open and free competition, without
> deception or fraud" (Friedman, 1962, p. 133).

Friedman is no moral neutralist in the absolute sense. He does not exclude
from business all moral concerns, but tries to restrict corporate morality to a
limited domain. The only legitimate goal of business, according to him, is
profit maximisation without deception or fraud (in the legal sense). Assuming
social or moral responsibilities, Friedman contends, is beyond the competence
of business executives. They are and should not be good judges of social interests. If corporate managers were to take on the social responsibilities of providing social welfare, the consequences could be disastrous. For Friedman, maximising profits is an inalienable right of persons in a free society. The economic freedom to pursue profit is essential for maintaining political freedom.
If people as stockholders voluntarily choose to form a corporation and estab-

lish the policy of profit-maximisation, denying them this freedom is to deny them one of their fundamental rights.

Loosely speaking, Friedman's view in effect can be unpacked into two standard arguments against the claim of corporate social responsibility – the utilitarian argument and the rights argument. For the purpose of this discussion, let us focus on the utilitarian argument.

III. The Utilitarian Argument

The utilitarian argument uses the consequences of an act to justify its moral acceptability. It states that adopting the policy of profit-maximisation and moral disinterest or neutrality can create, on balance, more social goods than bad ones when compared with adopting alternative policies. Some utilitarians even claim that profit-maximisation automatically transforms corporate self-interests into social welfare. One can readily detect some kind of invisible-hand mechanism assumed in the above argument. The central problem of this argument, however, is to show that profit-maximisation is in fact welfare-promoting for the whole society. There are two representative utilitarian views arguing for the welfare-promoting consequences of profit-maximisation (Donaldson, 1982, pp. 73–4):

(1) Welfare-promoting profit-maximisation requires a competitive and free market. In a free market, the pursuit of profit will help to increase a corporation's efficiency in order to gain advantage in competition with other corporations. Profit pursuit together with competition in a free market will bring about a situation where society is better off than pursuing other policies.

(2) A corporation may take either a short-term or long-term profit-maximisation strategy. Short-term profit-maximisation may bring profit to the corporation but may not necessarily be welfare-promoting in society as it may harm the public interests of society. However, the market is capable of punishing short-term profit-maximisation and of rewarding long-term strategies. Long-term profit-maximisation requires ongoing consumer trust in goods and services in order to maintain profitability. Long-term profit-maximisers therefore cannot afford to erode consumer trust by deception or fraud.

The utilitarian arguments depend on the truth of the assumption that the ideal workings of the free market are capable of bringing about better consequences than alternative policies if the corporate moral neutrality position is to be maintained. However, it is exactly the free-market assumption in the argu-

27

ments that is questionable. The chief difficulty of this assumption is, critics charge, that it represents only a highly idealised situation which is rarely empirically realisable. It fails to deliver the kind of good consequences the free-market proponents would like. Well-known market imperfections abound. Chief among these are imperfect information, external costs, imperfect competition, and consumer preferences ill-reflecting genuine needs, among other things.

It has been pointed out (Hollis and Nell, 1975) that perfect information and perfect rationality, notions presupposed by free-market theorists, are incompatible with each other. To acquire information about commodities has its cost, whether in the form of time, energy or money, which can be profitably used elsewhere. Therefore perfect rationality in the sense of acting rationally to advance self-interest, precludes perfect information.

For public goods such as public roads, market rationality tends to force people to underestimate them, hoping that the obligations can be passed off to others while we become richer and still retain the use of the good. As everyone is market rational, social welfare is therefore not maximised (Donaldson, 1982).

A free market presupposes a system of voluntary exchanges. However, a third party who is not part of the system may be made worse off as a result of the exchange. The market system itself is notoriously ill-equipped to solve this problem of externalities. Furthermore, the existence of monopoly and oligopoly renders the whole concept of perfect competition a myth. Finally, consumer preferences in the market crucially depend on their *ability* to buy and therefore do not necessarily reflect their genuine needs. Indeed, by using sophisticated modern methods of advertising and marketing, false needs can be created to guarantee product sales. In sum, the market mechanism, when left to itself, is not in general welfare-promoting. With the market assumption suspect, the utilitarian argument which centrally employs it, loses its apparent cogency.

IV. The Moral Agency Debate[2]

In close connection with this debate are further discussions of a more philosophical nature on the notion of corporate social responsibility. Let me briefly go through one major discussion which focuses on the question of corporate moral agency and responsibility.

The question raised was whether a corporation could meaningfully be said to be capable of discharging responsibilities. One line of reasoning runs as follows. Corporations are collective entities which are not capable of having intentions. Only persons, who have intentions, can be held responsible for certain deeds. When we say that corporations are responsible for their policies or actions, we are only saying *elliptically* that certain persons within the corporation are responsible. If a sophisticated machine lost control and killed and injured a number of people, it would be absurd or morally awkward if we condemned it for the tragedy. Our moral outrage and condemnations should be directed at the designers and operators of the machine, *not* the machine itself. Likewise, when a corporation causes harm to society, morally condemning it seems to be a rather perverse thing to do (Danley, 1984). If, due to shoddy work, a local construction company built unsafe buildings which one day collapsed and killed a large number of residents, could we say that the construction company itself was responsible? Yes, only elliptically. What we really mean is that the owner, top executives, designers, operators of the company should be held responsible, *not* the company itself.

Only entities which are capable of having intentions, the argument goes, can legitimately be attributed the ability to shoulder and discharge responsibilities. To the extent that a corporation is a collective entity having no intention of its own, it cannot be said to have the ability to discharge responsibilities, and therefore should not be treated as an object of moral praise or blame. When we say that a corporation is held responsible for its acts what we are *really* saying is that the *participating individuals* within the corporation is held responsible for the act.

V. The Attribute Argument

There is another view. Some philosophers (e.g., Ladd, 1983) use the *attribute argument* to the effect that a corporation cannot legitimately be said to be responsible for its acts. There are certain attributes which are *ascribable* to humans but not ascribable to corporations. Moral attributes, in particular, can meaningfully be ascribable to persons, but cannot meaningfully be ascribable to non-intentional entities like corporations. It makes perfect sense to say that a person is honest, kind, intelligent, conscientious, strong-willed, etc. However, to use these attributes to describe a corporation would be rightfully to be accused of misusing language.

Formal organisations, by virtue of their structure and nature, are perforce prescribed to pursue organisational aims and objectives independent of the individual's personal wishes. The aims and objectives constrain, as it were, how decisions have to be made in respect to them, and not the personal interests or wishes of those who make the decisions. Decisions within a corporation are made with regard to efficiency, not to morality. Hence it is inappropriate to expect corporations to conduct their business in line with human morality. In effect, the ordinary standards of human behaviour simply do not and ought not apply to corporations. Such a view, however, entails that persons working within the corporation may subscribe to one set of standards but conform to another set when they conduct their normal life outside work among friends and family members. This *double-standard* implication of the attribute argument invites criticism.

One objection to this view starts by arguing that a corporation can and should have a *conscience*, and persons working or making decisions within the corporation should be on a par with the man in the street with regard to moral responsibility (Goodpaster and Matthews, 1984, p. 150–62). If ordinary men can be held morally responsible for their acts, so can corporate agents. But why? Proponents of this view identify two key attributes of the corporation as a means of defence. It is argued that corporations are capable of displaying *rationality* and *respect*, two important attributes which enable the corporation to be responsibility attributable. To be able to act morally, one should be capable of a certain degree of rationality which includes self-control, the ability to deliberate alternative courses of action and their respective consequences carefully, and the ability to identify and have aims and objectives. To be able to demonstrate respect is tantamount to having the ability to be aware of and have concern for the effects of one's conduct on others. To respect others means, among other things, to treat people not merely as means but as ends, and to be cognisant of others' needs and concerns. The sharp line which is arbitrarily drawn between an individual's personal efforts and a corporation's institutional efforts is not tenable. In the real world, it is not possible to separate the two. It is therefore proper to propose that the rationality and respect that are displayed in humans be projected to organisations. As a result of such moral projection, what we demand of humans can also be demanded of corporations. There will be convergence of the standards we demand of ourselves and those we demand of corporations.

VI. More Discussion

The moral responsibilities of a corporation can be argued in other ways. One commentator (French, 1984) suggests that through the analysis of corporate *policies*, we can attribute a sense of moral responsibilities to corporations. Corporations formulate, develop and implement policies. These policies can be interpreted as generic rules and regulations governing courses of actions with respect to specific problems or tasks. Corporations don't make policies, it is the *persons* within the corporations that make them. Policies, regardless of their nature, are initiated, articulated, developed, implemented, by corporate persons. They are in effect the reflection of the collective wisdom and expectations of its people. Obviously, this collective wisdom and these expectations are due to many people, not to a single individual. To the extent that people within the corporation initiate, articulate, develop and implement these policies, they are responsible for them. At the same time, these policies are also subject to moral scrutiny like any other human conduct.

Policies are designed to meet certain objectives and to complete certain tasks. The impact of these policies very often has social and moral implications that corporations cannot deny. For example, a corporation may as a matter of policy choose not to hire woman employees for all its posts. Legal matters aside, this policy certainly has social and moral implications that the corporation has to face. Is the corporation in adopting this policy trying to discriminate against women? Is the policy a violation of women's right to equal opportunities? Does the policy have the social effect of endorsing and perpetuating the existing social inequalities of a given society? Is the policy, in depriving women of the chance of equal employment opportunities, creating injustice within society? These are important moral issues that corporations and society cannot choose to ignore. Other policies like fairness in competition, protecting consumer rights, respecting the environment, etc., equally have moral and social ramifications that the corporation cannot afford to shy away from.

1. Who is Responsible?

Granted that corporations have moral responsibilities, which their policies and the attendant consequences of those policies help to create, there is the question of how to allocate or distribute the responsibilities. As alluded to earlier, given the complex nature of decision-making processes within the corporation, it is through a group of persons that corporate policies are formulated

31

and implemented. Thus, it is a *collectivity* of persons and not a single individual that is to be allocated responsibilities. We may refer to this as *collective responsibility*, to be distinguished from *individual responsibility*. From its conception to its articulation, development and final implementation, a policy has to go through various stages of development, involving different persons. Persons in the Board of Directors, top management, middle management, committees and the personnel who implement the policy may be said to be involved. However, assigning responsibility to this group of persons indiscriminately seems not a reasonable thing to do. There should be some discrimination between, for example, those who formulate and initiate the policy and those who only enforce it according to orders. How responsibilities are to be fairly distributed among members of this group is not an easy and straightforward matter. In the Bhopal tragedy in India, or the Bangkok toy factory fire disaster, identifying those responsible is not simple or easy. To assign fairly the amount of responsibility among those who contributed to these tragedies is equally difficult.

In so far as corporations are perceived to be policy actors, they should be held responsible for the consequences of their policies. This view is different from the view that sees corporations as moral persons. It sees the corporation only as a collective agent acting within society to meet certain needs and to complete certain tasks. As agents they are responsible for their acts through their participation in the initiating, articulating and implementing of policies.

2. Cost, Benefits and Morality

In addition to these moral debates on a macro-level, there is a plethora of ethical issues directly related to the micro-level of ethical decision-making and practices in the corporate context. Businessmen making business decisions understandably take profit as their major concern. Very often cost-benefit analysis, whether in a crude and informal or a systematic and rigorous form, are undertaken to help decide the best course of action. This mundane process of business seems to be primarily rationality-based and has little to do with morality. Whether this is the case requires some detailed analysis. Let us focus on a concrete case (Beauchamp and Bowie, 1983, pp. 585–7).

VII. The Case

Bluebird Smelter is owned by a large, national mining company and located in Bluebird, a town of 2,000 in eastern Montana. The smelter, which has been operating profitably for 35 years with 125 employees, processes copper ore arriving by railroad. Bluebird Smelter is the only major industrial pollution source in the valley. On sunny days when the air is still and during periods of temperature inversion over the valley, the action of the sun on smelter emissions contributes to photochemical smog similar to that in urban areas. Car exhaust emissions and agricultural activities are also sources of photochemical oxidants, but smelter emissions are far more important.

A group of economists from a prestigious research institute in another city picked the Bluebird Smelter as a test case for a research project on the health effects of pollution. The figures they produced led to debate among various concerned local groups. The researchers looked at the operation of Bluebird Smelter in terms of costs and benefits to the community and to society. The following table shows their basic calculations.

Table 1
Annual Benefits and Costs of Bluebird Smelter

Benefits	*Value*
Payroll for 125 employees at an average of $15,000 each	$1,875,000
Benefits paid to workers and families at an average of S1,000 each	125,000
Income, other than wages and salaries, generated in the valley by the company..	4,600,000
Local taxes and fees paid by the company	100,000
Social services to community and charitable contributions	20,000
TOTAL	$6,720,000

Costs	
Excess deaths of 5 persons at $1 million each*	$5,000,000
Other health and illness costs to exposed population	450,000
Crop and property damage from pollutants...	1,000,000
Reduction of aesthetic value and quality of life	500,000
Lost revenues and taxes from tourism...	500,000
TOTAL	$7,450,000

* Calculated on the basis of recent court decisions compensating victims of wrongful death in product liability cases in Western states. The figure reflects average compensation.

The Earth Riders (a small local environmental group) seized upon the study, arguing that if total costs of smelter operation exceeded benefits, then a clear-cut case had been made for closing the plant. It was already operating at a loss; in this case a net social loss of $730,000. Thus, in the eyes of the environmentalists Bluebird Smelter was in social bankruptcy.

The smelter's managers and members of the Bluebird City Council, on the other hand, ridiculed the study for making unrealistic and overly simplistic assumptions. They questioned whether the costs were meaningful, citing estimates of the value of a human life that were much lower than $1 million, made by other economists. They argued that health risks posed by the smelter were less than those of smoking cigarettes, drinking or riding motorcycles and that benefits to the community were great. They even suggested that important costs had been left out of the calculations such as sociological and psychological costs to workers who would be laid off if the plant closed.

There are questions to be asked about the completeness and relevance of the cost-benefit analysis, and also about how some parameters are to be measured and compared with each other. One question of the first kind may read like this: are all the relevant items being included in the cost-benefit calculation? When making decisions of this nature, a pertinent question is about the dollar value of a life. This in turn brings up another, more basic, question, namely, whether and how one can decide the value of a human life. A related issue that needed to be addressed seems to be this: if one refuses to put a price tag on the value of human life, on what basis can we decide that a certain amount of money be allocated to certain medical research, on say cancer or AIDS, in order to save life? If one is willing to put a dollar value on the value of a human life, how much should be given, and on what basis? Suppose that when compared with another type of public hazard, like cigarette smoking, it is found that the smelter posed a lower health hazard, can we then draw the conclusion that the smelter should be allowed to continue to be run? Or that cigarette smoking should be banned? Or, more generally, whether the kind of analysis offered by cost-benefit analysis is an adequate tool in aiding us to decide whether the smelter should be closed at all? (Beauchamp and Bowie, 1983, p. 587.)

What appears to be a mundane case in business decision-making in effect conceals a Pandora's box of moral perplexities and methodological problems. I suppose that not until one has a better grasp of the intricacies of the case presented can one begin to appreciate the complexity and difficulty of problems involved. Yet this is a fairly typical case in business ethics of the kind that both business practitioners and students of business ethics often need to confront. There are myriad cases of different degrees of complexity which demand sober analyses and rational solutions.

34

Despite the diversity of these cases, one thing seems certain. There are important connections between the practices, policies and conduct of business institutions and morality that any rational human society cannot afford to ignore. Morality should not be seen as something peripheral to business, but should be seen as an integral part of a decent business. Recognition of this fact by the business community and society may help to contribute to a fair and enlightened understanding of the role business ought to have in society. However, this is not enough for both practitioners and the public at large, if the complex and difficult issues involved are not adequately analysed and solutions to the dilemmas business and society have to face are not offered. This indeed raises a fundamental question that this article intends to address: what is the task of business ethics? What is its scope? What are the major issues in the field? What are the prospects of business ethics in Hong Kong?

I propose to give a brief review of the issues raised here within the confine of this essay.

VIII. Defining the Field

Business ethics can mean a field of study as well as concerns and activities about morality and business. What this essay is concerned with is business ethics as an academic field. It aims at investigating the relationships between morality and business. As an intellectual pursuit, it is to be distinguished from moralising or ethical exhortations. Its distinctive contribution is to provide rational analyses and justifications of the relationship between morality and business, which may lead to normative prescriptions.

The objects of investigation range across different levels: system, organisation and the individual level. On the system level, the whole economic system will be under investigation. For example, the question of the relationships of business ethics in capitalism and in socialism is very interesting with regard to the diverse nature of the ideology and structure of the two systems. Issues like economic justice and freedom in connection with these two systems are also important. On the organisation level, the primary object is the corporation and its policies and processes. Issues like whether corporations should have social responsibilities and whether corporations should have obligations to protect the environment have aroused much debate and discussion. The third level relates to individual behaviour and conduct within a business setting – how individuals as employees, consumers, managers or co-workers react or respond to moral dilemmas in their everyday as well as business life. Issues like whistleblowing, ethical hiring and firing, discrimination, sexual harassment, ethical consuming have attracted much attention.

These three levels of investigation are by no means merely discrete, bearing no relationship to each other. In fact, they are interconnected and their respective analyses often overlap. There are three main approaches of investigation. The first is the empirical study of business practices, institutions, policies and individual agents' conduct and behaviour. Empirical studies undertaken by sociologists, economists, anthropologists, political scientists and management or organisation experts contribute to our factual understanding of business. Such a factual basis is vitally important for the ethical analyses that follow. Without these empirical inputs, ethical analyses may be accused of being armchair speculations which have little practical relevance to the real world of business. As the field involves different disciplines, it inherently has a highly multidisciplinary orientation. Such a multidisciplinary approach may enhance interdisciplinary investigation over time, effectively promoting cross-fertilisation of ideas across disciplines. The second kind of investigation is theoretical studies. Closely connected to and utilising the findings of the first kind, students of business ethics try to construct theories about business ethics to enable us to explain and eventually to forecast events and situations in the field. The third kind of inquiry focuses on normative studies. Unlike the previous kinds of inquiry which primarily concern the IS question, a normative study takes the OUGHT question as its major concern. Its aim is to investigate the problem of what and how business should be conducted and the moral justifications involved (De George, 1987).

What has been discussed can be summed up by the matrix in Figure A.

IX. Institutionalising Business Ethics

Like any other basic social institutions, business as an institution should not be exempted from taking social responsibilities, and hence is not immune to moral scrutiny and criticism. Rawls (1971) has proposed a theory of justice defining the morality of basic social institutions. Whether such a theory can effectively be applied to business is not a question to be answered here. However, lack of a general theory of this sort need not prevent us from proposing institutional responses to this problem. The following are some suggestions (Davis and Frederick, 1984; Buchholz, 1989):

Figure A: Topology of Inquiry in Business Ethics

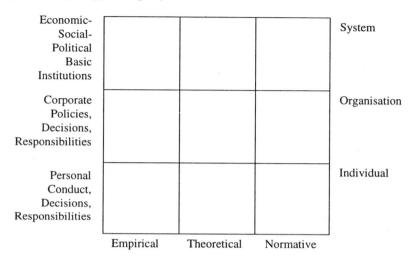

(1) A business *code of ethics,* which serves to explicitly define corporate goals and values and helps to establish a uniform framework for action, should be introduced. Caution: ethical codes, however, can only provide general guidelines for action and should not be blindly adhered to, because of the existence of unanticipated cases or complicated or ambiguous cases that defy simple analysis. Should such cases occur, ethical codes should be carefully interpreted and critically followed. To ensure that these codes are effectively implemented, it is suggested that employees should be consulted in designing them. Self-developed codes of ethics tend to enhance and facilitate the ethical conduct of employees (Brenner and Molander, 1977).

(2) A board-level committee should be created to examine the moral aspects of company policies and conduct. Similar committees charged with analogous functions should be formed to handle specific ethical issues. These committees function on a policy formation level to ensure that ethics, along with legal, financial and marketing factors, is an important policy component which deserves serious consideration.

(3) Courses or workshops and seminars in business ethics should be treated as a part of a corporation's regular training programme (staff development programme) for managers and employees. These courses or workshops may be run by experts teaching managers and employees to be aware of ethics issues in their work situation. They can be used to educate employees in rational ethical reasoning that they can apply in their work situations.

(4) The teaching of business ethics should be a part of the curriculum in business schools. In fact, more and more business schools have begun to recognise the significance of business ethics as a part of the educational process for future business executives and managers.[3] These courses can not only make students aware of ethics in business, but also train them to be competent in making ethical decisions in business. Business ethics education need not be confined solely to tertiary education. Similar curricular inclusions can be provided wherever practicable in middle schools or primary schools to alert students to these issues.

(5) Professional business bodies should take the lead in sensitising members about ethical issues in business. Seminars and conferences highlighting important and community-relevant ethical issues should be held regularly for both members and the public.

(6) Research Centres or Learning Resource Centres should be established to facilitate and promote research and learning in business ethics.

(7) The media should take a more active role in informing and sensitising the public about ethical issues in business.[4]

X. Concluding Remarks

People in Hong Kong are now beginning to recognise the importance and urgency of business ethics. The business community's recent initiative in organising a conference on business ethics is only one such clear indication. Despite the rather confined focus of the conference, such an initiative itself is a reflection of an enlightened concern on the part of business groups. Academic institutions are now beginning to take a more active role in this regard as well. The recent establishment of a Centre of Business Values at the University of Hong Kong is a welcome addition to such a concern and initiative. Despite their belated responses, the significance of such efforts should not be underestimated. Certainly, there is much to be done in both the academic and business communities in areas of teaching, research, education and corporate ethical development and reform. However, without the joint effort and close cooperation of both the academic and business communities, it is difficult to have a sustainable and viable programme which will enhance and facilitate both the minds and deeds of corporate personnel as well as the general public in matters relating to business ethics.

PROBLEMS IN BUSINESS ETHICS

Notes

1. A survey (Dolecheck and Bethke, 1990) provides valuable information about how business personnel view business ethics.

2. The discussion on the Moral Agency Debate has benefited from Buchholz (1989).

3. The teaching of business ethics at tertiary education institutions began very late. In the business curriculum of a number of institutions, business ethics has been taught not as a course, but only as a small part of the course. I initiated, developed and taught a half-year course in Business Ethics in 1987 at Lingnan College. The course since then has become an integral part of the General Education Programme there. It was probably the first full course on business ethics to be taught in Hong Kong. Very few business schools in Hong Kong have offered a full course in business ethics as part of their curriculum.

4. To my knowledge, only the *Hong Kong Economic Journal* has a weekly column, "Business and Professional Ethics", where I have been penning articles for the last two and half years. The establishment of this column was the result of the foresight and support of the *Journal*'s proprietor Mr. Lin.

Selected References

Beauchamp, T., and N. Bowie, 1983, *Ethical Theory and Business*, 2nd ed., Englewood Cliffs, New Jersey, Prentice-Hall

Bowie, N., 1982, *Business Ethics*, Englewood Cliffs, New Jersey, Prentice-Hall

Brenner, S.N., and E.A. Molander, 1977, "Is the Ethics of Business Changing?", *Harvard Business Review* 55, Jan.–Feb., pp. 57–71

Buchholz, R.A., 1989, *Fundamental Concepts and Problems in Business Ethics*, Englewood Cliffs, New Jersey, Prentice-Hall

Chan, A., K.F. Lau and P.K. Ip, 1988, "Factors Affecting Business Ethics: An Exploratory Study in Hong Kong", *Proceedings of the 1988 Academy of International Business South-east Asia Regional Conference*, E121–37, Bangkok

Danley, J.R., 1984, "Corporate Moral Agency: The Case for Anthropological Bigotry", in *Business Ethics: Readings and Cases in Corporate Morality*, W.M. Hoffman and J.M. Moore (eds.), New York, McGraw-Hill

Davis, K., and W.C. Frederick, 1984, *Business and Society*, 5th ed., Tokyo, McGraw-Hill

De George, R.T., 1986, *Business Ethics*, 2nd ed., New York, Macmillan

— (1987) "The Status of Business Ethics: Past and Future", *Journal* of *Business Ethics* 6, pp. 201–11

Dolecheck, M.M., and A.L. Bethke, 1990, "Business Ethics in Hong Kong: Is There a Problem?", *Hong Kong Manager*, Sep.–Oct., pp. 13–23

Donaldson, T., 1982, *Corporations and Morality*, Englewood Cliffs, New Jersey, Prentice-Hall

Drucker, Peter F., 1964, *The Concept of the Corporation*, New York, Mentor Books

Fisse, B., and John Braithwaite, 1983, *The Impact of Publicity on Corporate Offenders*, Albany, State University of New York Press

French, P.A., 1984, "Corporate Moral Agency", in *Business Ethics: Readings and Cases in Corporate Morality*, W.M. Hoffman and J.M. Moore (eds.), New York, McGraw-Hill, pp. 163–71

Friedman, M., 1962, *Capitalism and Freedom*, Chicago, University of Chicago Press

Goodpaster, K.E., 1984, "The Concept of Corporate Responsibility", in *Just Business: New Introductory Essays in Business Ethics*, Tom Regan (ed.), New York, Random House

— and J.B. Matthews Sr., 1984, "Can a Corporation Have a Conscience?", in *Business Ethics: Readings and Cases in Corporate Morality*, W.M. Hoffman and J.M. Moore (eds.), New York, McGraw-Hill, pp. 150–62

Hofstede, G., 1980, *Culture's Consequences: International Differences in Work-related Values*, London and Beverly Hills, Sage

Hollis, M., and E. Nell, 1975, *Rational Economic Man*, London, Cambridge University Press

Ip, P.K., 1987, "Should Managers be Moral?", in *Proceedings of the Conference on the Changing Environment of Management in Hong Kong*, Hong Kong, Hong Kong Baptist College, pp. 39–43

— with A. Chan and K.F. Lau, 1987, "Towards a Framework for Understanding Business Ethical Decisions", in *Proceedings of the Conference on Marketing and Management into the 90s*, Nov., pp. 43–9

Keeley, M., 1983, "Organizations as Non-Persons", in *Ethical Issues in Business: A Philosophical Approach*, 2nd ed., Thomas Donaldson and P.H. Werhane (eds.), Englewood Cliffs, New Jersey, Prentice-Hall

Ladd, J., 1983, "Morality and the Ideal of Rationality in Formal Organizations", in *Ethical Issues in Business: A Philosophical Approach*, 2nd ed., Thomas Donaldson and P.H. Werhane (eds.), Englewood Cliffs, New Jersey, Prentice-Hall, pp. 125-36.

Mokhiber, R., 1988, *Corporate Crime and Violence – Big Business Power and the Abuse of the Public Trust*, San Francisco, Sierra Club Books

Peters, T.J., and R.H. Waterman Jr., 1982, *In Search of Excellence – Lessons from America's Best-Run Companies*, New York, Harper & Row

Rawls, J., 1971, *A Theory of Justice*, Cambridge, Mass., Harvard University Press

Regan, T., 1984 (ed.), *Just Business: New Introductory Essays in Business Ethics*, New York, Random House

PROBLEMS IN BUSINESS ETHICS

Shaw, W., and V. Barry, 1989, *Moral Issues in Business,* Belmont, California, Wadsworth

Velasquez, M.G., 1982, *Business Ethics: Concepts and Cases*, Englewood Cliffs, New Jersey, Prentice-Hall

Werhane, P.H., 1985, *Persons, Rights, and Corporations*, Englewood Cliffs, New Jersey, Prentice-Hall

Chapter 3

Comparative Ethical Perceptions of Australian and Hong Kong Managers

GAEL M. MCDONALD, RAYMOND A. ZEPP AND PAK CHO-KAN

I. Introduction

Within the last two decades there has been a profusion of cross-cultural studies examining general population values and culture dimensions (e.g., England, 1975; Hofstede, 1980), and increasingly the investigative focus has moved to the business manager as a common unit of analysis. In relation to the field of business ethics, more recently a few studies have been performed on differences in ethical perceptions between Western managers and their Asian counterparts. A comparison of the ethical perceptions of Chinese businessmen in Singapore and the United States was undertaken by Mehta and Kau (1984), who found that across-the-board generalisations concerning ethics are impossible in the cross-cultural context: one type of behaviour may be more accepted by Singaporeans, while another type may be more readily accepted by Americans. For example, Americans regarded the heavy padding of expense accounts to be more unethical than did the Singaporeans, but the Singaporeans found the use of company time for personal business to be more unethical than did the Americans. The major conclusions of the study were: the higher the age or income of executives, the more unethical are the situations perceived, the higher the education, the less unethical was the situation perceived, and a comparison of Singapore and U.S. marketing managers indicated that American executives used stricter standards of evaluation.

Examining ethical beliefs of salespeople in the United States, Japan and South Korea, Dubinsky *et al.* (1991) concluded that nationality influences salespeople's beliefs about the ethics of selling practices and the need for company policies to guide those practices.

White and Rhodeback (1992) compared American and Taiwanese business students on the extent to which cultural differences bear on perceptions of ethical Organisational Development consulting behaviours. Subjects from the United States tended to provide higher ethicality ratings than the Taiwanese respondents (White and Rhodeback, 1992, p. 666).

Hong Kong has an international business reputation, fostered perhaps by such novels as Clavell's *Noble House*, as a moral jungle where no ethical standards exist and where any behaviour is permissible. This view has not been examined under the scrutiny of systematic research. The few studies undertaken to date (Kam Hon Lee, 1980, 1981; Dolecheck and Dolecheck, 1987; Chan and Lee 1986; Chan *et al.* 1988; McDonald and Zepp, 1988a; Armstrong *et al.* 1991) hint that the situation is more complex than the existing stereotype.

In one of the earlier cross-cultural studies Dolecheck and Dolecheck (1987) compared ethical perceptions and attitudes of Hong Kong and U.S. personnel. Differences were found to exist in seven of the eight circumstances posed. It was concluded that Hong Kong managers were more likely to define business ethics as simply operating within the law, felt greater loyalty to protect the organisation by which they were employed, less likely to "whistleblow", and felt compelled to compromise personal principles to conform to their organisation's expectations. It was also concluded that the behaviour of one's superiors was deemed to be the most influential factor on ethical behaviour in both Hong Kong and United States.

A purely intra-cultural focus was taken by Kam Hon Lee (1980, 1981), who compared the ethical perceptions of Chinese and British managers working in Hong Kong. He found no significant differences between the two groups, but was quick to point out the possibility that British businessmen in Hong Kong may not typify Western business ethics, and may experience acculturation to an ethic of "when in Rome, do as the Romans do".

In Australia, the literature tends to focus on the philosophical side of ethics (e.g., Swanton, 1987), on medical ethics (e.g., McCaughey, 1986), and to a lesser extent on business ethics (e.g., Benton, 1986; Hennessy, 1987). In business, the writing is still grounded in guidelines for professional conduct, particularly in the occupational areas of accountancy (Breakspear, 1987) and journalism (Road, 1985). In recent years there has been an increased interest in the subject of business ethics as reflected by the number of articles in both the academic and popular press. For example, a well-known Australian headhunter, Egon Zehnder, expressed the importance of integrity in the choice of CEOs (Lynch, 1985) and Williams (1985) has cited statistics on employee dishonesty in Australian business. Empirical research is still in its infancy. In reference to ethical perceptions, Kelly (1985) compared accounting students and practitioners according to differences which they perceived in ethical situations. Armstrong (1992) and Armstrong *et al.* (1990) have identified and categorised ethical problems encountered by Australian international business managers with large-scale bribery the most important ethical problem perceived.

While cultural values are often examined, the actual ethical attitudes of Australian business personnel have not been measured systematically, and with little comparison with managers of other cultures. Utilising the Preble and Reichel (1988) research instrument, Small (1992) compared West Australian undergraduates with their U.S. and Israeli counterparts and concluded that U.S. and Australian undergraduates tended to share similar or identical values in their attitudes toward business ethics. When the West Australian and Israeli students were compared, 19 of the 30 variables were found to be significantly different, although not particularly meaningful. Small concluded that the similarity of responses indicated a high commonality of views towards business ethics by Western Australian, U.S. and Israeli students.

Abratt *et al.* (1992) have also undertaken cross-cultural research and compared the ethical beliefs of managers operating in South Africa and Australia and despite differences in socio-cultural and political factors no statistically significant differences between the groups were identified. The ethical beliefs of South African and Australian managers differed slightly at the 0.05 level in only three of the 20 scenarios studied. Australian managers appeared to be more concerned with offering potential clients fully paid holidays, giving a client a bottle of whisky, and insider trading. Differences in the latter instance of insider trading could be attributed to differences in the South African and Australian laws governing insider trading. In general with limited empirical research the ethical literature in Australia appears to be standing on the sidelines of the issue; this attitude results in rather generalised discussions which generate "a lot of heat but very little light".

In the studies mentioned above, as well as in the present study, an important distinction must be made between ethical perception and morality. To state, for instance, that Singaporeans find certain behaviour more or less unethical, in no way makes a moral judgment about Singaporeans. Similarly, the present study will not comment on the morality of behaviour in Hong Kong or in Australia, but rather attempts to investigate whether certain behavioural situations are perceived as ethical or unethical. A second distinction must be made between ethics and "social responsibility". The latter term refers to collective organisational accountability, while "ethics" fundamentally relates to individual behaviour.

This distinction applies in both the East and the West, as noted by Drucker (1981):

> For the Confucian – but also for the philosopher of Western tradition – only law can handle the rights and objectives of collectives. Ethics is always a matter of the person.

Finally, any study of ethics must consider the relative perception of ethical behaviour. Simply to ask whether an action is perceived as right or wrong would be fruitless; rather, one must ask how right or wrong the action is perceived. For example, different cultures will probably agree that the padding of an expense account is unethical, but one culture might perceive such an action as a heinous sin, while another might view it only as a venial misdemeanour. A third culture might find small levels of expense account padding tolerable, but large levels repugnant.

II. Method of the Study

A questionnaire on ethical decisions was given to businessmen in Australia and in Hong Kong. In Perth, Australia, data were collected from two groups representing advertising practitioners: personnel from advertising agencies at the account executive/client servicing level, and members of business organisations at the marketing/advertising/sales/manager level. Both the advertising agencies and corporations were selected randomly from the Perth Yellow Pages. Of the 80 available advertising agencies, 24 companies were approached. As the research was only an exploratory study a total of 111 questionnaires were sent, of which 63 responses were returned. The mean age of respondents was 37.3 with a standard deviation of 9.5, and 92 per cent of the respondents were male. In Hong Kong, businessmen* were selected from mature age, part-time students attending a weekend residential statistics course within a Masters of Business Administration program at the University of Macau. The sample consisted of middle-level managers from a variety of industries in Hong Kong. The convenience sampling of four M.B.A. classes and the administration of the questionnaire as part of a class exercise ensured a 100 per cent response rate. The mean age was 33, with a standard deviation of 5.6

The sample of 107 represented a wide spectrum of business activity in Hong Kong.

A limitation of this research study also provides a research opportunity. The data was collected some time ago, although not reported in this comparative format, in Australia in 1982 and in Hong Kong in 1987. The delay in reporting these findings provides a current and unique opportunity for longitudinal replication.

The questionnaire contained 12 situational statements, incorporating elements from two previous studies. Eight of the original 10 ethical statements used by Kam Hon Lee (1981), based on a collection of morally difficult marketing situations by Kotler (1972), were modified. In addition, 10 of the 16 ethical concepts used by Ferrell and Krugman (1981) were given operational definitions by way of a situational context. A nine-point Likert scale with indicators of "strongly disagree", "neutral", "strongly agree", etc., was employed.

Section One of the questionnaire asked the respondent to state his personal beliefs on the ethical situations in question, while Section Two asked the respondent to estimate the probable beliefs of peers in the same situations. The specific issues intent in each statement were the following:

1) Truth in advertising
2) Obtaining trade secrets
3) Ethical sales practice
4) Irritation in advertising
5) Using company time for personal business
6) Taking credit for another's work
7) Taking longer than necessary for a job
8) Deceptive advertising
9) Padding an expense account
10) Gaining of competitor information
11) Falsifying reports
12) Offering and accepting bribes

(Details of ethical scenarios are contained in the appendix).

The final component of the questionnaire requested common biographical data such as gender, age, level of education. In the Hong Kong sample, consistent with an ancillary research objective, the respondent was asked if he/she worked for a multinational or a local company, and if he/she was educated overseas or locally.

III. Results

Means and standard deviations were recorded for each question and for each group (Australia and Hong Kong). Multiple t-tests were performed to compare the two group means on each of the ethical items. The results are described in Table Two, with significant t's marked with an asterisk.

1. Personal Beliefs

Concerning statements of personal belief, on seven of the 12 questions, means for the Hong Kong group were significantly higher than those for the Australians. The higher means indicate that Hong Kong businessmen found the possibly unethical actions more acceptable than did the Australians.

The greatest differences between the groups were found in the areas of deceptive advertising, ethical sales practices, bribery, and falsifying reports: in each of these four tests a t value of over 6.0 was measured, indicating a high degree of significance. On average Hong Kong businessmen agreed (mean 6.5) with the practice of adding the statement "new and improved" to a package when the product was not really new or improved, while the Australians disagreed with the practice (mean 4.1). Similarly, Hong Kong businessmen agreed (mean 5.6) with the practice of sending salesmen into houses under the pretence of taking a survey, while Australians disagreed (mean 3.1). Also, the Hong Kong group agreed (mean 5.2) with giving and receiving "gifts" to clients, while the Australians did not (mean 2.7). Both groups disagreed with the practice of falsifying reports, but the Australians' level of disagreement was much higher than the Hong Kong group's (mean of 1.5 as compared with 3.5 for the Hong Kong group).

Areas where the two groups were virtually identical were in irritating advertising and in padding an expense account. In the former case, both groups expressed a high degree of agreement with choosing a "noisy, irritating commercial" over a "soft-sell, honest, informational campaign" if it was thought to produce higher sales. In the latter case, both groups disagreed with the practice of padding an expense account.

When comparing with previous research it is interesting to note that in the current research for Australian managers bribery received a ranked place of 10 out of the 12 scenarios and was therefore perceived as an unethical activity and one that we presume managers would like to see averted. This finding is consistent with Armstrong's (1992) research which concluded that large-scale

47

bribery followed by cultural differences were the ethical problems of importance to Australian general managers.

Table 1
Ranking of Ethical Statements: Self-perceptions

Ranking of statements from (1) perceived as unethical to (12) perceived as acceptable.

		Chinese		Australian	
Ethical Statements		*Ranking*	*Mean** *Agreement*	*Ranking*	*Mean** *Agreement*
1.	Truth in Advertising	9	5.0	7	3.9
2.	Obtaining Trade Secrets	4	5.9	5	4.2
3.	Unethical Sales Practices	7	5.6	9	3.1
4.	Irritation in Advertising	2	6.7	1	7.0
5.	Using Company Time for Personal Business	6	5.6	3	4.4
6.	Taking Credit for Another's Work	12	3.2	11	1.6
7.	Taking Longer than Necessary to do the Job	5	5.7	4	4.3
8.	Deceptive Advertising	3	6.5	6	4.1
9.	Padding One's Expense Account	10	3.5	8	3.4
10.	Gaining of Competitor Information	1	7.0	2	6.1
11.	Falsifying Reports	11	3.5	12	1.5
12.	Bribery	8	5.2	10	2.7

*Means are based upon a nine-point scale (1 = Strongly disagree through 9 = Strongly agree).

Table 2
Self Versus Peer Comparisons

Ethical scenarios	Self		Peers	
	Australia	Hong Kong	Australia	Hong Kong
1. Truth in advertising				
mean	3.984	5.019	4.541	7.252
st. dev.	2.910	2.624	2.913	7.287
t		2.304		2.810
2. Obtaining trade secrets				
mean	4.254	5.925	5.426	6.804
st. dev.	2.753	2.593	2.604	2.187
t		4.087*		3.217*

Table 2 (continued)

Ethical scenarios	Self		Peers	
	Australia	Hong Kong	Australia	Hong Kong
3. Unethical sales practices				
mean	3.175	5.607	4.100	6.776
st. dev.	2.618	2.314	2.809	2.085
t		6.477*		6.718*
4. Irritation in advertising				
mean	7.081	6.729	6.700	6.897
st. dev.	2.190	1.984	2.242	2.095
t		0.612		0.567
5. Using company time for personal business				
mean	4.403	5.636	4.917	6.215
st. dev.	2.983	2.418	3.044	2.449
t		1.226		3.052
6. Taking credit for another's work				
mean	1.689	3.234	2.933	5.271
st. dev.	1.232	2.239	2.393	2.749
t		4.902*		5.516*
7. Taking longer than necessary to do job				
mean	4.333	5.710	4.283	5.729
st. dev.	3.090	2.379	2.525	2.276
t		3.310*		3.713*
8. Deceptive advertising				
mean	4.115	6.514	5.533	7.234
st. dev.	2.709	2.186	2.813	1.836
t		6.579*		4.762*
9. Padding one's expense account				
mean	3.443	3.570	4.250	5.766
st. dev.	2.896	2.477	2.808	2.619
t		0.239		3.513*
10. Gaining of competitor information				
mean	6.164	7.026	6.633	5.493
st. dev.	3.067	1.657	2.518	1.465
t		2.381		3.915*
11. Falsifying reports				
mean	1.532	3.533	2.700	5.345
st. dev.	1.183	2.368	1.968	2.492
t		6.250*		7.080*
12. Bribery				
mean	2.742	5.234	3.433	6.439
st. dev.	2.547	2.486	2.733	2.241
t		6.280*		8.269*

* Significant at $p < 0.05$

Table 3
Ethical Problems in International Marketing: Importance Ranking*

Ethical Problem	Hong Kong Ranking	Mean** Agreement	Australian Ranking	Mean Agreement
1. Gifts/Favours/ Entertainment	1	3.17	7	2.96
2. Pricing Practices	2	2.86	3	3.20
3. Tax Evasion Practices	3	2.70	8	2.94
4. Illegal/Immoral Activities	4	2.54	5	3.16
5. Questionable Commissions	5	2.45	6	3.08
6. Traditional/Small Scale Bribery	6	2.42	10	2.42
7. Large-scale Bribery	7	2.42	1	3.65
8. Inappropriate Use of Products/ Technology Transfer	8	2.21	9	2.56
9. Cultural Differences	9	2.19	2	3.43
10. Involvement in Political Affairs	10	2.01	3	3.00

* Armstrong *et al.*, (1991), and Armstrong (1992).
** Means are based on an 8-point scale (0 = not important through 7 = great importance)

When the Armstrong study was replicated in Hong Kong interesting comparison were noted (see Table Three, Ethical Problems in International Marketing). Large-scale bribery, which is perceived to be of considerable importance to Australian general mangers, is ranked only seven by Hong Kong managers. A possible explanation for this finding is the existence of the Independent Commission Against Corruption in Hong Kong. The high-profile activities of the I.C.A.C. may lead managers in Hong Kong to view the problem as "under control" and therefore not warranting a significant level of importance. Alternatively gifts, favours and entertainment followed by pricing practices and tax evasion were seen to be of importance. The mention of gifts and entertainment by Hong Kong managers is not surprising given the ambiguities of business entertainment in Asia which could extend to free trips and escort services (Asian Images, No. 3, 1993).

The Australian abhorrence of large-scale bribery is also supported by the results of a *Far Eastern Economic Review* study which determined that of 10 Asian groups Australians (17 per cent) were least likely to offer a bribe (*Asian Images* 3, 1993).

2. Peer Perceptions

Perception of peers' ethical views followed the same pattern as the personal beliefs. In eight of the 12 categories, Hong Kong managers agreed significantly more readily that their peers would accept the unethical actions. Seven of those eight categories were identical with the situations where significant differences were measured in personal beliefs. The eighth was in padding an expense account. Apparently, Hong Kong managers believe more strongly than their Australian counterparts that their peers would pad their expense accounts, although neither group would accept the practice personally.

By far the largest difference in peer perception between groups was recorded in the category of bribery. Hong Kong businessmen apparently believe strongly (mean 6.4) that their colleagues would give "gifts" while Australians do not share that view of their peers (mean 3.4). In almost all cases both groups expressed a more negative view of their peers than of themselves, i.e., they agreed that peers would undertake unethical activities more readily than they themselves would. This finding is consistent with many other studies (e.g., Pitt and Abratt, 1986). The only notable exception to this pattern was in the area of gaining competitor information, where the Hong Kong group personally agreed at the high level of 7.0, while they felt their peers would agree at a level of only 5.4. The Australians, on the other hand, followed the usual pattern: they agreed personally at a level of 6.2, while they felt their peers would agree at a slightly higher level (6.6).

The ethical perceptions of managers and their comparative perceptions of peers have previously been an important element of numerous studies (e.g., Newstrom and Ruch, 1975; Ferrell and Weaver, 1978). Baumhart (1961, p. 7) noted that although the respondents professed a lofty level of ethical aspiration for themselves, they revealed a lower opinion of the practices of the average businessman.

Brenner and Molander (1977) also concluded that respondents were somewhat cynical about the ethical conduct of their peers. The belief held by individuals that they are more ethical than their peers has been replicated internationally with similar findings also being reported in South Africa (Pitt and Abratt, 1986), and in Hong Kong (McDonald and Zepp, 1988a). The general conclusion from numerous studies is that executives view the ethical standards of their peers less optimistically than they view their own; however, believing that everyone is less ethical appears to have little impact on work behaviour (Tyson, 1992, p. 707).

It might be possible to compare composite scores of the two groups, i.e., to compute a total score for each subject, and to compare means of total scores for the two groups. This method would therefore compare the two groups' overall ethical behaviour. We suggest, however, that this not be done, for the reason that individuals' scores displayed very little internal consistency. A correlational analysis was done on the Hong Kong scores, and very low correlations between the various questions were recorded. This finding illustrates that an individual who agreed strongly with one unethical practice might disagree strongly with another. Thus, an individual should not be labelled "unethical" in an overall sense; each circumstance should be examined separately. Acceptance of unethical behaviour in one situation cannot be used as an indication of likely agreement to unethical behaviour in another situation, nor can it be taken as a measure of overall agreement to unethical behaviour.

IV. Conclusions

One must resist the temptation to pat Australians on the back for generally perceiving potentially unethical actions less acceptable than the sample of Hong Kong managers. The size of the Australian sample is an obvious limitation in this preliminary study. In addition, while the levels of agreement on seven questions were significantly lower than those of the Hong Kong managers, overall agreement was, however, expressed by Australian managers to a number of unethical practices, particularly the gaining of competitor information. Similarly, the possibly inaccurate perception of the lower ethical beliefs of peers could act as an unrealistic pressure on managers to commit unethical actions.

The findings of this study have implications for management (McDonald and Zepp, 1988b), and several practical suggestions can be made:

1. As potentially unethical situations are perceived independently, supervisory management should not evaluate or prejudge the overall ethical standards of employees on the basis of isolated incidents.

2. Basic awareness programmes could be initiated which incorporate exposure to current ethical issues, and published material could be circulated on relevant ethical topics, thereby heightening concern for ethical action.

3. Specific ethical training programmes could be set up which assist managers in recognising the possibly ethical dimensions of business decisions. Managers should be made aware that decisions may have ethical consequences which can adversely affect the individual as well as the organisation. When designing programmes, trainers should bear in mind that ethical situations are

not always black and white issues, but rather, a series of possible rationalisations which could be used to justify unethical behaviour. The content of many existing programmes emphasises the use of case studies posing difficult ethical decisions, and they encourage discussion by participants. Dilemma workshops, such as those used by Polaroid, assist participants in applying ethical concepts to cases drawn from actual events in the corporation (Lee, 1986).

4. A company which seeks to preserve its ethical reputation may use psychological testing as a preliminary step in the selection of ethical employees. Bommer, *et al.* (1987) suggested several instruments which can be used to identify differences in cognitive style which may affect ethical or unethical decision-making. In addition, hypothetical situations with ethical implications could also be posed during preliminary and final interviews with prospective employees.

5. It appears that ethical policy statements can promote ethical behaviour (Hegarty and Sims, 1979). Such policy statements should not, however, be confused with codes of ethics, which are more general indicators of behaviour. The term "ethical policy statement" appears to be used to mean "ethical rule", which is both prescriptive and enforceable.

6. Companies may wish to reconsider the ethical implications of activities such as management by objectives, the inherent pressure to surpass past years' accomplishments, cost savings plans, and pay-for-performance schemes. Unrealistic performance expectations and reward plans may unwittingly be applying pressure on employees to act unethically.

7. The establishment of ethical corporate cultures is a rather ambitious and somewhat overused suggestion. Still, the corporate culture will naturally affect the ethical values of its personnel. The more an employee feels himself to be a member of the company team, the stronger will be the tendency to conform to the ethical standards of the company.

8. Companies which operate internationally should be cognisant of potential differences in ethical perceptions held by managers of other cultures with whom they interact. What is considered unacceptable behaviour in the home context might be deemed quite appropriate in another, and *vice versa*. The dimension of ethical perceptions needs to be added to acculturation programmes, particularly for those managers who are considering entering an international corporation or participating in international trade.

This situation highlights the essential thesis of the theory of *Ethical Relativism* and also alludes to what is commonly considered the antithetical theory of *Ethical Absolutism*. At the core of ethical relativity is the question: do moral principles apply universally, or are all values and ethical judgements relative to their context, particularly cultural contexts? Ethical relativity does not simply highlight the fact that different people have different sets of moral ideas, the theory goes further and asserts that these differences may in fact be significant, and that the very same kind of action which is right in one country or period may be wrong in another. The advocates of ethical relativism appear to be most adamant that moral standards differ between groups, within a single culture, between cultures, and across time. They also believe that the ethical systems of belief supporting those moral standards of behaviour will differ according to the time and circumstance, as will ethical behaviour.

A critique of the literature in business ethics highlights a significant research deficit – that while interest has centred predominantly on descriptive research the newer perspective of cross-cultural ethical research and investigation of the strength of ethical relativity have received relatively little attention.

To conclude, to view business ethics as simply operating within the law is far too simplistic; nor should one view ethical issues as lofty and pious matters that affect merely an individual's reputation. Rather, an internal and external perspective should be taken. Internally, corporations need to raise the general level of ethical awareness as well as to isolate specific areas which pose potential ethical pitfalls within the business environment, e.g., the gaining of competitor information. Externally, corporations should be conscious of differing cultural perceptions in the ethical arena if successful transactions are to be initiated and accomplished. Company image, performance, international trade, and the degree of government intervention are all bound to a discussion of business ethics, and it is hoped that in the future, empirical examination, discussion, and practical proposals will ensue.

Given the growth in the number of multinational organisations and the increased expansion of world trade there appears an evidential need for more detailed cross-cultural empirical investigations. Fortunately this need for more extensive cross-cultural research has been recognised and, as De George has commented from the American perspective, "the growth of multinationals and the closer integration of U.S. and non-U.S. firms makes all the more necessary the development of business ethics on an international scale" (De George, 1987, p. 209). Clearly Asia is an area of growing importance in international trade and yet only a limited number of general ethics studies have now been conducted in the Asia-Pacific Region. In regard to Asia, Wong referred to the "dearth of systematic studies" in this field, and declared, "Chinese business ideology is largely an uncharted field" (Wong, 1983, p.137).

Over the last decade a limited number of general ethical attitudinal studies have started to emerge in the Asia-Pacific region; however, considerable effort is still needed in order for the literature in business ethics to go further than generalised statements of distaste that merely lament the erosion of ethical standards in business, or sermonise on the consequences of increasing unethical behaviour. While this type of discussion may initially prompt ethical awareness, such an inactive stance is hardly conducive in a formal sense to disciplined academic research, data evaluation, and theory development. What is needed in ethical research is a building on existing methodologies and findings, and the expansion of research efforts to ensure the accuracies of research conclusions, particularly in differing cultures.

(It should be noted that while the term businessmen has been used throughout this paper, some women responded to the Australian Survey. All Hong Kong respondents were male.)

V. Appendix

Questionnaire

General Instructions

This questionnaire requests you to contemplate each of the following statements, relate it to your own work situation and respond as frankly as possible.

Example

If you strongly agree with the statement, you would circle 9. If you strongly disagree with the statement, you would circle 1. If your disagreement lies somewhere in between these extremes, circle the number which best describes this. Use as much of the scale as possible and please circle one number for each statement.

Strongly Disagree				Neutral				Strongly Agree
1	2	3	4	5	6	7	8	9

Please ensure that you answer the three sections and all questions within each section.

Section One

In this section, please indicate the degree of your personal agreement or disagreement with the following hypothetical situations.

You produce/hold an account for an anti-dandruff shampoo that is effective

55

with one application. Your assistant points out that the product would turnover faster if the instructions on the label recommended two applications. To the recommendation of two applications, would you:

Strongly Disagree				Neutral			Strongly Agree	
1	2	3	4	5	6	7	8	9

1. You are interviewing a former product manager/account executive who just left a strong competitor company with similar product interests. He is similar in qualification and experience to other candidates and he would be more than happy to tell you all the competitor's plans for the coming year. To the proposal to hire him, would you:

Strongly Disagree				Neutral			Strongly Agree	
1	2	3	4	5	6	7	8	9

2. Your client is/you are sales manager in an encyclopaedia company. In discussing sales approaches, a common way for a company salesman to get into houses is to pretend they are taking a survey. After they finish the survey, they switch to their sales pitch. This technique seems to be very effective and is used by most of the competition. It has been suggested that this technique should be used. Would you agree to the adoption of this technique?

Strongly Disagree				Neutral			Strongly Agree	
1	2	3	4	5	6	7	8	9

3. You have to make a choice between two advertising campaigns outlined by your agency for a new product. The first (A) is soft sell, honest, informational campaign. The second (B) involves a noisy, irritating commercial that is sure to gain audience attention. Interestingly, the preliminary tests show the second (B) commercial is more effective. Would you agree to sue the second (B) commercial?

Strongly Disagree				Neutral			Strongly Agree	
1	2	3	4	5	6	7	8	9

4. Due to the nature of your work, it is possible to take longer than normal lunch breaks, depart early or occasionally conduct personal business on company time. Do you agree that this is acceptable?

Strongly Disagree				Neutral			Strongly Agree	
1	2	3	4	5	6	7	8	9

5. An unusually perceptive junior member of your organisation was assigned to you for your direction in investigating a specific area of concern to your company. Upon completion of the highly commendable study, you present

the findings to upper management/client, but make no mention of the junior's contribution. Under these circumstances, do you agree that this is acceptable?

Strongly Disagree				Neutral				Strongly Agree
1	2	3	4	5	6	7	8	9

6. In relation to your own work scheduling, do you agree with the axiom that work expands to fit the time available?

Strongly Disagree				Neutral				Strongly Agree
1	2	3	4	5	6	7	8	9

7. The R & D department has modernised one of your products. It is not really "new and improved", but you know that putting this statement on the packaging and in current advertising will increase sales. Do you agree that the "new and improved" statement should be used?

Strongly Disagree				Neutral				Strongly Agree
1	2	3	4	5	6	7	8	9

8. Due to the position you hold in the company, you are provided with an expense account. One of the unique aspects of your own work situation is that you feel no guilt in using the expense account to take an occasional non-business associate out to dinner.

Strongly Disagree				Neutral				Strongly Agree
1	2	3	4	5	6	7	8	9

10. You have heard that a competitor has a new product feature that will make a big difference in sales. The competitor will have a hospitality suite at the annual trade show and unveil this feature at a party thrown for the dealers. You can easily send a snooper to this meeting to learn what the product advantage is. It is suggested that your company would send a snooper to this meeting. To this you would:

Strongly Disagree				Neutral				Strongly Agree
1	2	3	4	5	6	7	8	9

11. At your personal recommendation, your company/client invests considerable resources in a creative new media form. Later, you discover that the new media was by no means as effective or cost-efficient as you originally anticipated. The error is easily recognised as yours, but if brought to the attention of others, further losses could be avoided. Do you feel this information should be made available to your company colleagues/client?

Strongly Disagree				Neutral				Strongly Agree
1	2	3	4	5	6	7	8	9

12. Recently, a colleague in your company conducted some market research. Upon conclusion of the study, it was found that the response rate was too low and consequently no valid conclusions could be drawn. Your colleague is expected to present his findings in an extensive report to parties external to the firm. In his discussions with you, he mentions his intentions to slightly modify the results in an effort to gain credibility. Do you agree with his intentions?

Strongly Disagree				Neutral				Strongly Agree
1	2	3	4	5	6	7	8	9

13. You have a chance to win a big contract/account that will mean a lot to you and your company. The person with whom you are dealing has hinted they will be influenced by a "gift" or any "special deals". With finance at your disposal, your assistant recommends sending a colour television or making other arrangements. Do you agree with your assistant?

Strongly Disagree				Neutral				Strongly Agree
1	2	3	4	5	6	7	8	9

References

Abratt, R., D. Nel and N.S. Higgs, 1992, "An Examination of the Ethical Beliefs of Managers Using Selected Scenarios in a Cross-Cultural Environment", *Journal of Business Ethics,* Vol. 11, pp. 29–35

Armstrong, R.W., 1992, "An Empirical Investigation of International Marketing Ethics: Problems Encountered by Australian Firms. *Journal of Business Ethics.* Vol. 11, pp. 161–73

—, B.W. Stening, J.K. Ryans, L. Marks and M. Mayo, 1990, "International Marketing Ethics: Problems Encountered by Australian Firms", *Asia Pacific Journal of International Marketing*, Vol. 2, No. (2), pp. 6–15

—, C.F. Chan, N.B. Holbert and T. Pecotich, 1991, "An Exploration of Ethical Perceptions of Hong Kong International Marketing Managers: Their Attitudes Toward the Organisation, Industry and Country", *Hong Kong Journal of Business Management*, Vol. 9, pp. 75–90

Asian Images 3, 1993, "A Study of Business Practices and Corporate Images in Asia", *Far Eastern Economic Review.* Hong Kong

COMPARATIVE ETHICAL PERCEPTIONS

Baumhart, R.C., 1961, "How Ethical are Businessmen?", *Harvard Business Review*, July-August, pp. 6–31

Benton, S., 1986, "Do Commercial Ethics Still Exist?", *Computer Control Quarterly*, Spring, pp. 40–4

Bommer, Michael, *et al.*, 1987, "A Behaviour Model of Ethical and Methodological Decision Making", *Journal of Business Ethics*, Vol. 6, pp. 265–80

Breakspear, Ken, 1987, "Pirates or Planners? A Spotlight on Ethics" (for financial planners), *Chartered Accountant in Australia*, Vol. 57, June, p. 50

Brenner, S.N., and E.A. Molander, 1977, "Is the Ethics of Business Changing?", *Harvard Business Review*, Vol. 55, No. 1, pp. 57–76

Chan, C.F., K.F. Lau and P.K. Ip, 1988, 1991, "Factors Affecting Business Ethics: An Exploratory Study in Hong Kong", in *Proceedings of the 1988 AIB Southeast Asia Regional Conference*, Chira Hongladarom, Vatchareeya Thosanguan, Preecha Jarungidanan and Kulpatra Wethyavivorn (eds.), Bangkok, Thammasat University

—, and K.H. Lee, 1986, "Organisational Culture and Salesperson's Ethical Position", in *Proceedings of the Academy of International Business SEA Regional Conference*, R.T. Hsieh and S. Scherling (eds.), Taipei, National Chiao Tung University

De George, R.T., 1987, "The Status of Business Ethics Past and Future", *Journal of Business Ethics*, Vol. 6, pp. 201–11

Dolecheck, M.M., and C.C. Dolecheck, 1987, "Business Ethics: A Comparison of Attitudes of Managers in Hong Kong and the United States", *The Hong Kong Manager*, April-May, pp. 28–43

Drucker, P., 1981, "What is Business Ethics?", *The Public Interest*, Vol. 64, Spring, p. 18

Dubinsky, A.J., M.A. Jolson, M. Kotabe and C.U. Lim, 1991, "A Cross National Investigation of Industrial Salespeople's Ethical Perceptions", *Journal of International Business Studies*, Fourth Quarter, Vol. 22, No. 4, pp. 651–70

England, G.W., 1975, *The Manager and his Values: An International Perspective*, Cambridge, Ballinger Publishing

Ferrell, O.C., and K.M. Weaver, 1978, "Ethical Beliefs of Marketing Managers", *Journal of Marketing*, July, pp. 69–73

— and D. Krugman, 1981, "The Organisational Ethics of Advertising: Corporate and Agency Views", *Journal of Advertising*, Vol. 10, pp. 21–30

Hegarty, W.H., and H. Sims, 1979, "Organisational Philosophy, Policies, and Objectives Related to Unethical Behaviour: A Laboratory Experiment", *Journal of Applied Psychology*, Vol. 64, pp. 331–8

Hennessy, E., 1987, "An Agenda for Business Ethics", *Australian Accountant*, Vol. 57, April, pp. 40–3

Hofstede, G., 1980, *Culture's Consequences*, Beverly Hills, CA, Sage Publication

Kam Hon Lee, 1980, "Ethical Beliefs in Business in Hong Kong", *The Hong Kong Manager*, June, pp. 8–13

— 1981, "Ethical Beliefs in Marketing Management: A Cross Cultural Study", *European Journal of Marketing*, Vol. 15. No. 1, pp. 58–67

Kelly, C., 1985, "Do Accounting Students Perceive Ethical Situations in the Same Way as Practitioners?", *Chartered Accountant in Australia*, Vol. 55, No. 7, February, 36–9

Kotler, P., 1972, *Marketing Management Analysis, Planning and Control*, (2nd ed.), New Jersey, Prentice-Hall

Lee, C., 1986, "Ethics Training: Facing the Tough Questions", *Training*, Vol. 30, March, pp. 30–40

Lynch, A., 1985, "Getting Integrity Back into Management", *Rydges*, December, p. 49

McCaughey, D., 1986, "Ethics at the Growing Edge of Medicine", *Australian Health Review*, Vol. 9, April, pp. 243–50

McDonald, G.M., and R.A. Zepp, 1988a, "Ethical Perceptions of Hong Kong Chinese Business Managers", *Journal of Business Ethics*, Vol. 7, pp. 835–45

— and R.A. Zepp, 1988b, "Business Ethics: Practical Proposals", *Journal of Management Development*, Vol. 8, No. 1, pp. 55–6

Mehta, S.C., and Kau Ah Keng, 1984, "Marketing Executive's Perceptions of Unethical Practices: An Empirical Investigation of Singapore Managers", *Singapore Management Review*, Vol. 6, No. 2, pp. 25–35

Newstrom, J.W., and W.A. Ruch, 1975, "The Ethics of Management and the Management of Ethics", *M.S.U Business Topics*, Winter, Vol. 23, pp. 29–37

Pitt, L.F., and R. Abratt, 1986, "Corruption in Business – Are Management Attitudes Right?", *Journal of Business Ethics*, Vol. 5, No. 1, pp. 39–44

Preble, J.F., and A. Reichel, 1988, "Attitudes Towards Business Ethics of Future Managers in the U.S. and Israel", *Journal of Business Ethics*, Vol. 12, pp. 941–9

Road, T., 1985, "The Ethical Values of US and Australian Journalists", *Australian Journalism Review*, Vol. 7, pp. 19–21

Small, M.W., 1992, "Attitudes Toward Business Ethics Held by Western Australian Students: A Comparative Study", *Journal of Business Ethics*, Vol. 11. pp. 745–52

Swanton, C., 1987, "The Rationality of Ethical Intuitionism", *Australian Journal of Philosophy*, Vol. 65, No. 2, pp. 172–81

Tyson, T., 1992, "Does Believing that Everyone Else is Less Ethical Have an Impact on Work Behaviour?", *Journal of Business Ethics*, Vol. 11, pp. 707–17

White, L.P., and M.J. Rhodeback, 1992, "Ethical Dilemmas in Organisation Development: A Cross- Cultural Analysis", *Journal of Business Ethics*, Vol. 11, pp. 663–70

Williams, K., 1985, "Employee Dishonesty in Business", *Business Bulletin*, December, pp. 29–32

Wong Siu-lun, 1983, "Ideology of Chinese Industrial Managers in Hong Kong", *Journal of the Royal Asiatic Society* (Hong Kong Branch), Vol. 23, pp. 136–71

Chapter 4

Ethical Challenges of the Market for Health Care

FRANCES K.Y. WONG AND RANCE P.L. LEE

I. Introduction

The introduction of market mechanisms to the system of health-care services has emerged as a major trend in many countries around the world. This is mainly due to the steeply rising cost of health care in recent decades. Progress in medical technology and the growth in health-care demand are key factors in the escalation of medical costs, which has far outrun the general increase in cost of living (Coe, 1970, Chapter 13). In many countries, the ever-rising cost of health care has made an increasing number of people unable to obtain adequate care for their health needs. It has also made it increasingly difficult for governments to finance public sector health-care services.

A widely accepted method of containing the rising cost is to create a competitive market for health-care services (Roemer, 1989; Hay, 1992). It is expected that market forces would increase competition in the health-care sector, resulting in proper pricing of health-care services and productive utilisation of the limited resources for health care. In other words, competitive market forces could help to enhance the cost-effectiveness of health-care services.

The market approach may be an effective way of rationalising the organisation and delivery of health-care services, and may thus contribute to the containment of medical costs. However, whether or not this would improve the "efficiency" of health-care services is a matter that requires further investigation (Williams, 1992). The question is: efficiency for what? To improve efficiency, one must contain medical costs, but one must also ensure that the methods to be used allow the different segments of the population to have their health needs adequately met. The purpose of this paper is to argue that even if competitive market forces can help to improve the cost-effectiveness of health-care services, they fail to ensure that the needs of people can be adequately met by the health-care providers in a complex modern society.

II. Health-care Reform in Hong Kong

Hong Kong has emerged as a modern industrial city in the Asia-Pacific region. Its recent reform in health care can be used as a case illustrating the problems arising from the introduction of market mechanisms to the health-care sector.

For many decades, the government of Hong Kong has cherished the policy that no one should be denied adequate medical treatment through lack of means. As a result, a comprehensive range of medical and health-care services are subsidised by public funds and are provided to the public at low-charges (see Hong Kong Government, 1993). For instance, a patient in the general ward of a public hospital is charged $43 a day, while a consultation at general outpatient clinics costs $21.

The private sector of health care in Hong Kong also provides a wide range of both outpatient and institutional care. As of 1993, about 11 per cent of the 27,038 hospital beds and almost 58 per cent of the 6,493 registered doctors were in the private sector. In general, private health-care services in Hong Kong are of good standard and would compare favourably with those in many OECD countries. However, while the fees charged for public health-care services are very low, the fees charged by private physicians and private hospitals are among the highest in the world (Hay, 1992; Hong Kong Government, 1993). As pointed out by Hay (1992), this indicates the existence of an anti-competitive market structure in the private health-care sector of Hong Kong.

In recent years, there have been rising concerns about the substantial increase in medical costs in both public and private sectors. It was estimated that public expenditure on health care had increased three times over the five years from 1987/88 to 1992/93 (Hong Kong Government, 1993). Public health-care spending in Hong Kong is now roughly 6 per cent of the GDP, which is similar to the levels of spending in many OECD countries (Hay, 1992). Nevertheless, both the government and the people have been proud of the fact that Hong Kong residents generally maintain a good level of health. As of 1993, the crude death rate was 5.1 per 1000 population; the infant mortality rate was 4.7 per 1000 live births; the maternal mortality rate was 0.04 per 1000 total births. Nowadays, the average life expectancy at birth is around 75 years for males and nearly 81 years for females. These vital statistics suggest that the health of Hong Kong residents is among the best in the world.

The good health of Hong Kong people could be due to a number of extra-medical factors, such as the traditional Chinese lifestyle and the substantial economic progress in Hong Kong since the early 1970s. The contribution of the health-care service system, however, cannot be ignored. As mentioned above, the government provides a comprehensive range of low-charge health-care services for all people. The economically better-off can also choose to use the more convenient and more comfortable, though much more expensive, private health-care services.

The vital statistics mentioned above are indicators of the objective health status of the general population in Hong Kong. How do people subjectively assess their own health? And how do they evaluate the health-care services in Hong Kong? From the end of 1992 to the middle of 1993, a Hong Kong-wide survey was conducted by Lee, one of the authors of the present paper. A random sample of 361 Chinese residents aged 18 and over was successfully interviewed. From the preliminary results, nearly six out of 10 respondents were very satisfied or satisfied with their health conditions, whereas only one out of 10 respondents felt dissatisfied or very dissatisfied. Similarly, over one half of the respondents perceived that their health status was very good or good, while about one-third considered their health fair and less than one-tenth considered it poor. These survey data together with the previously reported vital statistics firmly indicate that Hong Kong residents generally enjoy a good level of health both objectively and subjectively.

Meanwhile, the people of Hong Kong tend to be quite happy with the current health-care services. The above-mentioned 1992-93 survey revealed that about four out of 10 respondents were very satisfied or satisfied with the health-care services, while less than three out of 10 felt dissatisfied or very dissatisfied. Respondents were also asked to assess the seriousness of various social problems in Hong Kong, including the problems of youth, environmental pollution, the elderly, law and order, morality, housing, the brain-drain (i.e. the loss of professionals through emigration), transportation, social welfare, and education. It was found that only two out of five persons considered the medical and health problem a very serious or serious problem. More important, the

63

medical and health problem was ranked as one of the least serious social problems in Hong Kong.

The medical and health-care system in Hong Kong appears to have performed quite well. Among the general population, there is a high level of satisfaction with their own health status and with the existing health-care services. Nevertheless, as mentioned above, the sharp rise in medical costs has come to make the government and the public increasingly concerned with the effectiveness of the present organisation of health-care services for meeting the changing needs and the growing demands for health care. Attempts have been made to reform the present system of health-care services (Thong, 1987).

In a recent consultation paper, the Hong Kong government (1993) suggests five possible options for restructuring the financing of public health-care services. They are (1) the percentage subsidy approach, (2) the target group approach, (3) the co-ordinated voluntary insurance approach, (4) the compulsory comprehensive insurance approach, and (5) the prioritisation of treatment approach. While these options have yet to be decided, the government has already taken some action to reform the health-care service structure.

One of the most serious attempts was initiated in 1984. The government invited a consultant panel to review the hospital sector, as it was apparently the most expensive area with the most rapidly increasing costs in the health-care service system. A report was prepared for public consultation in March 1986. Major suggestions were directed towards the development of the Hospital Authority as an independent statutory body to integrate and control all public hospitals in Hong Kong. It was expected that new management initiatives would be introduced for better utilisation of health-care resources.

The Provisional Hospital Authority was formed in 1989, and then the Hospital Authority was established in December 1990. *Cost-effectiveness* has been the catchword throughout, and a market strategy is to be adopted. This policy was reconfirmed and elaborated in the 1994 Hospital Authority Convention. In his opening address to the Convention, the Governor of Hong Kong highlighted the need for market mechanisms in achieving the objective of quality health care. It was strongly believed that a freely operating market would be the most efficient mechanism for identifying the needs of patients and for directing resources to meet those needs (Hospital Authority, 1994). Strategic directions were thus pledged towards the efficient use of resources. Value-for-money was defined as an essential component of "best practice" (Yeoh, 1994).

The change in government policy makes the adoption of market incentives for health-care services imminent. In the framework of a market economy, the value of health needs to be converted to measurable economic terms. This policy, however, gives rise to a battery of ethical questions: Should the value of health be priced? Are the clients genuine consumers in the health-care market? Do the clients know what they need? Can the clients freely choose what they want even if they know what they need? And, if the clients were given a free choice of what they want, what would be the social consequences?

III. The Price of Health

When we say something is priceless, we normally mean that its value is too great to be measured in any terms. If something can be priced, then its value is finite, no matter how high a price we are willing to pay (Kelman, 1992). The introduction of a competitive market for health-care services requires that all the costs and benefits related to health and health care are measurable and can be expressed in monetary terms. Health and human life do not enjoy a priceless status. They are evaluated and priced for market exchange and for determining the efficiency of the health-care system. The question is: How do we assess the value of a person's life?

There are at least four possible methods for estimating the value of life: (1) the expected future earnings of the person concerned; (2) the expected losses to others due to the person's death; (3) the value placed by the person on his own life, such as the insurance premium one is willing to pay for; and (4) the value placed on the life of the individual by the existing policies and practices in society (MacIntyre, 1992). In other words, the value of a person's life depends upon one's ability to earn, one's own value of life, one's contribution to others, or the will of policy makers. When individuals differ in value of life, they do not have equal rights to health and health-care services. In a health-care system guided by competitive market forces, the rights of health care are more for those who are able and willing to pay for it, or for those who are highly valued by others. The health economists who argue for the market approach to health care are, in effect, philosophers on the value of human life. Their proposals to solve health-care problems by maximising benefits and minimising costs represent a classic answer given by utilitarians (Kelman, 1992).

Is utilitarianism an adequate principle for organising and providing health-care services? When the principle underlying health-care policies is reduced to economic rationality as in utilitarianism, it is cost-effectiveness rather than health itself that becomes the major concern. However, whether or not cost-effectiveness can ensure good health for people depends a great deal on the existence of a competitive market truly based on supply and demand. The question is: Can patients be "genuine" consumers in the market of health-care services?

The classic law of supply and demand does not fully operate in the health-care market, for it is doubtful if the clients are genuine consumers. Some patient-consumers are covered by insurance. They should be more accurately called claimants, as they are concerned with their rights more than the price of health-care services. More important, a vast majority of Hong Kong residents are not covered by health insurance. When they are sick, they cannot afford to take time and to shop around just for bargains. They tend to spend as much and as fast as they can to maintain health, especially in times of serious illness.

Furthermore, the patient-clients are generally not in the position to decide on what they need. They are expected to rely on the technical judgment and advice of the health-care providers. Even if they know what they need, can they have complete freedom of choice in the health-care service sector?

IV. Freedom of Choice in Health Care

Besides the cost-benefit consideration, another justification for the development of a market system is personal freedom in the exchange of goods and services. In a truly competitive market, individuals are presumably allowed to have complete freedom in the choice of goods or services. Personal autonomy is generally regarded as an ethical appeal of the market system, as it promises to result in the greatest utility of outcome (Gillroy, 1992). To what extent can this be honoured in the health-care market?

In many modern industrial societies, including Hong Kong, health policy-makers have become the sovereign princes in the health-care empire. They constitute the most powerful group for making assessments and decisions on the wealth-maximising allocations in the health-care system (Gillroy, 1992). What the Hong Kong Hospital Authority has claimed to do is an example. The Authority has explicitly proclaimed itself to act as a health-care purchaser and as a consumer advocate (Hospital Authority, 1994). It sees itself "equipped with information and knowledge of health-care products, as well as expertise in evaluating quality of health care" (Yeoh, 1994). It could thus help consumers to get the best possible value for money. Because of this proclaimed knowledge and expertise, the health policy-makers have gained the legitimacy in health care to dominate the presumably less informed lay public.

ETHICAL CHALLENGES OF THE MARKET FOR HEALTH CARE

In capitalist societies, the power of control over health affairs has been traditionally in the hands of health elites, i.e. the medical practitioners (Freidson, 1986). It has come to be increasingly shared by the business corporations and executives who claim to act as purchasers and advocators of health care. This is a natural result of introducing market incentives to health-care services. However, it is conceivable that these business elites will work with the health elites to form an elite alliance to control the health-care system and to shape the health-care market for their own material interests. In the health-care market, the prospects for patient-consumers to fully exercise their personal autonomy is not as promising as it appears. The choice is limited to what is for sale or what is bestowed on them.

The alliance of business elites and health elites is a dominant force in the health-care market of many modern industrial societies. It has been referred to as the "new medical-industrial complex" (Relman, 1980). Unfortunately, these elites tend to be so preoccupied with medical efficacy and cost-effectiveness that they may not duly recognise the importance of cultural factors in the choice and utilisation of health-care services. As social scientists, we consider it important for the health-care providers to realise the close relationship between culture and medicine. In particular, it should be recognised that the cultural tradition in society plays a key role in defining what the patients should do for their health and illnesses (Kleinman, 1980). To illustrate this point, let us examine two health-care issues in the Chinese community of Hong Kong. One is patient non-compliance, and the other is medical pluralism.

1. The Problem of Patient Non-compliance

In its Patients' Chapter, the Hospital Authority (1993) of Hong Kong clearly states that it is a responsibility of the patients to "follow the prescribed and agreed treatment plan, and conscientiously comply with the instructions given". If a patient does not follow the prescription or advice of the medical practitioner, he would be labelled non-compliant. Non-compliance is a form of deviance, which is regarded by medical practitioners as undesirable behaviour; it may be harmful to the patient's health. Such behaviour, however, has been quite prevalent in the Chinese community of Hong Kong (Lee, 1994).

It should be emphasised that the interpretation of illness lies ultimately in the patient himself, not the practitioners of medicine. What the illness means to the patient and what he should do about it depend upon not only what he has learned from doctors, but also the cultural tradition in which he was brought up. Wong, one of the authors of this paper, has been a lecturer in nursing in

Hong Kong. An encounter her student reported in a clinical case discussion can be employed to illustrate this argument.

A woman contracted tuberculosis. She went to a chest clinic for treatment at a rather late stage. The initial reaction of the clinical staff was anger. The client was blamed for the delay in seeking treatment, as not only herself but also her family members might be infected. The woman had three children, including a new-born baby who had suffered from recurrent fever. The woman explained that the health of her baby took precedence over her own health. Her obligation to take care of the baby as well as the family as a whole deferred her decision to seek medical help. Of course, little did she realise the impact of her disease on herself and her family members. Nevertheless, her behaviour is understandable, for the ideal of womanhood in Chinese culture is to serve as an able and virtuous wife and also a loving and supportive mother. She is expected to take care of all the household work without complaints and to protect her children even at the expense of her own wellbeing.

The contribution of cultural factors to patient non-compliance can also be illustrated by the findings of a random sample survey of 550 adult residents in the urban areas of Hong Kong (Lee, 1982a). It was found that doctor-shopping behaviour, a form of patient non-compliance, was quite prevalent among the Chinese. As many as 64 per cent of the respondents reported that they frequently or sometimes switched from one doctor to another without professional referral. More important, such behaviour was closely associated with the long tradition in Chinese culture of treasuring family cohesion and social relations. It was also affected by the deep-rooted cultural belief in "*yuan*", i.e., predestined affinity. More than two-fifths of the respondents would consult their friends and relatives about what medicine to take or which doctor to see when they were sick. About half of the respondents believed that a doctor's success or failure in treating a patient would depend upon not only his technical competency but also his affinity with the patient. The survey results indicated that both the dependency on lay advice and the belief in affinity were factors contributing to the widespread existence of doctor-shopping behaviour among Hong Kong Chinese.

Apparently, the interpretation of illness varies among individual patients, depending upon their social and cultural backgrounds. It should also be pointed out that individuals are active, capable and creative agents in the understanding of their own situations and in the pursuit of their own interests. The interpretation of illness is, therefore, not static. In the process of seeking medical interventions, patients may continually reinterpret professional advice and medical treatments in order to suit their own life situations and cultural beliefs. Their ideas about health and illnesses are formulated in a dynamic, interactive process, shaped and re-shaped particularly by their significant others. To many patients, the professional health workers are significant others, but so are their family members, neighbours, co-workers and close friends. Patients may also learn from mass media and from their past illness experiences.

The social world in which the patients live and work with others provide them with a cultural framework for understanding their health and illness conditions (Hunt, Jordan and Irwin, 1989; Donovan and Blake, 1992). The advice of doctors is only one of the many factors in their decisions on how an illness should be dealt with. Their own cultural beliefs and the opinions of their friends and relatives may make them consciously or unconsciously deviate from the doctor's instruction. It is these patients who are portrayed by the medical regime as non-compliants.

In a competitive market system, patient-consumers are expected to make rational decisions on the use of health-care services. The question is: What is a "rational" decision? It has been suggested that a decision is rational if it "appraises the likely consequences of alternative courses of action and chooses the course of action that leads to the most desirable or least undesirable consequences" (Hoffmaster, 1990). In the views of health professionals, patients are rational if they follow professional instructions and keep on using the seemingly most cost-effective medicine for treating their illnesses. Patient non-compliance is thus labelled by health professionals as a kind of irrational behaviour.

Health and illness are matters of important concern to individuals. Naturally, patient-consumers would do their best to make rational decisions on the use of health-care services. Patient non-compliance, however, has been a recurrent behaviour in Hong Kong for many decades. This fact indicates that what is defined as irrational or abnormal by the health professionals may be considered by the patients as rational or normal activity. This is because to many patients, a rational decision involves more than economic rationality and professional-medical judgment. It has to take into account their special social situations and their deep-rooted cultural beliefs. To develop a health-care service system that is based on professional judgment and cost-effectiveness can hardly do justice to patient-consumers.

2. The State of Medical Pluralism

A number of studies in recent years (Lee, 1980; Koo, 1987; Wong, Wong and Donnon, 1993) have consistently revealed that the Chinese in Hong Kong tend to use modern Western health-care services, particularly in the initial stage of illness. However, many of them also use traditional Chinese health-care services during the same or different episodes of illness, particularly when they are suffering from chronic or terminal diseases. This is the case among different sex, age, educational and income groups. The existence of pluralistic health-care practices has been a fact of life in Hong Kong, despite the rapid modernisation and Westernisation of social and economic life. Can this be regarded as a sign of freedom of choice in the health-care sector of Hong Kong?

Western medicine and Chinese medicine have coexisted in the territory of Hong Kong, with their distinct systems of concepts, skills and organisation of services. However, as Lee (1982b) has pointed out, the health-care service sector in Hong Kong is not just pluralistic; it is in the form of "hierarchical pluralism". Traditional Chinese medical practices have been widespread throughout the territory and have been widely utilised by the Chinese residents, but Western medicine has been superior to Chinese medicine in terms of all the major dimensions of hierarchy, i.e. power, prestige, and wealth.

The lack of government support for Chinese medicine seems to have played the most crucial role in the formation of a hierarchical pluralistic health-care structure in Hong Kong. Up to now, the government has not provided nor subsidised any Chinese health-care services. The government has also been reluctant to regulate the practice of Chinese medicine. Any person can practice Chinese medicine and any shop can sell Chinese medicinal materials. As a consequence, there are numerous practitioners of Chinese medicine with varying qualifications. Chinese medicinal materials are also of varying qualities, some of which may be toxic and hazardous to health.

There have been social pressures on the government to exert control over Chinese health-care services. But, as David Combes (1985), a former Secretary of the Medical Examination Board, has rightly explained, the reluctance of the government to interfere with the various practices of Chinese medicine is due to a clause in the 1840 Nanjing Treaty between Britain and China. The clause stated that the customs and usages of the Chinese people in the Colony of Hong Kong would be preserved and not disturbed. As Chinese medicine is part of Chinese customs and usages, it has been allowed to exist without intervention by the colonial government. Moreover, as Combes has also pointed out, in many quarters it is still felt that Chinese healers should have the right to practice and that the public should be free to choose a form of medicine – Western or Chinese – when they get sick.

Pluralistic health-seeking behaviour among Chinese patients could be due to deep-rooted cultural beliefs (Lee, 1994). For instance, the Chinese concept of equilibrium and harmony may encourage patients to believe that the various forms of Chinese and Western health-care services are complementary to each other, rather than mutually exclusive, in the treatment of illness. The traditional belief in predestined affinity may make Chinese patients try out both Western doctors and Chinese healers in order to find one with the "affinity" to treat the illness. Pluralistic health-seeking behaviour may also be facilitated by the great dependency on lay referral, as different laymen may recommend different health practitioners or medicinal materials. Whatever the reasons, the widespread consumption of Chinese medicine and particularly the varying qualities of both practitioners and medicinal materials deserve serious consideration by health policy-makers.

The government's non-interference policy concerning Chinese medicine has recently been under challenge. Hong Kong is approaching the year 1997 and will soon become a Special Administrative Region of China. Article 138 in the Basic Law (drafted in 1990) of the Region stipulates that the Region shall, on its own, formulate policy to develop Western and Chinese medicine. The pressure on the government to take action was also aroused by an unfortunate incident in February 1989. A man and a woman lapsed into a coma after consuming poisonous herbal medicine. The incident was widely reported by the mass media.

As a result of political considerations and community concerns, the government decided to set up a Working Party on Chinese Medicine in August 1989. Its terms of reference are to examine the present practice of and training in Chinese medicine, including herbal medicine, acupuncture and bone-setting, and to identify any widespread abuse of Chinese medicinal materials in the community. It aims at finding measures for promoting the good practice of Chinese medicine and for preventing the abuse of Chinese medicinal materials. The public is generally in favour of the government's attempt to look into traditional Chinese medicine, as it may help to ensure the quality of both medical practices and medicinal materials. The practitioners of Chinese medicine and their associations also welcome such a move by the government, as it may result in official recognition of their work.

The Working Party produced an Interim Report in October 1991, for the purpose of making further consultations with different segments of the community. The consultation period was supposed to end on 16 April 1992. By June 1994, the final report had yet to be released. A number of technical and political issues might be involved, making it difficult to arrive at a consensus. The criteria for registration and the mechanism for assessment of standards, for instance, are not easy to work out. It is envisaged that the practitioners of Chinese medicine will be involved in the formulation of a system of registration or regulation. But an adequate list of the numerous Chinese medical practitioners with varying qualifications has yet to be compiled, and the long-standing factionalism among the various groups of Chinese medical practitioners has to be skilfully resolved.

Whatever the difficulties involved, the government has to come up with a policy to ensure acceptable standards for both Chinese medical practitioners and Chinese medicinal materials. The government should also consider introducing Chinese medicine of high standard to the public sector of health care. Unless these steps are taken, the freedom given to patient-consumers in a competitive health-care market can hardly ensure safety and equity.

As mentioned above, the various forms of Chinese medical practices and the various kinds of Chinese medicinal materials are widely utilised by Chinese people in Hong Kong. When the patients have a felt need for Chinese medicine, they have to resort to the private sector. The public sector does not provide them with low-cost Chinese health-care services. The fees charged by Chinese medical practitioners and the costs of Chinese medicinal materials vary a great deal. But reputable practitioners of Chinese medicine and high-quality Chinese medicinal materials are usually too expensive for average people. In order to develop a health-care market in which patient-consumers can have free choice of adequate services, the government must move to support and control the various forms of traditional Chinese health-care services as soon as possible.

3. Social Consequences of Free Choice

In a market situation, consumers should have the right to choose whatever products or services they want and can pay for. In the market for health care, however, such freedom of choice by consumers may cause undesirable and even disastrous consequences for society. The establishment of the Gender Choice Centre in Hong Kong in 1993 can serve as an example.

The Centre operates as a commercial undertaking. It is difficult for its work to be clinically monitored, because there is no guiding code of practice enforced by the community. The operation of this Centre gives rise to at least two ethical concerns. One is directly associated with the process of gender selection. The other is related to the endeavour of turning a health matter into a business venture.

An apparent issue arising from people's pursuit of gender selection is: What should or could be done if the selection process goes wrong (Leong, 1993)? In this situation, a battery of questions may be asked. For instance, how should a foetus of unwanted gender be treated? Should the pregnancy be terminated?

Can the disappointed consumers file their complaints and demand compensation? Where can they do that? These are some of the questions that have to be resolved by the government in consultation with health professionals and the lay public. Ethical codes and regulations need to be well-formulated to monitor both the providers and the consumers of gender selection.

A more fundamental question about gender selection is: Should we simply take it as a choice of the couples who can afford it in the free market of health care? Or, should we take it as a complex issue that could affect the welfare of the entire society? We are of the opinion that gender selection should not be treated as an individual choice, for its implications for society can be far-reaching. Free choice in the gender of babies is likely to be, for instance, disruptive to human ecology. In many contemporary societies, including Hong Kong, people generally prefer boy to girl babies. Personal freedom in the selection of gender would lead to the male population greatly outnumbering the female population, at least in the foreseeable future.

As the above example has illustrated, the selection of gender ought to be constrained by social and ethical considerations. The stability and growth of our society is likely to be jeopardised if the choice is to be decided entirely by economically motivated providers and those consumers who can afford it in the free and competitive market of health-care services.

Equity is another issue of concern. The turning of a health matter into a business venture by the Gender Choice Centre is a natural process in a capitalist society emphasising market incentives. Under the ideology of capitalism, whoever can afford it should have the privilege of obtaining what they want, including the gender of one's baby. In a capitalist society, health-care organisations could and should perform a profit-making function. What is at issue is that the price of a product or service in a market economy normally fluctuates according to the golden rule of supply and demand. It is the economically better-off who are better able to obtain what they want, especially those goods or services that are in limited supply such as the service for gender selection. Average people and particularly the poor can hardly afford to choose what they want, including the gender of their offspring. The introduction of a free market for health-care services may, in some instances such as gender selection, function to reinforce and perpetuate inequality in society (Waitizkin, 1983).

Furthermore, in a society with a general preference for boys, is it fair or right to allow the economically advantaged segments to have a greater proportion of males than the under-privileged classes? How would this affect the future form, especially the class structure, of our society in the next few decades? These are also issues that deserve our reflection before introducing a market system for health-care services. The case of gender selection indicates

73

that the social consequences of market forces have to be well thought out, in addition to their contribution to cost-effectiveness in health care.

V. An Ethical Framework for Health Care

The system of health-care services in modern industrial society has become increasingly complex. It has been moving from a single physician model to a multiple professional model involving a team of general and specialised physicians plus a number of other health professionals. An increasing number of patients are now treated in a comprehensive hospital setting rather than an isolated outpatient clinic. Of no less importance is the emergence of the so-called "new medical-industrial complex" (Relman, 1980) involving not only health elites but also business elites. The ever-increasing complexity of the health-care sector makes the consideration of medical ethics a complex task in modern industrial society (Jonsen and Hellegers, 1976). Nevertheless, we will venture to outline a conceptual scheme for considering medical ethics. The scheme consists of three orders of ethics.

The first order of ethics is related to the conduct of the physician and his obligation to the patient. It corresponds to the theory of virtue and the theory of duty. The theory of virtue is a discourse about moral characters, such as honesty and benevolence. It prescribes what is required of a medical practitioner. The theory of duty includes the conditions, the intentions and the consequences of medical practice. The point of interest is centred on the interactions of medical practitioners with the sick and their families. Questions commonly asked on this level include: To treat or not to treat the patient? To inform or not to tell the truth?

The second order of ethics deals with the relationships among physicians and other health professionals. Traditionally, a typical therapeutic situation involves one physician and one patient, with the former playing an active role while the latter takes a passive attitude. This one-to-one and asymmetric therapeutic relationship is gradually fading away. The increased participation of patients and their family members as well as health professionals other than physicians has created a dilemma in therapeutic situations. For instance, the close relatives of a patient who has suffered brain-death may request that the respirator be removed. The attending doctor, seeing the continuing anguish of the patient's relatives, may agree to the request for terminating the artificial life support. However, he would be caught in a dilemma if his opinions were different from other members of the health-care team. Ethics are required for guiding the working relationships among physicians and other health professionals. This order of ethics entails the issues of power and prestige among the various types of health-care workers (Horacio, 1990). It would affect the decision to be made in regard to what constitutes adequate care for the patient.

The third order of ethics is related to the role of health institutions and the government. The growth of the new medical-industrial complex and the need for effective management of health-care services confound both the first and the second order of ethics. Clinicians who are committed to provide the best care for their patients are, for instance, finding themselves increasingly in a conflicting situation, as the hospital administrators or the government have become more determined to contain medical costs (Lidz and Mulvey, 1990).

Ethics are required in the setting up of social policies and institutional strategies for health care. This order of ethics corresponds to the theory of common good. Questions to be asked include, for instance, how should the limited health-care resources be distributed in society? Or, to what extent should cost-effectiveness be considered in dealing with patients of minimal life chances? These questions become more difficult to resolve, if the incident is politicised or if the concept of human rights is advocated. In a clash between individual interests and social values, institutional ethics will be called for. As Jonsen and Hellegers (1976) have rightly argued, institutions are "vehicles for the distribution of benefits and burdens of social life, and it is the function of the principles of justice to determine fair and equitable assignment of rights and duties and fair and equitable distribution of benefits and burdens".

The aforementioned three spheres of ethics should be considered concurrently and should be introduced to reinforce each other (Horacio, 1990). This is important, particularly in the present age of biomedical revolution. Technological innovations will continue to open up new possibilities for treatment and prevention of diseases, to result in a new balance of risks and benefits, to create new definitions of life and death, and to produce new concepts of social responsibility (Kunstadter, 1980). To deal with these complex and ever-changing situations, health-care policy-makers would have to consider ethical issues in all three spheres outlined above. Health-care policies should not be formulated and implemented merely on the basic of cost-effectiveness.

VI. Need for Ethical Concern and Research

The market approach may help to improve the cost-effectiveness of health-care services. However, this should not be taken as an end in itself. It is a means for achieving the ultimate goal of providing quality health-care services for all people in society. To achieve this goal, policy-makers in health care must undertake two critical tasks in addition to the task of cost-effectiveness.

The first task is to emphasise the need for considering moral principles, such as social obligation, equality and distributive justice. In the view of many economists, a good criterion for policy choice is cost-effectiveness, i.e. the ability to obtain the most benefit with the least cost. However, cost-effectiveness is an economic principle based on utilitarian considerations. It does not have a moral concern, and it may not be justifiable on ethical or moral grounds (Gillroy, 1992; Williams, 1992). As an instrumental value, cost-effectiveness should be taken as a lower-order criterion when applied to policy judgment (Anderson, 1992).

Some acts may result in benefits greater than costs, but such acts could be morally wrong. In a rape situation, for instance, the rapist might have gained enormous pleasure from his act, while the victim might have experienced only minor displeasure. Whatever the benefits and costs, such an act cannot be accepted on moral grounds (Kelman, 1992). Similarly, the efficiency of health-care services in Hong Kong may be improved by introducing some form of health insurance scheme (Hay, 1992). But, unless a vast majority of the population recognises the need for health insurance and is willing to pay for it, the government should continue to provide a comprehensive range of high-quality but low-charge public health-care services for most people in society. In striving for efficiency, some higher-order moral principles are needed for protecting the health of individuals and for safeguarding their right to adequate health care.

The second task to be undertaken by health policy-makers is to reveal the "contextualist morality" (Hoffmaster, 1990), i.e. the specific content of moral concerns and cultural values that are commonly shared by people in a particular society at a given time. Once identified, contextualist morality should serve as a base for the formulation and implementation of health-care policies.

Social science methods and perspectives can be employed to discern the contextualist morality by studying how decisions are actually made by individuals in society (Hoffmaster, 1990). When individuals make decisions, they usually take into account the various social, political and economic constraints imposed by the social context in which they live. An objective and systematic examination of their actual processes of decision-making on important matters such as health and illness would be able to reflect the moral concerns and cultural beliefs prevailing in their own social groups or in the society as a whole (Etzioni, 1988).

Attention should be paid to the concept of ethical or moral relativism. Cultural values and moral standards are products of dynamic interaction among different socio-political forces and historical circumstances (Markova, 1990). They differ from one society to another at a given time, and they also change over time within the same society. It is important for health-care policies and services to be reviewed periodically. This is to ensure that current policies or services are congruent not only with economic development and technological progress, but also with the prevailing cultural values and moral standards in society. The review panel should include selected people from all walks of life, not just the health-care policy-makers and practitioners. Social scientists should be engaged in analysing economic efficiency as well as the contextualist morality in health care. The introduction of a competitive market for health-care services may help to enhance cost-effectiveness. Such a market, however, might not do justice to the people unless its operation is consistent with the cultural traditions and moral concerns of society.

References

Anderson, Charles W., 1992, "The Place of Principles in Policy Analysis", pp. 387–410 in *The Moral Dimensions of Public Policy Choice*, J.M. Gillroy and M. Wade (eds.), Pittsburgh, University of Pittsburgh Press

Coe, Rodney M., 1970, *Sociology of Medicine*, N.Y., McGraw-Hill Book Company

Combes, David, 1985, "Plea for Register of Herbalists Renewed", *South China Morning Post*, 11 December

Donovan, Jenny L., and David R. Blake, 1992, "Patient Non-compliance: Deviance or Reasoned Decision-making?", *Social Science and Medicine* 34, pp. 507–13

Etzioni, Amitai, 1988, *The Moral Dimension: Toward a New Economics*, New York, Free Press

Freidson, Eliot, 1986, *Professional Powers*, Chicago, University of Chicago Press

Gillroy, John M., 1992, "The Ethical Poverty of Cost-benefit Methods: Autonomy, Efficiency, and Public Policy Choice", pp. 195–216 in *The Moral Dimensions of*

Public Policy Choice, J.M. Gillroy and M. Wade (eds.), Pittsburgh, University of Pittsburgh Press

Hay, Joel W., 1992, *Health Care in Hong Kong: An Economic Policy Assessment*, published for the Hong Kong Centre for Economic Research by the Chinese University Press, Hong Kong

Hoffmaster, Barry, 1990, "Morality and the Social Sciences", pp. 241–60 in *Social Science Perspectives in Medical Ethics*, G. Weisz (ed.), Dordrecht, Kluwer Academic Publishers

Hong Kong Government, 1993, *Towards Better Health: A Consultation Paper*

Horacio, Fabrega Jr., 1990, "An Ethnomedical Perspective of Medical Ethics", *The Journal of Medicine and Philosophy* 15, pp. 593–625

Hospital Authority, 1993, *Your Introduction to the Patients' Charter: Putting Patients First*, Hong Kong, Hospital Authority

— 1994, *Hospital Authority Newsletter*, Issue 12, April 1994

Hunt, L.M., B. Jordan and S. Irwin, 1989, "Views of What's Wrong: Diagnosis and Patients' Concepts of Illness", *Social Science and Medicine* 18, pp. 945–56

Jonsen, Albert R., and Andre E. Hellegers, 1976, "Conceptual Foundations for an Ethics of Medical Care", pp. 17–34 in *Ethics and Health Policy*, R.M. Veatch and R. Branson (eds.), Cambridge, Mass., Ballinger Publishing Company

Kelman, Steven, 1992, "Cost-benefit Analysis: An Ethical Critique", pp. 153–64 in *The Moral Dimensions of Public Policy Choice*, J.M. Gillroy and M. Wade (eds.), Pittsburgh, University of Pittsburgh Press

Kleinman, Arthur, 1980, *Patients and Healers in the Context of Culture*, Berkeley, University of California Press

Koo, L.C., 1987, "Concepts of Disease Causation, Treatment and Prevention Among Hong Kong Chinese: Diversity and Eclecticism", *Social Science and Medicine* 25, pp. 405–17

Kunstadter, Peter, 1980, "Medical Ethics in Cross-cultural and Multi-cultural Perspectives", *Social Science and Medicine* 14B, pp. 289–96

Lee, Rance P.L., 1980, "Perceptions and Uses of Chinese Medicine Among the Chinese in Hong Kong", *Culture, Medicine and Psychiatry: An Interdisciplinary Journal of Comparative Cross-Cultural Research* 4, pp. 345–75

— 1982a, "Social Science and Indigenous Concepts: With 'Yuan' in Medical Care as an Example", pp. 361–80 in *The Sinicization of Social and Behavioral Science Research*, K.S. Yang and C.I. Wen (eds.), Taipei, Institute of Ethnology, Academia Sinica (in Chinese)

— 1982b, "Comparative Studies of Health Care Systems", *Social Science and Medicine* 16, pp. 629–642

— 1994, "Cultural Tradition and Health-seeking Behaviour", pp. 26–37 in *Principles and Practice of Primary Care and Family Medicine: Asia-Pacific Perspectives*, J. Fry and N. Yuen (eds.), Oxford, Radcliffe Medical Press

Leong, C.H., 1993, "No Safeguards for Sex Selection Parents", *South China Morning Post*, 10 November

Lidz, Charles W., and Edward P. Mulvey, 1990, "Institutional Factors Affecting Psychiatric Admission and Commitment Decisions", pp. 83–96 in *Social Science Perspective on Medical Ethics*, G. Weisz (ed.) Dordrecht, Kluwer Academic Publishers

MacIntyre, Alasdair, 1992, "Utilitarianism and Cost-benefit Analysis: An Essay on the Relevance of Moral Philosophy to Bureaucratic Theory", pp. 179-194 in *The Moral Dimensions of Public Policy Choice*, J.M. Gillroy and M. Wade (eds.), Pittsburgh, University of Pittsburgh Press

Markova, Ivana, 1990, "Medical Ethics: A Branch of Societal Psychology", pp. xx in *Societal Psychology*, H.T. Himmelweit and G. Gaskell (eds.), Newbury Park, Sage Publications

Relman, Arnold S., 1980, "The New Medical-industrial Complex", *The New England Journal of Medicine* 303, pp. 963–5

Roemer, Milton I., 1989, "National Health Systems as Market Interventions", *Journal of Public Health Policy* 10, pp. 62–77

Thong, K., 1987, "Medical and Health Systems with Special Reference to Hong Kong", *Journal of the Hong Kong Society of Community Medicine* 17, pp. 17–40

Waitizkin, 1983, *The Second Sickness*, New York, Free Press

Williams, Alan, 1992, "Cost-effectiveness Analysis: Is it Ethical?", *Journal of Medical Ethics*, 18, pp. 7–11

Wong, T.W., S.L. Wong and S.P.B. Donnon, 1993, "Traditional Chinese Medicine and Western Medicine in Hong Kong: A Comparison of the Consultation Processes and Side Effects", *Journal of the Hong Kong Medical Association* 45, pp. 278–84

Yeoh, E.K., 1994, Address at the Opening Ceremony of the Hospital Authority Convention 1994, 6 January 1994, Hong Kong Convention Centre

Chapter 5

The Possibility of Administrative Ethics in Hong Kong

TERRY T. LUI

I. Introduction

Within the realm of applied ethics, one of the areas which has captured the attention of scholars and practitioners relates to the moral responsibility of public officials. The subject has appeared in the literature on politics and public administration under different labels, such as "administrative ethics", "bureaucratic morality" and "public service ethics". As a burgeoning field of inquiry, the study of administrative ethics is still in a state of flux. Nonetheless, in the midst of an "identity crisis" (Sheeran, 1993, p. ix), it is possible to discern some general themes which have characterised mainstream academic discourse on the subject.

The purpose of this chapter is to use these common themes as a starting point for analysing whether, and to what extent, the concept of "administrative ethics" as it has developed in the West could be applied to Hong Kong. The discussion will be organised into four parts. The first part provides a brief historical account of the emergence of administrative ethics as an area of concern in the analysis of government in general and public administration in particular. This will then be followed by an exploration of the assumptions which underlie the mainstream study of bureaucratic responsibility. The third part of the chapter focuses on the situation in Hong Kong, where, it will be argued, the assumptions that have guided the "Western" approach to public service ethics may not be entirely applicable. Finally, the chapter will end on a section examining the prospects for the meaningful, albeit selective, adoption of Western standards of administrative ethics in the local context.

II. The Emergence of Administrative Ethics as an Area of Concern

Academic interest in the relationship between ethics and government is by no means a recent phenomenon: the works of the classical Greek philosophers (and, for that matter, the ancient Chinese sages) were constructed on the premise that ethics and politics are inseparable. Although the contemporary view is inclined towards the Machiavellian notion that morality and effective governance are incompatible, the concern for ethics (defined broadly as proper standards of behaviour expected of those in public office) has remained an integral part of any informed debate on the conduct of public affairs.

Hence, ethics in government is firmly rooted in the philosophical tradition. However, if one were to draw a distinction between the *political* aspects of governance (i.e. the process of making value judgments regarding the ends of government and the distribution of goods, benefits, rights and responsibilities to different groups in society) and the *administrative* aspects (i.e. the bureaucratic process of implementing policy-decisions), there has clearly been an imbalance in the development of the literature on the subject.

Over the centuries there has been an abundance of ideas relating to questions of political morality. The parallel issue of what constitutes responsible administrative behaviour was, however, largely left unexplored. This imbalance can be attributed to two interrelated causes. The first is that the role of public administration in the process of government did not receive serious scholarly attention before the end of the 19th century. The second consideration is that the problematical nature of bureaucratic ethics was not formally recognised until well after the Second World War.

Modern conceptions of public administration are often traced back to the publication of Woodrow Wilson's famous article on "The Study of Administration".[1] In that article, Wilson not only laid the foundation for the establishment of a "science" of administration, but also provided the theoretical justifications for the separation of "politics" from "administration":

> The field of administration is a field of business. It is removed from the hurry and strife of politics ...
>
> ... administration lies outside the proper sphere of *politics*. Administrative questions are not political questions. Although politics sets the tasks for administration, it should not be suffered to manipulate its offices (Wilson, 1887).

In the event, the dichotomisation of politics and administration dominated the early study of public administration. As a result, difficult value choices involving ethical reasoning were considered to belong to the exclusive province of politics. Administration, by contrast, was reduced to a purely technical process of selecting the most rational courses of action to attain desired ends. Consistent with such a view of administration was the notion that a responsible public servant is one who need only ascribe to such values as efficiency, impartiality, formalistic impersonality, and, most important of all, loyalty to hierarchical authority:

> The honour of the civil servant is vested in his ability to execute conscientiously the order of the superior authorities, exactly as if the order agreed with his own conviction. This holds even if the order appears wrong to him and if, despite the civil servant's remonstrances, the authority insists on the order. Without this moral discipline and self-denial, in the highest sense, the whole apparatus would fall to pieces (Weber, 1991, p. 95).

This "Weberian" conception of bureaucratic responsibility, coupled with its attendant simplification of the moral universe of public administrators, persisted until around the 1940s. By that stage, some scholars began to question whether traditional methods of ensuring accountability were sufficient to control a bureaucracy that was playing an increasingly influential role in the process of government (Friedrich, 1935; Gaus, White and Dimock, 1936; Leys, 1943). Central to the concern of these scholars was the realisation that administrative discretion had become an inevitable fact of life if efficient and effective governance were to be sustained in a rapidly changing environment. Discretion required independent value judgments on the part of officials. The problem was therefore how an individual sense of responsibility, informed by some kind of personal or institutional ethics, could help to guide the exercise of discretionary powers. To date, the issue of administrative discretion remains at the heart of academic analyses of public service morality.

Over the years, the study of administrative ethics has undergone several phases of development. In many ways, the process of evolution can be perceived as linear, as scholars have been steadily building on the premises established by, and loopholes inherent in the works of, their predecessors (Denhardt, 1988). In other ways, however, each phase can be regarded as a departure from the previous one, as new assumptions, themes and concerns have been brought in, cumulating in the "diversity" and "vitality" (Rohr, 1990) characteristic of the current state of the discipline.

Despite the growing complexity of the subject, Cooper identifies six major themes in recent administrative ethics literature in the United States. These are, respectively, "citizenship and democratic theory", "virtue", "founding thought and the constitutional tradition", "the organisational context", "ethics education" and "philosophical theory and perspectives" (Cooper, 1994, pp. 17–22). These themes revolve around several salient questions, including, *inter alia*, whether a consensual normative basis for administrative ethics could be established; whether such a foundation could be grounded upon the notions of "citizenship", "democracy" and/or the "public interest"; whether political tradition and/or the values of the regime could inform the search for a "proper" bureaucratic ethos; whether "character" and "virtue" have a place in the definition of administrative responsibility; whether organisations have a positive or negative effect on ethical behaviour; whether and how ethics in public administration could be taught; and whether philosophy could contribute to the development of a coherent concept of public service morality.

Although Cooper's analysis is derived from the American literature on administrative ethics, a survey of published material on the subject relating to other countries (for example, Chapman 1988, 1993; Jabbra and Dwivedi, 1988; Kernaghan and Dwivedi, 1983) shows that many of the above-mentioned issues are also central on the agenda of the international academic community. There are variations in focus, emphasis and orientation among scholars from different cultural and socio-political backgrounds, but the quest for a morally responsible civil service appears almost to be a universal concern.

III. Underlying Assumptions of the Contemporary Academic Approach to Administrative Ethics

Given the wealth of material on administrative ethics, it is tempting for someone who is intent on improving public service morality in any given context to consider a wholesale adoption of ideas and solutions that have been developed in the literature. However, to follow such a path would run the risk of ignoring the Euro-American bias which is inherent in the dominant academic approach to the subject. The crux of the matter is that public administration is a discipline that has flourished primarily in democracies in the West.[2] Consequently, many Western democratic precepts have crept into the mainstream discourse on administrative ethics. For our present purpose, two sets of precepts are particularly relevant. One concerns the role of public administration in the process of government, and the other relates to the role of individual officials in the bureaucratic setting.

1. Public Administration in the Process of Government

Despite Wilson's attempt to draw a conceptual distinction between politics and administration, there was never any question that public administration was an important aspect of governance in a democratic polity. Indeed, analysts have postulated that one of the considerations underlying Wilson's dichotomy was to free the civil service from political interference so that the ideals of democratic government could be better achieved (Kirwan, 1987, p. 396). Paradoxically, following Wilson's legacy of the "science of administration", the early study of public administration tended to be dominated by an approach that could be aptly described as "managerial" (Rosenbloom, 1992). However, the rise in administrative discretion inevitably refocused scholarly attention on the role of administrators as *political* actors. Academic works which sought to place the bureaucracy in a wider political context began to reappear in the 1940s (for example, Appleby, 1947, 1949; Waldo, 1948). Since then, there has been a sustained interest in the question of how administrative powers could be balanced against, or justified in terms of, the requirements of democratic governance (Burke, 1986; Mosher, 1968; Ostrom, 1973).

While there has been an obvious shift in the perceived role of public administration in the process of government, the assumptions underlying the conception of democracy have remained fairly constant. In almost all cases, democracy is understood as entailing a system in which policy decisions should, at least in theory, rest with political representatives who are elected by the people. Career bureaucrats are supposed to be hierarchically subordinated to, and therefore held accountable for their actions by, the politicians. Administrators may have become increasingly influential in the policy-making arena, but since they lack popular mandate, they must not be allowed to usurp the authority of their political superiors.

Contemporary scholars of administrative ethics are sceptical of the adequacy of traditional forms of control in containing bureaucratic powers. Rather than seeking to curtail discretion, their preferred solutions to the problem of the "administrative state" are, first, to explore the different ways whereby the exercise of discretion can be guided by some consensual values, and second, to legitimise the political role of the administration by according the bureaucracy formal status in the constitutional set-up (Richardson and Nigro, 1987, 1991; Rohr, 1986). Put in another way, public administrators are morally obliged to uphold the constitution (or, in the case of countries like the United Kingdom, they are obliged to maintain the conventions of government); their powers could accordingly be justified in terms of how their actions and decisions actually contribute to the advancement of the spirit of the constitution and/or the established values of the regime.

2. The Role of the Individual in a Bureaucratic Setting

Thompson (1985) has argued persuasively that it is impossible to attribute moral responsibility to an individual unless that individual can actively undertake to make ethical choices, and that he/she can be the object of moral appraisal. The conventional Weberian conception of bureaucratic responsibility does not permit either of these conditions to be fulfilled. The emphasis on hierarchical loyalty essentially denies officials latitude in making individual moral decisions. Furthermore, the requirements of formalistic impersonality, coupled with "the problem of many hands" (Thompson, 1980), inevitably mean that individuals in an organisation cannot be expected to foresee the outcome of their actions. Any moral blame which arises from such an outcome should therefore be apportioned to the organisation as a collectivity rather than to individuals within it.

Thompson rejects the conventional view on the ground that it is neither realistic nor desirable. Indeed, the starting point for many scholars of administrative ethics is that individuals do have the freedom to make choices, that their decisions often have significant moral consequences, and that they must transcend organisational constraints if necessary in order to pursue their ethical ideals. In short, public service is not purely a matter of obeying orders imposed from above; it involves a sense of "individual responsibility" (Wakefield, 1976) which must in turn be founded on some personal "mental" and "moral" attributes (Bailey, 1965) or on some personal virtues internal to government service as a "practice" (Cooper, 1987; Tong, 1986).

3. Democracy and Individual Responsibility

Paradoxical as it may seem, the assumptions of democracy – which entail the subservience of public administrators to institutionalised political authority and/or communal values – and the requirements of individual responsibility – which imply autonomy on the part of civil servants, not only at the attitudinal level but also at the behavioural level – are by no means incompatible. The analytical coherence between the two sets of considerations is best encapsulated in Warwick's concept of "dialectical accountability", which he defines in the following terms:

> ... public officials are neither fully rational in their administrative actions nor totally lacking in rationality. They rarely if ever seek all the possible alternatives for action, search for all the information relevant to each alternative, and weigh the advantages and disadvantages of each option for choice. But at the same time they are not blindly driven by organisational routines and by self-interest, so that reason can influence their decisions. *Accountability is thus dialectical in the sense that moral choice involves the competing pulls of routine and reason, obedience and initiative, narrow interest and the public interest* (Warwick, 1981, p. 115; emphasis mine).

Hence, a moral civil servant must on the one hand be aware of the obligations which the external environment (political, legal, sociological) has placed upon him. On the other hand, he must develop the capacity to challenge those obligations if they go against his informed ethical judgment of what is best for the community. However, for dialectical accountability to be practicable, certain preconditions must be met. These are: first, the presence of a politico-administrative system in which the roles and responsibilities of the actors in the different institutions of government are fairly clearly delineated and well understood; second, the entrenchment of a legal-bureaucratic tradition which is generally tolerant (if not downright supportive) of individual dissent on moral grounds; and third, the possibility of identifying a core set of values which are definitive of the ethos of the polity.

IV. The Hong Kong Scene

Using these three conditions as points of departure, one would immediately see how the accepted approach to administrative ethics may not be readily applicable to Hong Kong. In the first place, Hong Kong does not have a political system that can be regarded as "democratic" in the Western sense. Moreover, the administrative culture of the local civil service is not conducive to the assumption of "individual responsibility". Finally, Hong Kong is currently undergoing a critical period of political change. The corollary of this is that the old set of values which has hitherto provided the polity with a distinct identity is gradually disintegrating. In the meantime, a new consensus has yet to be created. In the midst of this transition, notions such as "citizenship", "public interest" and "regime values" may be of limited use to the conceptualisation of a bureaucratic ethic that is appropriate for the territory.

1. The Political System

Unlike the case of Western democracies, the administration in Hong Kong has always occupied a disproportionately prominent position in the governance of society. Until the mid-1980s, when the first attempts to introduce semi-democratic reforms to the central level of government were made by the British colonial authorities, the political institutions were relatively weak and assumed only an inconsequential role in the policy-making process (Miners, 1991).

The relationship between politics and administration is therefore dissimilar from the superordinate-subordinate model of Western democracies. Furthermore, until 1991, members of the Legislative Council in Hong Kong were not directly elected on the basis of universal franchise. Even after 1991, those legislators who could claim popular mandate only comprise a minority in the legislature. The situation is likely to remain unchanged in the foreseeable future.[3]

There is therefore little in the way of political tradition in Hong Kong which can form the basis for the meaningful adoption of "citizenship" as a normative foundation for administrative ethics and a justification of bureaucratic powers. To the extent that colonial governance has conventionally been grounded on consultation and consensus, it might make sense to talk about a "public interest" in the territory. In most instances, however, this "public interest" tends to be articulated by an appointed bureaucratic elite who do not necessarily share the sentiments of the populace. Under these circumstances, the Western idea of a democratic polity where citizens participate in the definition of the common good that could ultimately inform the conduct of administrative affairs is not strictly applicable.

Since the instigation of constitutional reforms in 1985, the Legislative Council has become relatively more "representative" of the community. There are also signs that bureaucratic hegemony is gradually eroding in the face of a more assertive legislature.[4] Whereas in the past civil servants were generally averse to politics (Lau, 1984), senior-level bureaucrats now appear to be more receptive of the inevitable politicising effects that accompany the progress towards representative government (Lee, 1994). Despite these changes, however, Hong Kong's political system still lags behind its counterparts in Western democracies. Elected representatives are still unable to hold public administrators accountable. What is more important, politicians and senior bureaucrats are still struggling to carve out their respective jurisdictions in the policy arena. A workable relationship between the legislature and the executive has yet to be established. In this process of transformation, there is considerable uncertainty over the proper limits of administrative authority and the precise nature of bureaucratic obligations *vis-a-vis* other actors in the polity. The first precondition for Warwick's dialectical accountability is therefore not yet met.

2. Bureaucratic Culture and Tradition

A second reason why dialectical accountability cannot be easily transplanted to Hong Kong relates to the problem of "individual responsibility". Owing to the colonial nature of the government, civil servants in the territory are not encouraged to exercise reflective choice in the discharge of their duties. The entire public personnel management system is designed to institutionalise the Weberian values of neutral competence and organisational loyalty (Lui, 1988, 1994). There is as yet little public debate on the virtues of whistleblowing, let alone the formal enactment of legislation to protect conscientious objectors in the administrative hierarchy.

Given the pervasive mentality of professional detachment and adherence to organisational directives, public administrators are not predisposed to behaving as autonomous moral agents in the workplace. This is borne out directly and indirectly by the findings of a number of empirical studies on the civil service. For instance, a survey conducted in the early 1970s shows that most government employees adopted a disinterested attitude towards their office (Wong, 1972). Another study, undertaken in 1989 (Cooper and Lui, 1990), also reveals that loyalty to the hierarchy was a value firmly rooted in the minds of many public officials.[5] What is even more interesting is that respondents in that same study (who were mostly senior civil servants) were reluctant to utilise their positions in the government to push for more democracy even though they believed that democracy was important in safeguarding Hong Kong's interests under Chinese rule.

Results of a more recent study, which involved a questionnaire survey of over 200 senior public servants in early 1994, appear to lend further credence to the argument that the capacity of administrators to resist hierarchical pressures is rather restricted. For example, in their answers to one question, a majority of respondents (61 per cent) indicated that the opinions of their superiors were either "very important" or "important" in guiding how they should conduct themselves at work. This reliance on their superiors seems however to be independent of their private assessment of the moral standing of their bosses.[6] Similarly, in response to a vignette in the questionnaire, a significant majority (62 per cent) expressed approval for the action of an official who followed the instructions of his supervisor and engaged in an act which he considered as morally wrong. It appears therefore that compliance with hierarchical orders is deeply entrenched in the collective ethos of the public service.

3. Political Change and the Shift in Regime Values

Underlying the Euro-American (particular American) emphasis on constitutionalism as a basis for administrative ethics is the belief that there is a set of values which is central to the identity of a political community. Hence, Rawls (1985, 1993) talks about an "overlapping consensus" in modern liberal democracies; Rohr (1989) proposes the adoption of "regime values" as a source of reference for bureaucrats engaged in ethical decision-making; and Cooper (1991) draws on the notion of "citizenship" as a model for the public administrative role in the polity. In all cases, the assumption is that civic order ultimately rests on a plethora of shared values.

In Hong Kong, analysts have also tried to explain the relative stability which has marked the long years of British colonial rule in terms of some communal values. It has been argued, for instance, that Hong Kong people are fundamentally concerned with economic prosperity, that they are politically apathetic, that they cherish harmony over confrontation, and that they are unlikely to challenge a regime that can offer them opportunities for self-betterment. These generalisations might have been valid for the period up to the 1970s. However, the local political landscape has been undergoing dramatic changes since the early 1980s, when the question of China's resumption of sovereignty over the territory was first publicly mooted. The process of political transformation appears to have had a subtle but discernible effect on the psychology of the populace. Whereas previously the orientation of the society was primarily consequentialist, certain sectors of the community (especially the younger, better educated, middle-class professionals) have begun to consider social and political events from a deontological standpoint. Instead of focusing only on results, there is now a greater public readiness to examine the impact of alternative policies on human rights and individual freedoms.[7]

This does not mean, however, that a new set of regime values has emerged to replace the old consensus. From a sociological perspective, the influences of Westernisation and economic progress have brought about a considerable level of attitudinal ambivalence among the Hong Kong people over a range of issues (Lau and Kuan, 1988). From a political perspective, an agreement over the new order which should prevail as China takes over the governance of the territory in 1997 has yet to be reached (Scott, 1989). In short, the value orientation of the community is in a state of flux. Until the turbulence calms down, there is little solid ground for the founding of an integrated concept of bureaucratic ethics.

V. The Application of 'Administrative Ethics' in Hong Kong: Opportunities and Prospects

The foregoing analysis seems to suggest that the mainstream academic approach to administrative ethics is of limited utility to the local context. Does this mean that Hong Kong should adopt a different model for the conceptualisation of its public service ethics? Does it also follow that one should discard the various prescriptions which have been put forward in the literature?

The formulation of an ethic for the Hong Kong civil service is a vast topic which cannot be adequately covered within the confines of this chapter. Nevertheless, some general observations can be made. The first of these is that the discourse on administrative ethics is still an ongoing scholarly enterprise. The frontiers of the subject are continuing to expand. Judging from the growing volume of comparative research in recent years, scholars of administrative ethics now appear to be more aware of the limitations of any general "theory" of administrative ethics. There are some prospects therefore that cross-cultural analyses will gradually be incorporated into the framework of study. When that happens, the difficulties arising from the application of accepted ideas to diverse bureaucratic settings may be alleviated.

A more important consideration, however, is that the politico-administrative system in Hong Kong is also evolving very rapidly. The change is not only restricted to the institutional level, but it can also be found at the attitudinal level. As the community leans closer towards the ideals of democracy,[8] there are corresponding signs that the administration is beginning to embrace liberal democratic values. The survey of senior civil servants in early 1989 undertaken by Cooper and Lui (1990) has revealed a rather strong democratic sentiment at the top echelons of the bureaucracy. The results of the 1994 study further reinforce this finding. Although the majority of respondents attached great importance to conventional bureaucratic precepts such as "respect of organisational rules and regulations", "the reputation of one's organisation", "respect of the law" and "duty to one's organisation" as guides to the conception of ethical behaviour, they were prepared to accord secondary importance to factors like "respect for individual freedom and autonomy", "respect for individual privacy", "respect for human dignity", "fairness" and "equality". Putting this piece of evidence in the context of political change, it could be argued that Western democratic ideas are slowly finding their way into the collective ethos of the bureaucracy.

There is another fascinating aspect to the 1994 survey, and it relates to the significance of personal ethics as a factor which influences moral decision-making in the workplace. Among the 271 respondents who were asked to rank the relative importance of their own conscience as a guide to conduct, an overwhelming majority (91 per cent) expressed the view that conscience was either "very important" (59 per cent) or "important" (32 per cent). The same group of respondents also regarded "honesty" as "very important" (48 per cent) or "important" (42 per cent). The significance attached to personal integrity is further demonstrated in the respondents' answers to an open-ended question aimed at gauging their opinions on the qualities that an "ethical" public servant should possess. Attributes such as "honesty", "integrity", "sense of justice" and "adherence to one's conscience", or words to that effect, kept reappearing. In general, therefore, the concern for personal ethics was quite remarkable.[9]

The ethical disposition of the Hong Kong civil service cannot be fully determined without the support of further research evidence. In the meantime, however, there is some cause for optimism. Hong Kong is not a fully-fledged democracy, but there are indications that the subjective value orientation of the public administration (at least at the senior levels) may be heading towards that direction. Officials in the territory are embedded in an organisational culture which stresses hierarchical loyalty and formalistic impersonality, but there appears to be a latent capacity for personal moral judgment. The political scene is extremely volatile, but some consensual values may eventually emerge to provide the parameters for the conception of a bureaucratic ethic.

If one takes these considerations into account, the "Western" notion of administrative ethics may not be as irrelevant as it may seem. It is conceivable, for instance, for ideas like "regime values", "public interest", "constitutionalism" and even "citizenship" to take shape as normative foundations for the establishment of an administrative ethos. Given the divergences in political traditions, the substantive content of these concepts cannot be expected to be the same as that in Western democracies.[10] Furthermore, as the path of political development in Hong Kong is likely to be dissimilar from that in the West, there may also be a need to be selective in the use of such concepts. However, the fundamental *approach* to administrative ethics could and should be the same. The essence of this approach is that whatever standards are devised to guide bureaucratic conduct, they must conform to the norms of the body politic and of the community. Unless this unity of ethics is attained, the *raison d'être* of public administration as a vehicle for the pursuit of common goals and interests could be compromised.

Notes

1. There is some dispute over whether the modern study of public administration should be attributed to Wilson and whether he intended to separate "politics" from "administration". These issues will not be addressed in this chapter.

2. This is a generalisation which may arouse some objections, but the criteria being used here are first, the volume of published works on public administration; second, the accessibility of such works to the international academic community; and third, the focus of empirical research and theory-building. On the basis of these considerations, one could reasonably argue that the study of public administration has largely taken place in North America, Continental Europe and Australasia.

3. The post-1997 political system is circumscribed by the provisions of *The Basic Law of the Hong Kong Special Administrative Region of the People's Republic of China* (April 1990).

4. The *Hong Kong Hansard*, which is the official records of proceedings of the Legislative Council, clearly shows that there have been more prolonged debates and

critical challenges of the administration in the Council since 1985.

5. Of the 234 respondents who were asked to express their views over the proposition that "a civil servant should obey all lawful orders", a total of 206 (88 per cent) either agreed or strongly agreed with the statement.

6. There was another question in the questionnaire gauging the respondents' opinions on whether their bosses were concerned about ethics and morality. The responses show that there was considerable ambivalence over their superiors' moral standing. However, an analysis of correlation between the two sets of responses has shown that the respondents' answers to this question did not seem to affect the way they ranked the relative importance of the opinions of their superiors.

7. This is reflected in recent public debates over such issues as: the abolition of capital punishment; the decriminalisation of homosexual conduct among consenting adults; the powers of law-enforcement agencies (especially the Police Force and the Independent Commission Against Corruption) in relation to the Bill of Rights; and the Hong Kong government's relations with China in connection with matters like the pace of democratic reform and the treatment of political dissidents from the Mainland.

8. A number of opinion polls conducted over the last few years have consistently shown that the majority of people in Hong Kong favour a more democratic form of government. This sentiment is particularly pronounced among the younger and better educated groups in the community.

9. There is no inconsistency between this and the finding in the same survey that respondents were attitudinally disposed to complying with hierarchical orders. What has emerged from the survey results is that respondents generally saw no conflict between loyalty to their organisation and superiors on the one hand and adherence to their personal moral convictions on the other hand.

10. One promising area of research for the future would be to explore the possibility of basing administrative ethics on some elements of Chinese moral and political philosophy.

References

Appleby, Paul H., 1947, "Toward Better Public Administration", *Public Administration Review*, 7, pp. 93–9
— 1949, *Big Democracy*, New York, Alfred A. Knopf
Bailey, Stephen K., 1965, "Ethics and the Public Service", pp. 283–98, in *Public Administration and Democracy*, Roscoe C. Martin (ed.), Syracuse, New York, Syracuse University Press

Burke, John P., 1986, *Bureaucratic Responsibility*, Baltimore, Maryland, the John Hopkins University Press

Chapman, Richard A., 1988, *Ethics in the British Civil Service*, London, Routledge

— 1993, *Ethics in Public Service*, Edinburgh, Edinburgh University Press

Cooper, Terry L., 1987, "Hierarchy, Virtue, and the Practice of Public Administration: A Perspective for Normative Ethics", *Public Administration Review* 47, pp. 320–8

— 1991, *An Ethic of Citizenship for Public Administration*, Englewood Cliffs, New Jersey, Prentice-Hall

— 1994, *Handbook of Administrative Ethics*, New York, Marcel Dekker

— and Terry T. Lui, 1990, "Democracy and the Administrative State: The Case of Hong Kong", *Public Administration Review* 50, pp. 332–44

Denhardt, Kathryn G., 1988, *The Ethics of Public Service*, Westport, Connecticut, Greenwood Press

Friedrich, Carl J., 1935, "Responsible Government Service Under the American Constitution", Monograph No. 7 in *Problems of the American Public Service*, editors Carl J. Friedrich and others, New York, McGraw-Hill

Gaus, John M., Leonard D. White and Marshall E. Dimock, 1936, *The Frontiers of Public Administration*, Chicago, University of Chicago Press

Jabbra, Joseph G., and O.P. Dwivedi, 1988, *Public Service Accountability: A Comparative Perspective*, Connecticut, Kumarian Press

Kernaghan, Kenneth, and O.P. Dwivedi, 1983, *Ethics in the Public Service: Comparative Perspectives*, Brussels, International Institute of Administrative Sciences

Kirwan, Kent A., 1987, "Woodrow Wilson and the Study of Public Administration", *Administration and Society* 18, pp. 389–401

Lau Siu-Kai, 1984, *Society and Politics in Hong Kong*, Hong Kong, Chinese University Press

— and Kuan Hsin-Chi, 1988, *The Ethos of the Hong Kong Chinese*, Hong Kong, Chinese University Press

Lee, Jane C.Y., 1994, "Political Accountability of Senior Civil Servants in Hong Kong: A Study of the Bureaucrat-Politician Relationship", paper presented at an international conference on "The Quest for Excellence: Public Administration in the Nineties", jointly organised by the Department of Public and Social Administration, City Polytechnic of Hong Kong and the Hong Kong Public Administration Association, February 1994

Leys, Wayne A., 1943, "Ethics and Administrative Discretion", *Public Administration Review* 3, pp. 10–23

Lui, Terry T., 1988, "Changing Civil Servants' Values", pp. 131–66 in *The Hong Kong Civil Service and Its Future*, Ian Scott and John P. Burns (eds.), Hong Kong, Oxford University Press

— 1994, "Administrative Ethics in a Chinese Society: The Case of Hong Kong", pp. 487–503 in *Handbook of Administrative Ethics*, Terry L. Cooper (ed.), New York, Marcel Dekker

Miners, Norman, 1991, *The Government and Politics of Hong Kong*, 5th edition, Hong Kong, Oxford University Press

Mosher, Frederick C., 1968, *Democracy and the Public Service*, New York, Oxford University Press

Ostrom, Vincent, 1973, *The Intellectual Crisis of American Public Administration*, 2nd edition, Alabama, University of Alabama Press

Rawls, John, 1985, "Justice as Fairness: Political not Metaphysical", *Philosophy and Public Affairs* 14, pp. 223–51

— 1993, *Political Liberalism*, New York, Columbia University Press

Richardson, William G., and Lloyd G. Nigro, 1987, "Administrative Ethics and Founding Thought: Constitutional Correctives, Honor, and Education", *Public Administration Review* 47, pp. 367–76

— 1991, "The Constitution and Administrative Ethics in America", *Administration and Society* 23, pp. 275–87

Rohr, John A., 1986, *To Run a Constitution: The Legitimacy of the Administrative State*, Kansas, University Press of Kansas

— 1989, *Ethics for Bureaucrats*, 2nd edition, New York, Marcel Dekker

— 1990, "Ethics in Public Administration: A State-of-the-Discipline Report", pp. 97–123 in *Public Administration: The State of the Discipline*, Naomi B. Lynn and Aaron Wildavsky (eds.), Chatham, New Jersey, Chatham House Publishers

Rosenbloom, David H., 1992, *Public Administration: Understanding Management, Politics, and Law in the Public Sector*, 3rd edition, New York, McGraw-Hill

Scott, Ian, 1989, *Political Change and the Crisis of Legitimacy in Hong Kong*, Hong Kong, Oxford University Press

Sheeran, Patrick J., 1993, *Ethics in Public Administration: A Philosophical Approach*, Westport, Connecticut, Praeger

Thompson, Dennis F., 1980, "Moral Responsibility of Public Officials: The Problem of Many Hands", *American Political Science Review* 74, pp. 905–16

— 1985, "The Possibility of Administrative Ethics", *Public Administrative Review* 45, pp. 555–61

Tong, Rosemarie, 1986, *Ethics in Policy Analysis*, Englewood Cliffs, New Jersey, Prentice-Hall

Wakefield, Susan, 1976, "Ethics and the Public Service: A Case for Individual Responsibility", *Public Administration Review* 36, pp. 661–6

Waldo, Dwight, 1948, *The Administrative State*, New York, Ronald Press

Warwick, Donald P., 1981, "The Ethics of Administrative Discretion", pp. 93-127 in *Public Duties: The Moral Obligations of Government Officials*, Joel L. Fleishman, Lance Liebman, and Mark H. Moore (eds.), Cambridge, Massachusetts, Harvard University Press

Weber, Max, 1991, "Politics as a Vocation", pp. 77–128 in *From Max Weber: Essays in Sociology*, translators and editors Hans H. Gerth and C. Wright Mills, Cornwall, Routledge

Wilson, Woodrow, 1887, "The Study of Administration", *Political Science Quarterly* 2, reprinted pp. 10–24 in *Classics of Public Administration*, Jay M. Shafritz and Albert C. Hyde (eds.), 3rd edition, California, Brooks/Cole Publishing Co

Wong, Aline K., 1972, "The Study of Higher Non-expatriate Civil Servants in Hong

Kong", Hong Kong, occasional paper, Social Research Centre, Chinese University of Hong Kong

The Basic Law of the Hong Kong Special Administrative Region of the People's Republic of China, April 1990, Hong Kong, the Consultative Committee for the Basic Law of the Hong Kong Special Administrative Region of the People's Republic of China

Hong Kong Hansard, Reports of the Sittings of the Legislative Council of Hong Kong, Hong Kong, Government Printer

Part Two

Ethical Issues in Society

Chapter 6

Chinese Philosophy and Human Rights: An Application of Comparative Ethics

CHAD HANSEN

I. Introduction: The Normative and the Descriptive

For the past several years a controversy has raged about the applicability of ethical concepts like "human rights" to non-Western or developing societies and specifically to China. It is a debate with particular urgency in Hong Kong where past and future history complicate matters. A 1993 meeting among Asian nations in Bangkok turned on this one issue. The 1993 "Bangkok Declaration" compromised on the following formulation:

8. Recognise that while human rights are universal in nature, they must be considered in the context of a dynamic and evolving process of international norm-setting bearing in mind the significance of national and regional particularities and various historical, cultural and religious backgrounds...

Scholars of comparative philosophy have contributed to the implicit worry that something may be wrong with "imposing" human rights on Asian societies. Many Western students of Chinese thought have noted striking and deep differences between our respective views of moral personality. The individualism of the West, looked at from a Chinese perspective, begins to look like a cultural peculiarity. Historians, such as Theodore DeBary and Roger Ames, have reminded us of the historical context surrounding the emergence of Western individualism. The evaluative attitude toward the individual meshes with unique beliefs emergent in enlightenment-period Christianity. Other social changes accompanying the rise of industrial capitalism, science, the conflict of church and state and so forth, all help tell the story of how individualist moral values emerged.

Most authors, e.g., Ames (1988), rest with the descriptive claim about Chinese thought. What normative conclusion should we draw? One tempting response is to treat these scholarly reports as supporting the anti-rights position of some Asian governments. Let us call any appeal to the historicity of values to undermine the normative moral status of rights a *Bangkok attitude* or *Bangkok objection* to human rights.

Ostensibly, drawing a normative conclusion from historical premises is an example of Hume's is-ought fallacy. Using descriptive claims to support a Bangkok objection to human rights runs the danger of confusing moral truth with moral knowledge. People have rights whether or not they know about them or historically acknowledge them. Normally, we assume ethical truths, like scientific ones, are true independently of whether or not a society believes them.

In this paper, I will examine whether we can draw any normative conclusions from these descriptive, interpretive or historical premises concerning Chinese thought. I will first address how these historical observations bear on the live issue. I will accept that, properly put, they have some normative force. That force, however, is extremely tangential and heavily dependent on questionable rhetorical strategies. Then I will ask whether, understood in ways that give them even this minimal normative bite, the historical claims are sound. I conclude that they are not – although they do alert us to some interesting differences in ways of reasoning about human rights.

100

II. Comparative Ethics and Critiques of Individualism

One legitimate indirect way to use comparative ethics to get normative conclusions is to show that another culture's arguments against individual rights and human liberty are sound. Henry Rosemont has been surprisingly outspoken in challenging the hegemony of Western "rights individualism". He, however, does not draw his conclusion directly from interpretive claims. He points toward independent arguments against ethical individualism. It is, he hints, not merely a cultural peculiarity; it is a morally dubious bias.[1] Western individualism rests on a flawed conception of the individual – flawed because it is unrealistically abstract. Rosemont presents Confucianism as having a more acceptable conception of human nature. Confucianism recognises the inherent involvement of social relations in the idea of a person.

> For the early Confucians there can be no *me* in isolation, to be considered abstractly: I am the totality of roles I live in relation to specific others. I do not *play* or *perform* these roles; I *am* these roles. When they have all been specified I have been defined uniquely, fully and altogether, with no remainder with which to piece together a free, autonomous self (Rosemont, 1988, p. 177; see also his 1991, p. 71).

So for Rosemont, a Chinese perspective is important because it reveals the error at the heart of Western ethical thought, i.e., its conception of the autonomous individual. It is not easy to find an attack of Western conceptions in Chinese writings. His critical observations echo a line of argument found within contemporary Western philosophy. It is sceptical of orthodox deontological individualism. We have come to identify that position with John Rawls. Rawls has tried over several decades to derive principles of justice. His moral system exemplifies the conception of individual autonomy. The centre-piece of that derivation is his famous first principle.

> "... each person is to have an equal right to the most extensive basic liberty compatible with a similar liberty for others".[2]

Critics, especially communitarians, argue Rawls's framework presupposes a human personality that is so abstract we can hardly recognise it as a real human being. They worry that the autonomous individual is an individual denuded of all human characteristics except his pure individuality and his autonomy. This accompanies an accusation that Rawls's derivation of extensive liberty is circular. They doubt the soundness of standard arguments in the Rawlsian tradition (which, with Donagan, 1977, most take to stem from Christian and Kantian conceptions of a person).

CHAD HANSEN

1. The Structure of Normative Reasoning

To enter this complicated dispute would take us too far afield from the subject of this paper. I shall not address whether the Confucian conception of our humanity is superior to the Western Kantian conception (though I share some of Rosemont's appreciation of that alternative). In any case, I do not think Rawls's argument is a deduction from a conception of the autonomous person.[3] The normative process that Rawls made famous was "reflective equilibrium". It does indeed have presuppositions, but Rawls does not start simply from a specific conception of a person. It starts from all of our standing "considered moral judgments". The idea is that normative reasoning is an attempt to bring these attitudes into a coherent system. He justifies the first principles primarily because they yield such an equilibrium. Rawls's method strikes us as giving ethical reasoning a touch of objectivity – a structure a little like our modern understanding of science.

> By going back and forth, sometimes altering the conditions of the contractual circumstances, at others withdrawing our judgments and conforming to principle, I assume that eventually we shall find a description of the initial situation that both expresses reasonable conditions and yields principles which match our considered judgments duly pruned and adjusted. This state of affairs I refer to as reflective equilibrium. It is an equilibrium because at last our principles and judgments coincide and it is reflective since we know to what principles our judgments conform and the premises of their derivation (Rawls, 1971, p. 20).

> There is a definite if limited class of facts against which conjectured principles can be checked, namely, our considered judgments in reflective equilibrium. (*ibid.*, p. 51).

This use of reflective equilibrium in moral reasoning gives us a clue to the moral relevance of comparative ethics. Moral reasoning is dependent on a given starting point of moral attitudes and judgments. A conception of the person is one of these, but not the only one. The task of normative reasoning is to bring existing moral attitudes into overall consistency or equilibrium. It shares a feature of coherence theories of truth. The set of beliefs the definition marks as true depends on the set from which your reasoning began.

We can further sense the normative tug of the Bangkok position by focusing on the more social character of normative reasoning. We *can* strive for coherence in moral attitudes or scientific beliefs *individually*. Still the content of morality is social and we objectify the results in the sense of expecting wide sharing of the attitudes we eventually adopt. We are reasoning about the standards that guide our praising, blaming, excusing, feeling guilty or angry and so on. Morality consists of idealised *standards* governing our *evaluation* of each other's behaviour. We praise or blame from what we take to be a public point of view, not merely individual preference. When we disagree, we naturally discuss matters and seek to resolve the disagreement.

We can locate part of our sense of morality's *objectivity* within this more social conception. Morality is not simply how I *feel*, but how the standards and language of evaluation my linguistic-moral community shares *guide* my feeling. We expect the norms guiding moral intuitions to gather wide support and yield agreement in attitudes. We characterise as "moral" only those normative reactions that we expect community discourse to justify. Purely individual standards we regard as taste, religious or subjective norms.

In principle, we expect universal agreement. Descriptively, however, we can hardly avoid noticing that the standards are more similar within historical communities than across them. What is the moral relevance of these differences? Even *idealised* descriptions of *actual* social behaviour in different societies do not concern us. We are looking at the systems of attitudes, norms, and values that influence their thinking about praise, blame, moral guilt and anger. Further, we are looking at the actual standards at work in a community's reasoning, not the pronouncements of their leaders.

This means that morality is distinct from *mores*. We distinguish morality by its more reflective character. Morality is characterised by what Gibbard (1990, pp. 201–3) calls "modest objectivity" or what Blackburn (1984, ch. 6) calls "quasi-realism". Moral reasoners in a community do not simply agree on evaluative attitudes. They also discuss and share second-level standards for justifying those attitudes and they presuppose deeper reasons for those standards and so on. We understand right and wrong as depending on how norms *justify* people in feeling, not by what people happen to feel.

The standards of justification are themselves social, but, again, we do not accept them as second-level norms *simply* because our society so uses them.[4] So this conception of morality can distinguish normative reasoning and reflective thinking from either sociology or history. Still, it accepts that "reasonable" as applied to moral attitudes, is a public, conventional concept. Different moral communities may have differing standards of moral reflection.

We thus bridge the gap between Rawls's reflective normative theorist and DeBary and Ames's sociological analysis. We accept the view that these standards are the outcome of normative discussion within moral communities.[5] We reason with our neighbours about ways (*daos*) to evaluate, guide and harmonise our actions. We carry on moral reflection in groups and naturally adjust our attitudes to harmonise with those of others in our community. Still, we wonder what follows from the differences themselves?

2. Universal, Innate Morality

One possible normative conclusion is this: such deep differences undermine the view of morality that assumes moral standards are innate, pan-human attitudes. Such variation supports the claim that moral dispositions are the product of variable, historical discourse. In this case, the Bangkok objection uses it to undermine the claim that evaluative approval of human freedom and liberty is natural or instinctive.[6] An innatist still has many responses. The observation merely calls for a more careful response since it cites a difference in deep underlying standards rather than resultant (possibly erroneous) judgments.

Again, I will not trace this line of argument far here. It cannot quite show there are no universal moral intuitions. Hume and Mencius (*Mencius*, 2A, p. 6 and 6A, p. 6) might not have been far off in their characterisation of these (on what I call the "weak interpretation" of Mencius: Hansen, 1992, pp. 168–74). Still, I doubt that innate dispositions are elaborate enough to yield reliable intuitions about this controversial issue.[7] Admittedly, culture largely shapes moral reactions and norms of discussion and it is hard to sort out natural from nurtured attitudes. The interpretive claim about deep differences between Chinese and Western moral systems would suggest that the value of liberty is nurture not nature. In allowing that, I do implicitly accept some of the thrust of the Bangkok, anti-universalist position. We probably best understand moral attitudes, including the priority of liberty, as socially agreed-on attitudes.[8]

3. Subjective and Objective Morality

The normative bite, however, is only to undermine appeal to innate dispositions in support of extensive liberty. Since we have accommodated the communitarians in viewing moral norms as standards arrived at in social discourse, we can still mount other attacks on authoritarianism, and defences of liberty. The Bangkok objection amounts to saying that no socially acceptable line of thinking can start from Chinese premises and conclude that liberty is morally right. Rosemont puts this form of the claim most distinctly: "... even if we assume that there is nothing wrong with the concept of rights, we must face the problem of exporting it, making it universally understood and appreciated" (Rosemont, 1991, p. 60).

Rosemont's worry thus ties into our social discourse conception of the development of moral attitudes. He observes that *arguments* for rights, which win over Western reasoners, would not have convinced Confucius. Ames suggests that the idea "rights" is unintelligible to someone within a *genuinely*

Chinese moral-conceptual framework. Now we can shift from the blunt normative issue of whether China should have human rights to a more neutral worry that is still reflectively normative. Would any argument for human rights "work" in a Chinese context? Could we make conceptual sense of and convince someone culturally Chinese (given their first-level intuitions and second-level norms) of the correctness of a system that maximises equal liberty and freedom from state coercion?[9] Could we imagine that conclusion emerging out of discussion *within* a Chinese community of moral reasoners? Would it follow from their initial shared attitudes, their first- and second-level norms of judgment?

Why does this question have normative bite? Would it not still be right to allow liberty even if we could not make the argument using premises available to a Chinese community of moral reasoners? Have we not simply blurred the difference between knowledge and truth again? I think the normative bite lies in the general region of the theory of excuses (the distinction between subjective and objective rightness). We understand people to have acted correctly while technically having done the wrong thing. When they act on the best motives and most rational procedure available to them, they act rightly. Even if events conspire to make their actions lead to a bad outcome, they acted as they should.

The question, thus, still has normative bite because we accept the second-level procedural norm implicit in Rawls's reflective equilibrium. People *should* judge as moral what accords with the standards of reasoning that best justify their existing considered moral judgments. A Westerner's own commitment to this version of rational autonomy requires her to respect different moral points of view as long as they are seriously and sincerely reflective. She still has room to say the other community is wrong but must grant they have reasoned rightly by their own lights and further grant that, by our lights, they ought (subjectively) to so reason. Western reasoners should conclude that Chinese moral agents who unreflectively accept Western standards would be *internally* wrong.

This need for respect in dealing with rival reflective moral communities is subtle and complex. It follows from liberal, Rawlsian values. On the one hand, Rawls assumes that if the two principles best justify one's considered moral judgments in reflective equilibrium, he ought to accept them as true. To accept them as true, however, is not to accept that their truth depends on what attitudes people have. To accept them as true is to accept them as true for those who engaged in the Spanish inquisition though they did not share a modern attitude. Similarly, to accept them as true is to accept them as true for Chinese governments although they do not share those intuitions.

However, the same applies to members of a Chinese moral community.

They should treat as morally correct the principles that best justify their judgments in reflective equilibrium. Further, they should accept them as binding on Western moral agents despite the agents' inability to recognise their truth. It is precisely because each culture treats its moral judgments as quasi-objective in this sense that the disagreements strike us as real.

We endorse a *second-level norm*. People should accept the moral principles that best justify their considered judgments in reflective equilibrium. Thus, we should agree that members of other communities who accept rival principles by an equally reflective process have judged rightly about moral issues *in a procedural sense*. This does not lead to massive incoherence because we already make a distinction between being objectively wrong (say because of lack of information) and being blameworthy or subjectively bad. Both agree that one side is wrong, but neither is being irresponsible in moral reasoning. We can, and should, continue to believe and advocate our own best moral judgment, but must acknowledge the equivalent authority and rationality of the other community. If we do not, we owe ourselves some coherent reason for thinking it has been less competent in reaching its equilibrium.[10]

This explains why the Greater China case particularly troubles Westerners. However a Westerner may react to anthropological studies of titillating sexual practices, she can hardly dismiss the awareness that Chinese normative attitudes have as long and as rich a tradition of literate discussion and reflection as has the West. Even if she disagrees with the norms that guided Chinese historical reflection, she must respect both its intellectual wealth and practical success. Thus, she must take Rosemont's challenge seriously.

III. Examining the Chinese Perspective

We have identified just how the Bangkok objection has normative bite – and how it fails. By itself, it fails to show that extensive liberty is either wrong or omissible. It does, however, justify the demand for equal respect for a rival reflective moral tradition and community. Their judgments on this issue might differ although they arrived at them validly. Now what that "respect" would require is another complicated question that I will not examine here. It is not obvious that the "respect" requires non-intervention. On the contrary, we would show respect by engaging in further moral argument. We support and urge our moral attitudes on the other in the hope and expectation of reaching some agreed principles.

My concern here shifts to the descriptive question. Are the historical claims *that have normative relevance* true? That certain key and influential people oppose democracy and "bourgeois liberty" should not satisfy us. The question is not about Chinese governments. It is not about what the leaders of countries in Greater China want or believe, or what position they take in international councils. As Christine Loh has said, "When attempts are made to justify tyranny on grounds of history or culture, such attempts are invariably made by those who are practising the tyranny. Never by the victims." We can only be pleased when leaders of government speak with the intelligence and lucidity of a Lee Kwan Yew, but the issue is not what judgments he makes. We found the objection to have normative bite only if it shows that, within a reflective Chinese community, *public standards would validly warrant* such a judgment.

It is similarly not sufficient to show that no period in China ever adopted or exercised democracy or human rights. Even showing a consensus of all *actual* moral judgments of the entire existing Chinese community will not, by itself, have that normative bite. Sociological *predictions* about what rights will survive in Hong Kong or be adopted in China are also irrelevant to the normative issue. Our focus is on the judgments that reflective equilibrium would *justify*. We address the underlying intuitions and second-level reasoning standards of the Chinese moral community, i.e., the point of view of idealised Chinese discussants.

Our question is, however, a crucial and practical one. It is not a detached intellectual issue. It is a question facing each member of the Chinese moral community when she wonders whether or not to support and work for greater freedom and democracy within her community. Any reflective moral thinker will have to address that question starting from the "considered moral judgments" she makes and the perspective she occupies. Chinese thinkers who discuss human rights in China are themselves in a situation of trying to achieve reflective equilibrium with their own set of initial moral intuitions and attitudes.

So Rosemont's way of putting the issue is instructive. Is it possible, consistent with traditional Chinese moral attitudes, to *justify* adopting a more robust scheme of individual liberty? Could it, like the Rawlsian theory, justify a scheme of liberty that is relatively invulnerable to restriction in the interest in other political goals such as national wealth and power? Rosemont and Ames, with many others,[11] suggest that it could not.

Chinese tradition, they note, has a radically different moral perspective and did not even have a word for "rights". They borrowed from Japan a term, *chuan-li*, manufactured for translating Western political thought about a century ago. Ames remarks that the initial Chinese response to it "must have been one of considerable bemusement" (Ames, p. 203). That term, *chuan-li*, suggests a combination of expedience, raw power, and even selfishness.[12] Any kind of individual rights program, he suggests, would have to strike Chinese thinkers as a form of selfishness. Confucians traditionally considered selfishness to be the opposite of morality.

1. Chinese Philosophy and Individualism

Rosemont and Ames are right. There are deep differences in Confucian and Western moral attitudes and in the conceptual structure guiding how we reflect on them. I have argued that the differences do go quite deep (Hansen, 1985a and 1985b). Our respective moral attitudes (our "intuitions") are not conceptual orphans. Different comprehensive philosophical outlooks support our respective attitudes. Each tradition has a view of human nature, society and the world that informs and reinforces its moral attitudes. Assuredly, Christianity, with its individual souls, a personal relation to God and individual quests for salvation, has had an effect on Western reasoning about values.

Many background features of European thought have also contributed to the difference in outlook. A general *methodological individualism* buttresses the sense that human individuals are evaluatively significant. It characterises both our metaphysical and scientific thinking. Western theorists have understood the world as made up of particulars. Chinese metaphysical theory analyses objects as parts carved out of a larger, more basic whole. Western traditional psychology and philosophy of language postulate a private, individualised mind as the locus of meaning, of thought, and of reason. Western epistemology focuses on the ways we go from the private, subjective, individualised beliefs to an abstract, objective, knowledge. It bypasses and denigrates social orthodoxy as "conventional wisdom".

Chinese theories locate meaning in historical conventions. They postulate no language of private symbols (ideas) scattered through all the minds of the community and derived from their contact with objects. They focus instead on conventional symbols that history and tradition bequeathed, derived from a "culture hero's" contact with objects. Language has meaning because we preserve and conform to the Sage King's original intention to refer to these (mereological) objects. Knowledge is primarily of this historical *dao* (the social guiding discourse).

So the differences in reflective moral attitudes about individualism are not isolated items. Normative discussion, in China or in the West, draws from and appeals to a wide range of other philosophical doctrines. The differences between Chinese and Western perspectives are, I agree, both broad and deep.

What we have to decide is whether they block, inhibit or otherwise render arguments for freedom and democracy unpersuasive or unintelligible.[13]

2. The Complexity of Chinese Tradition

Rosemont, Ames and DeBary concentrate on Confucianism and especially on ancient or medieval varieties. Such claims, even if true, would not have the normative bite required. The issue arises today in Hong Kong, Taiwan, Singapore and China, not 2,000 years ago in LoYang or Chang An. "Chinese tradition" is a rich and changing concept. Confucianism is only a part – however important a part.

Hong Kong now has a tradition of abiding by the rule of law that is nearly as old as is the abolition of slavery in America. China as a whole has had as long a history of contact with Western ideas as has North America. China has a literary and republican revolutionary tradition already almost a century old. The advocacy of "Western Ideas", from Mr. Science and Democracy to half a century of Marxist ideology, fills this century of Chinese history. Furthermore overseas Chinese with experiences in most countries of the world are members of the extended moral community. Kang You-wei, Tan Si-tong and Liang Qichao are now figures that have belonged to Chinese history as long as Abraham Lincoln has to American. Sun Yat-sen is called the George Washington of China. All of this history and tradition is now available to reflective Chinese reasoners in addressing the question of liberty and democracy. Ames and Rosemont's Classical Confucian is not the model of the idealised Chinese reasoner that is relevant to a normative issue today.

The existing base of moral attitudes from which a Chinese community would address this issue thus includes a lot of Western moral and cultural content. Despite the alleged isolation of China, Western values have penetrated it more than vice versa. The actual discourse milieu of this issue in China resembles the romantic challenge of finding the harmony of East and West more than of tracing out the implications of classical conceptions.

As we noted above, Chinese moral attitudes are like Western ones in a crucial respect. Both cultures assume that if there are moral disagreements, one side must be closer to correct than the other. Both share a quasi-objective conception of what is morally correct. The awareness of another reflective tradition with different equilibrium judgments on such important moral matters disrupts the internal equilibrium of both discourse systems. Thus both can imagine that a "bridging" morality might settle the conflict and blend the moral thinking of both cultures.

Again, I will not trace this rather complicated path here. Let me make three assertions. First, as I speculated above, some modern Chinese communities are better placed than Western ones are to engage in these kinds of reflections. Second, becoming permissive is a more natural and typical response to exposure to diverse reflective moral systems than is becoming more demanding. There is little doubt that many reflective contemporary Chinese thinkers can (and do) come to advocate freedom and democracy. Third, moral reason appears to supplement nature on this issue. Blackburn argues that a first approximation of any rational synthesis will normally be more permissive than either of the clashing traditions (Blackburn, 1984, pp. 201–2). According normative respect to another tradition is to treat it as a possible or permissible moral system. We thus accept that a permissible moral system permits X although our own morality forbids it. The first approximation of a synthesising position would say, accordingly, that it is permissible to make X permissible. Complexities abound,[14] but this suggests that any emerging "common" morality would normally expand permissions (freedoms) and reduce prohibitions and obligations.[15]

The conservative accusation that such an outcome is "polluted" by exposure to Western values has some rhetorical force, but negligible normative weight. It would have a mild retroactive normative implication. The objector would have to show that *correct* adherence to and reasoning in accord with purely Chinese principles would have prohibited allowing oneself (or one's community) to risk such exposure initially. Then it would merely follow that they made an earlier mistake. Having made that mistake, the situation has changed. We frequently make moral choices arising from situations that past blunders brought about. That doesn't allow us to reverse time and obliterate the consequences of those errors from our present moral reasoning.

The accusation has even less rhetorical and normative bite when we reflect that before the modern contact with the West, China already differed in conceptual structure from the pure classical Chinese view I described above. Buddhism is an Indo-European religious system which Nietzsche described as "a kindred religion" to Christianity. Around 200 AD it imported the idea of a private realm of consciousness, of Indo-European concepts of reason and truth, of religious goals of salvation of the individual soul. It even has the religious selfishness implicit in Christianity, i.e., being moral in contemplation of supernatural reward or punishment for the individual.

110

3. The Normative Relevance of Classical Chinese Thought

This almost reduces the issue to an academic one. We can understand Ames and Rosemont as making a claim with normative implications. It still has minimal relevance to the pressing issue and offers only rhetorical support to a Bangkok attitude. Even this academic point still lies in the region of excuses or subjective rightness. It bears in interesting ways on the normative project we touched on above, i.e., synthesising different moral traditions. It still has *some* rhetorical force. Conservatives may parade the *purity* of their reasoning base. They may take the internally normative position that from within the purely Chinese reasoning structure we cannot justify "polluting" the base with foreign attitudes.

Interpretively, one could also say that the Buddhist and Western attitudes have not permeated the reasoning structure of the community. This suggests that a member of the Chinese moral community who advocates greater freedom has defected to and become an agent of a rival moral consciousness. The academic point does give "aid and comfort" to the rulers' claims that talk of rights and freedom amount to an imposition of Western values on China. I will, thus, now join these academics in looking at the rather academic, quasi-descriptive historical claims that would be germane given these conservative attitudes.

4. Non-Confucian Counter-examples

First, we can object that we should not identify Confucianism with the "pure and unsullied" Chinese tradition[16] any more than we should identify orthodox Roman Catholic attitudes with Western morality. Confucianism is *an* authentic expression of that Chinese tradition, but the classical "Hundred Schools" philosophies are anti-Confucian in about the way Western philosophy is anti-religion! Further, for this debate, we should distinguish the correct interpretation of those other schools and the traditional Confucian interpretation. Confucianism does construe those other schools as in essence derived from Confucianism.

Chinese philosophy starts with Mozi's attack on Confucianism and Confucian theorists are on the defensive throughout the Warring States period. Daoism, Mohism, and Legalism are the best known philosophical rivals but a rich classical milieu floated alternatives to the Confucian *dao*. Any account of "pure, indigenous" Chinese attitudes and norms for argument must take account of these other schools. None is plausibly a Western import.[17]

I will not dispute the general features of Confucianism on which Rosemont and Ames rely. I agree that some apply to the whole classical period. Like Rosemont, I have argued that the debate about the moral *dao* does not use an equivalent to "ought" or "should" or even "duty" (let alone "rights") and that, in Confucius's own system, moral relations among individuals are a function of their social roles, not of their being persons.[18] "Should" and "ought" are key terms in any duty morality. Given the deeper points I made above about the absence of the individualism, I do agree that it is unlikely that Chinese ethics will resemble duty-based individualism – the Rawlsian position.

However, classical ethical thought does have pan-human reasoning and a fully general utilitarianism. Mohism's moral posture is explicitly "universal" and contrasts with what it takes to be Confucian partiality and conventionalism. Mozi is as committed as Confucius to the view that human attitudes are social and that a role-hierarchy is the natural form of society. Such a view does lead him to think the correct *dao* should guide only the society that develops it. The debate between Mohism and Confucianism is about what social guiding discourse to adopt in instilling moral attitudes in people.

Mohism, though authoritarian about social structure, is liberal in its view of tradition. It rejects the original Confucian position that the traditional code is binding on us today. In the debate about what code to use in society, the Mohists favour a universal utilitarian standard for constructing that idealised code.[19] Mozi suggested we could identify the optimum code and it would be the constant *dao*. That guiding discourse should always work optimally for society.

Mozi's political theory is striking for his use of a line of thinking associated with the individualist West. This is the hypothetical choice model. We treat the fact that we would make a choice in certain circumstances as justifying that choice now. Hobbes, Locke, and Rawls all exhibit varieties of this model. Mozi's justification of leadership follows a hypothetical choice model. Its logic relies on basing value on choice. The occurrence of such an argument at the birth of Chinese philosophy suggests strong similarities in moral attitudes.

So Mohist "authoritarianism" resembles democratic centralism more than the divine right of kings.[20] The leaders embody and enforce a consensus moral judgment. Many scholars have concluded that the leaders of Mohist branches and their military units were probably "elected".

Mencius (probably influenced by Mozi) shows a distinct tendency to interpret the "mandate of Heaven" as based on a mechanism of popular acceptance. Mencius further postulates a universal capacity to recognise moral qualities in a leader. Of course neither Mencius nor Mozi accepts a view of the leader as democratically delegated decision-maker. Both assume we select him because he is the wisest and best. The democratic component interacts with a natural meritocracy and an assumption that everyone has access to the correct moral attitudes or ultimate standards.

Daoism, notoriously, tends toward anarchism. It is anarchist, further, not only about government, but also in its relativism and scepticism of any *dao*. It denies that any *dao* would work in all situations, that any *dao* is constant. The Daoist position mirrors the relativist thrust implicit in Rawls's reflective equilibrium. Any judgment about which *dao* to choose presupposes some existing choice-guiding attitudes. The Confucians, for example, presuppose the authority of tradition, Mohists the value of utility.

Daoism, I would agree, is still not individualist (contrary to some characterisations). It is pluralist, but is no more based on private subjectivity than is Confucianism or Mohism. Daoists treat many *daos* as equipossible. It is not an individual mind (a private, internal meaning locus) that makes the envisioned selection of a moral *dao*. *Societies* make it from some actual social perspectives. Among the pantheon of allegedly Daoist thinkers we find Yang Zhu whom Mencius accused of being an egoist. He is – in one sense. He argues society should instil the *dao* that guides each to limit his moral concern to himself. He is, that is, an ethical egoist, but not a descriptive or psychological egoist. He does not think the natural human reaction *is* egoistic but tries to convince us it is an attitude we *should* instil.

Legalism, notoriously, is as authoritarian as is Confucianism. Interpreters commonly identify Legalist writers as advocating the rule of law. I doubt that. However, if Legalists had a clear concept of the rule of law, then the tradition would have a proven line of reasoning leading to human rights. A pro- attitude toward the rule of law is one of the considered judgments Rawls brought into "reflective equilibrium" by his theory of maximising human freedoms. The rule of law limits application of legitimate coercion to clearly pre-warned situations. People can then intelligently predict which actions will result in punishment. The implicit principle is: government ought to give such warning because it should allow people, planning creatures, to plan their lives. The right to liberty wherever explicit law does not constrain follows from this principle and the conceptual correlatively of rights and duties. If Chinese tradition had had a clear concept of the rule of law, then they would have the same reflective route Dworkin and Rawls have to "taking rights seriously".

I have doubted that they had the required theory of the rule of law.[21] Still, some Legalists gave arguments with a surprisingly familiar libertarian ring. Shang Yang argued that having clear, objective, measurement-like standards for the application of terms in social guiding discourse protected the people against arbitrary officials. Thus, it placated and pacified them. In other places, he argued that making the standards of interpretation explicit, clear, and publicly known will eliminate punishment. No one would risk it if they knew clearly what the ruler had forbidden (Hansen, 1992, pp. 359–61).

The target of these Legalist arguments was Confucianism, i.e., the Confucian gentry and other scholar bureaucrats. All threats to the ruler arise, Legalists argued, from his ministers. Scholar bureaucrats rely either on their cultivated scholarly *intuitions* for interpreting a traditional *dao* or on *appropriately* cultivated innate moral inclinations. The Confucians modelled their standard of *appropriate* cultivation on that of the sage-like moral-mystic. It was thus inaccessible to "normal" people. Legalists objected that allowing middle-level officials access to the handles of punishment and reward on such vague grounds lets them build a power-base. Using objective standards of punishment and reward ties the minister's hands and thus protects the ruler as well as the people.

5. Variety within Confucianism

Even within Confucianism, some strands exhibit crucial differences from Confucius's own original hyper-traditionalism. Confucius himself, famously, does not develop anything like a moral *system*. We do, however, find an implicit recognition that a "single thread" *should* tie the teachings together (although interpreters have struggled without much consensus to identify it). The most popular candidate for this "single thread" is the Confucian negative golden rule. It brings Confucius's deeper theory shockingly close to Mozi's normative position plus the subjective notion of "desire". Other candidates for the one thread are *reciprocity* and some version of *fidelity* or *loyalty*. The latter may or may not be hierarchical. Most informal interpretive suggestions of the justification for traditional standards are vaguely utilitarian. The sage kings intended the traditions for the *good* of the people.[22]

Still, fundamentally, Confucius *is* more authoritarian than the Legalists. His code derives from a now-dead authority. Political leaders (Prime Ministers) "rectify names" so that the traditional code gives the "right" ethical guidance. This capacity to rectify names and thus identify the correct course of behaviour in the traditional *dao* is the semi-mystical, difficult and rare capacity called *ren*[humanity]. Without the authoritarian man of *ren*[humanity] at the top, the state cannot run well even given our inheritance of the sage-kings' *dao*. The paradigm use of this ability is in being a magistrate.

Confucius *may* have been a hyper-traditionalist, as Rosemont argues, lacking any clear conceptual distinction between mores or propriety and morality itself. Mencius, however, was responding to the challenge of Mozi. He thus must and does distinguish traditional *mores* from *morality* and implicitly abandons tradition as the standard of identifying *dao*. He justifies Confucian moral attitudes as universal and natural dispositions.

Mencius's position, however, is not the Kantian position. He does not base it on our capacity to reason. Mencius does argue that every human has access to a reliable moral intuition. Everyone is sage-like in this capacity. We will *realise* it in the normal course of events if nothing hinders our moral heart's natural development. Hence, it does not depend on authority, teaching, or role in society. (Of course, its specific guidance is indexed by role. It tells each of us what we should do in our own situation, not what someone else should do. It is unerring moral intuition but not about particular acts, not principles or theory.) Although it will be a *different* basis for it, the Mencian position does give a ground for respecting every human being as a potential sage. It could ground an attitude of equal respect for each person as a potential source of access to the moral *dao*.

Mencius's political theory, as I hinted above, is also comparatively liberal. He saw the mechanism of getting the mandate of heaven as working through each person's natural moral insight. People can recognise and are inclined to align with moral models, teachers and leaders. Thus achieving the mandate comes about partly because people "vote with their feet".[23]

Mencius's version of Confucianism underwrites a powerful form of Chinese liberalism. It contradicts Rosemont's argument that Confucianism lacks any abstract conception of the human. His reworking of the Confucian position has been the orthodox and most influential version. So it is hard to see where the normative bite of Rosemont's position lies. He merely casts doubt on a belief that Confucius *himself* might have come to appreciate the importance of liberty. Its normative force perhaps rests on Confucius's deification.

Xunzi's version of Confucianism, to be sure, reverts to a more authoritarian, traditionalist posture. He insisted on taking tradition as per the interpretation of a class of Confucian "Gentlemen" as the ultimate standard. Furthermore, he advocated "shutting up" the rival philosophical voices who challenged or undermined that tradition and those authorities – all in the interest of social order and economic distribution. His attitudes fed into the Legalist position and thereby into Chinese imperial political attitudes. China's leaders still struggle with these attitudes.

However, his second-level attitudes, like those of Mozi, were pragmatic utilitarian ones. We affirm the authority of tradition and "gentlemen" so we can achieve the unity and order necessary for good government and economic wellbeing. His is the argument of the modern Asian ruler. Xunzi advocated forbidding philosophical debate in the interest of public order.

Now our normative question has to be, can we make a case for democracy and liberty from pragmatic, utilitarian assumptions? It is not enough to show that Xunzi drew the opposite conclusion or that rulers of China have followed him in doing so. The question is if his conclusion is soundly derived from his highest values.

Xunzi's position "won" in China only if by "winning" we mean getting the rulers to adopt and use our *dao*. Zhuangzi reminds us that winning in such a sense does not mean one is right. The crucial point is that *no* classical thinker *other than* Xunzi accepts the economic-cum-order justification for restricting public debate about *daos*. It hardly warrants saying it is *the* indigenous Chinese view.

What Chinese norms justify for most classic thinkers[24] is the use of pragmatic utilitarian reasoning in deriving the social *dao*. Pragmatic reasoning is sensitive to new information and depends on correctly judging the probabilities of each outcome. The question *we* have to ask from any temporary, artificial, "pure" Chinese moral perspective is whether Xunzi was right *by the lights of classical philosophy*. We do not simply ask if we can understand why he took the position he did (we can) or why it appealed to Chinese rulers at the that time (we can). Was he *right* that suppression of dissenting voices and competitive theorising was the most efficient way to achieve the broad pragmatic utilitarian goals (e.g., economic development and social order) which Chinese thinkers shared? Was he *right* to think those goals outweighed other widely shared ends that repression would sacrifice, e.g., growth in knowledge of *dao* and the humanly fulfilling dynamic process of distinguishing and refining it?

6. Utilitarian Arguments for Liberty and Democracy

Asking the question is different from answering it – both for us and for the Bangkok objectors. Asking it in the context of a pressing normative issue today allows us to add our current knowledge of economic, political, psychological and sociological facts that combine with pragmatic utilitarianism in testing Xunzi's conclusion. As we bring this classical perspective to the current debate, I want to draw attention to certain considerations. First, I have accepted that classical Chinese assumptions differ from a Rawlsian or Kantian perspective.[25] Rawls and Kant are explicitly hostile to utilitarian considerations of any sort. Some, however, mistakenly conclude from Rawls's arguments that utilitarian reasoning *cannot* justify equality or liberty. That is far from obvious. The argument from diminishing marginal utility, for example, does not create an *in principle* demand for equality in distribution, but it justifies far more distributive justice than most actual modern societies achieve.

Mencian intuitions about moral equality can buttress the resources of utilitarian theory in supporting equality. Dworkin has argued that Rawls's two principles follow from an ur-principle of "equal concern and respect" (Dworkin, 1977). That formulation would hardly look as alien in a classical Chinese context as the first principle itself might. The source of respect is different (reason versus moral intuition). The implications for political leadership (moral wisdom) do not derive directly from the consent of the governed. Still, respect for general opinion has a genuine classical Chinese base. Mao's "mass line" did not invent it.

Our concern here, however, is for liberty. The question is whether we can make successful utilitarian arguments for an extensive *personal liberty*. The answer is obvious. Arguments for free speech did not start with Rawls or Kant. The classic argument is John Stuart Mill's "On Liberty".[26] Mozi argues that the state of nature disorder causes us to "waste valuable *daos*". The classical awareness of the importance of not wasting valuable *daos* shows up again in the mythical story of Laozi. On his way out of China, a border guard (keeper of the pass) detains him to jot down his *dao* so it will not disappear with him.

A Chinese version, thus, would include a less abstract, more Darwinian claim that the most useful, social-utility producing doctrine will prevail in competition among *daos*. That kind of attitude was, as we saw, widespread in ancient China. It surfaces again in modern China among the "Westernisers" who are more attracted to Pragmatic or Marxist attitudes than to abstract truth systems. Even Maoists saw a social utilitarian argument for "letting a hundred flowers bloom".

Other utilitarian arguments are available for, e.g., freedom of the press. A standard economic analysis shows that corruption makes an economy inefficient. A free press is one (notoriously fallible and sometimes obnoxious) way to expose and inhibit corruption. It is also a good way to spread the information needed for quick and responsive business decisions. It is an efficient way to help economic units' decision-making and thus enhance overall wellbeing. This approximates the position of the students in Tiananmen. We do not always need truth-seeking arguments to justify allowing free discussion of political, cultural or scientific doctrines.

Consider some pragmatic goals shared in all corners of "greater China". All of them want to encourage market mechanisms and the capitalist creation of wealth (by whatever name they call it). All recognise that business requires a stable, predictable environment in which to plan and project in making business decisions. All the governments, therefore, express overt support for the rule of law. Now it is open to the pragmatist to observe that the rule of law and the independence of judges is easier to sustain and protect when there is real multi-party democracy. Authority pluralism, free and open political comment and discussion help preserve an independent judiciary.

As some clever statistician pointed out, the correlation between the wealth of a society and the place on the U.N. Freedom Ranking is higher than the correlation between intelligence and good grades in school.

> As is well known to every student of statistics, positive correlations range from 0.0 to 1.0. The correlation between the heights of husbands and wives, for example, is about 0.3. The correlation between IQ and elementary-school grades is 0.6 – suggesting that intelligence power-fully affects but does not totally determine the grades.

> Using U.N. data, we calculate the correlation between political freedom and gross domestic product per capita at a smashing 0.7. We assume that the Third Worlders will continue denouncing the freedom index as (in the *New York Times* summary of their complaints) "interference in their internal affairs and irrelevant to their development needs". Or at least the dictators' needs.

The statistics do not help the Asian rulers' argument that depriving people of freedom is a quick road to getting rich. A pragmatic argument with false probabilities loses. Even if we limit ourselves to economic considerations, utilitarian standards do support less control and decentralisation. Even China's communist leaders have appreciated this economic truth.

Notoriously, another of the serious practical, political problems facing China that threatens the stability needed for business confidence is the legitimacy of succession. Whatever satisfaction we get from the success of Deng Xiaoping's reforms, the uneasy awareness that the next leader could undo what he did as he undid Mao's policies undermines it. Mao and Deng have both recognised and struggled unsuccessfully with the problem of legitimate succession. The Communist Party faces a crisis of legitimacy. Following wave after wave of political education, the technique has ceased to affect the people.

There are many routes to legitimacy. The mandate of heaven and divine right of kings used quasi-religious grounding; the Long March generation stands for another approach. (Trial by combat was another component of the mandate of heaven.) The original, idealistic traditional rationale in China has always been merit. The best and wisest should rule. So writing philosophy and poetry helps give legitimacy. Still, as I argued, China has a tradition of fondness for identifying merit by popular acclaim. We hardly need to point out that the Communist Party has always based its claims to legitimacy on its democratic support. It distinguished itself from the old bad "republic" as the "people's republic" and still uses a formal mechanism of election as a legitimisation technique.[27]

Fair and open election is not the only way to get that legitimacy but it is an effective way. It demonstrably legitimises leadership in Chinese societies. We merely need to look at Hong Kong's own recent history to appreciate this. The element of surprise in a free election exercise is a considerable source of legitimacy. So is the perception of cheating a destabilising one. After years of imposed British executive leadership, Hong Kong held an election for a small minority of seats in the comparatively powerless legislative body. When one party won overwhelmingly, the leaders of that group grew in stature overnight. The British governor shrank in proportion. Almost from election day the elected figures in the dominant party have spoken with more authority and legitimacy than other public figures in the territory.

Dispatching a seasoned professional politician with skills at courting public opinion, shaping and expressing the popular will was, at that point, arguably a necessary condition for Britain's maintaining public order until 1997. His strong advocacy of more democracy for Hong Kong has still barely sustained his legitimacy. Another diplomat/bureaucrat governor without support of the democratically identified local leadership would have had almost no chance of gaining legitimacy within Hong Kong.

Recently, the communist world came to a view that utilitarian aims favour less control and decentralisation. The authoritarian's fondness for a single *dao* is not the obvious conclusion for a reflective, pragmatic Chinese reasoner. He could conclude that Xunzi was wrong, as his contemporary Daoists argued even then.

7. Possible Counter-arguments

a) Contingency of the Proof

Several objections still face pragmatic approaches to Chinese justifications of liberty. First, a duty individualist may argue that even if pragmatic, utilitarian arguments can justify a scheme of rights, they do not yield the Rawlsian priority of rights. It is an empirical, contingent fact about economies, psychology, society and the world that greater freedom, wider political participation lead to utilitarian results. Those *could* be different and if they were, the argument for human rights would vanish. It leaves rights contingent and thus vulnerable to counter-argument. For example, someone may say that a scheme of human rights will undermine public order and lead to crime and other horrors.

The Rawlsian allows no such response or counter-argument from the authoritarian. A utilitarian argument does. The challenge cannot, then, be to give a utilitarian justification of perfectly non-defeasible freedom. Utilitarian arguments depend on the real-world outcome of political principles. Still, we should insist that the mere assertion of *possible* effects is neither enough for the libertarian nor for the authoritarian. The challenge is to show that the best consequential reasoning justifies a scheme of political liberty, democracy and freedom. We meet that challenge as long as the statistics and consequential reasoning are sound. Authoritarians still must show that the good outcomes follow from restricting freedom. The weight of empirical evidence is against them. To allow a response is not to lose the debate.

We have argued that greater freedom fosters utility in the form of economic prosperity, but we have not conceded that the *only* utilitarian end that counts is economic prosperity. Utilitarianism, itself, is a variable "point of view". It varies as we consider a richer range of values to seek. Our Chinese base allows us to appeal to more complex goals than those on which Xunzi or Lee Kwan Yew rely.

The utilitarian "good" is under-defined in both China and the West. There are internal and comparative differences in both conceptions of the good. The classical Chinese conception places a higher value on the goals of order, social development, elegance in performance, skill or know-how. The Western conception comparatively stresses private satisfaction, pleasure, happiness or the accumulation of theoretical wisdom. Both value economic measures and in roughly the same degree. Mozi so excluded private enjoyment from his utility calculations that he opposed music. However, Confucians, starting from Confucius, valued the elegant performance of ritual and music. Daoists valued the spontaneity of wine drinking, poetry, painting, abstruse philosophy and occurrent whim. A valid authoritarian counter-argument based *solely* on economic prosperity is not available in either culture.

b) Internal Coherence: Rights Must be Non-contingent
A kindred objection, however, would be that the consequentialist position is *internally incoherent*. Society loses the utilitarian efficiency of liberty when the liberties are not secure. If people worry that government might remove their liberty whenever conditions change then we lose the utilitarian advantages (predictability, forward planning, etc.). Greater utility derives from liberties that are comparatively invulnerable to temporary circumstances. The best utilitarian outcome, a Rawlsian may argue, comes from valuing liberty above temporary economic advantage. Therefore, we should enshrine rights in higher law, less vulnerable to change. A scheme of freedom achieves greatest utility when it can veto even democratically designed economic policies aimed at general welfare.

This, of course, is not so much an objection as a utilitarian route to an argument for a more invulnerable scheme of liberties. The advocates of a Bangkok position miss the point that even classical Chinese ethics does have access to exactly this type of second-level justification. Chinese ethical disputes were not a simple matter of advocating different first-level attitudes about actions. Mozi originally raised utilitarian considerations in China as second-level considerations. He thought of a *dao* as the public moral stance and proposed utilitarian considerations as the higher-level standards for choosing a public *dao*. Xunzi's reactionary justification of tradition, as I noted, also starts from a higher-level standard of utility.

IV. Conclusion

Thus, this objection does not undermine a genuinely Chinese form of consequential reasoning in defence of *practically* secure liberty. Such an argument is available to reasoners from within Chinese tradition. It merely requires allowing that Xunzi miscalculated the probabilistic outcomes. Given modern awareness of the econometric arguments, Chinese liberals can easily update Mozi's claims. This would give a straightforward justification of a legal and moral priority and relative political invulnerability for a scheme of ordered liberty.

Taken in a way that gives it normative bite, therefore, the Bangkok objection distorts the Chinese tradition. Whatever some key figures in the tradition may have concluded or argued and whatever rulers may have favoured, there are argumentative resources within a *purely* Chinese reasoning base that can generate valid and persuasive arguments for democracy and an extensive and secure scheme of human liberty.

Notes

1. Rosemont's arguments are complicated not only by his challenge to Western background beliefs, but also by his way of characterising morality and his related argu-

ments about relativity. These are complicated issues which deserve fuller discussion but I will not be able to address these issues in the detail they deserve here. I will have to make do with noting where I agree with and depart from Rosemont on these deeper issues.

2. Rawls, 1971, p. 60. Rawls has continuously revised the wording of the two principles, the latest in 1993. Nothing in my argument will turn on subtleties in formulation.

3. It comes closest, I think, in his "Kantian constructivist" phase (1980). His use of a hypothetical choice model (1971) was not an argument as much as an expository device. Dworkin (1977) best exemplifies a Rawlsian approach of deriving the principles of justice from some higher principle – equal concern and respect for individuals.

4. Some may use this criterion to distinguish between moral and legal claims. Legal claims, they may argue, are justified by second-level standards, but those standards themselves have no justification. They are the standards of the legal system in virtue of their being institutionalised.

5. See Gibbard, 1990. Gibbard does not deny that some moral standards may be genetic adaptations, but the most important one is the adaptation to engage in moral discourse, to be moved by others' judgments and to expect them to be moved by ours. See Kitcher, 1993 for an excellent discussion of the evolutionary issues surrounding the genetic disposition to qualified altruism.

6. It is easy enough to claim that each person wants him or herself to be free, but it is harder to show that all people have a pro- attitude toward a scheme in which all are as free as they can be while still being equally free. One way to salvage the pan-human view is to combine the individual's alleged approval of her own freedom with a requirement of consistency/universalisation and a claim that the latter is a natural or inherent presupposition of moral reasoning.

7. For example, Mencius thinks humans are naturally inclined to benevolence. They are inclined to other moral behaviour by something like a social "shame" response. This suggests that there is a genetic sociability that underlies a range of possible conventional moralities. We are inclined to accept content included in our community morality.

8. Arguments in favour of a universal attitude of moral autonomy would normally take the form of those offered by Piaget (1932) for a parallel conclusion about physical concepts. The main reference here is Kohlberg (1981, 1984). For an interesting presentation of the view that traditional Confucian thinkers do have strong conceptions of moral autonomy, see Roetz 1992.

9. Careful readers will note that I am not focusing on the conceptual structure of rights claims but on the normative support for extensive liberty. If we can defend a normative conclusion that we should allow extensive liberty from within a Chinese moral framework, I take that as normative success. Whether they use a strict equivalent to "a right" is a conceptual issue. I appreciate that some would argue that it has normative implications. I touch on this in the last section when I discuss how Chinese justifications of liberty might differ from the liberties the West emphasises.

10. In the case of the Confucian orthodoxy, one could claim that while Chinese philosophy was suitably reflective in its classical period, the Medieval and Early Modern forms of Confucianism were too much like religious ethics to count as reflective in the appropriate sense. Another might be to deny that it is in equilibrium – there is a substantial portion of that moral community (the people *v.* the rulers) who advocate greater freedom and democracy.

11. Some include me among those "others". As I note below, I have joined Ames and Rosemont in drawing attention to the depth of the differences in moral and philosophical outlook. I am here anxious, however, to avoid the questionable *normative* inference that this makes it permissible for Chinese governments to restrict individual liberty.

12. This stems partly from Mencius's use of the term and his interpretation of utilitarianism as inherently selfish.

13. Neither Ames nor Rosemont directly claims that the concept is baldly unintelligible. Rosemont only notes that there would be no way to get to the conclusion from classical Confucian premises.

14. We need to avoid a purely syntactic conception of permissions to rule out the following kinds of permissions: "Governments are permitted to exile nuns from religions that oppose its rule."

15. This can only be an approximation, not a final judgment. One of the interesting differences between Western and Chinese moral attitudes involves the optimism about how much moral suasion can achieve and thus how aggressively the social mechanisms of moral anger/guilt-shame/blame/praise can be used. Western morality tends to be, in Gibbard's words (1990 pp. 303–9), a "diffident" morality. Confucianism and Daoism split partly on this issue, but Confucianism, certainly, tends toward the "imperious" ambition to get more from moral mechanisms. In a synthesis, Westerners might decide that moral mechanisms are more effective than traditionally thought (hampered by unreasonably pessimistic views of human psychology) and choose a more "imperious" moral stance. One reason for this might be to reduce the reliance on legal and other sanctions.

16. As an intellectual point, Rosemont's challenge seems to be carefully limited to Confucius himself. Would there be a way to show Confucius that his conception was wrong and that it should include elements of human rights? I still think the answer is yes and that the way to do it is found in the Chinese tradition itself. Mozi shows that on Confucian assumptions about the goals of moral guidance (family wellbeing) one can conclude that we should favour a *dao* of universal concern to one of Confucian, partial (based on social relations) concern. See my discussion in Hansen, 1992, pp. 112–5.

17. I leave this conclusion in place despite now-growing literature stemming from, among others, Victor Mair insisting that Chinese civilisation came from Indo-European roots and Daoism from Buddhism. At some point the issue becomes terminological. If we count among Western influence migration patterns of 3,000 BC then there is no point in even thinking of a Chinese moral perspective.

18. See Hansen 1972. For my reasons for agreeing with Rosemont on these differ-

ences but thinking that they do not warrant his conclusion that Confucianism has no concept of morality, see Hansen 1992, pp. 81–3.

19. Here I disagree with Rosemont who rejects use of the concept "morality" in discussing China. He does, admittedly, limit himself to Confucianism – specifically to Confucius – and I accept that it is not obvious that Confucius had a clear conception of morality. However, Rosemont can conclude that Mozi and other classical Chinese thinkers lack such a notion only if he limits morality to deontological moralities with a focus on individual choice. Such a limit would not reflect the range of the term even in Western use. Western usage recognises utilitarianism as a (perhaps false) moral theory and recognises virtue moralities as alternative moral perspectives. The term that marks the distinction between traditional rules or mores and the ideal *dao* that Mozi seeks, *yi*, is a workable Chinese counterpart of "morality". Its crucial identifying feature is evidenced in Mozi's arguing that the fact that a whole society always has agreed on some action or behaviour does not make it *yi*. Thus, even if Confucius's theory did not mark the distinction between propriety/mores and morality, the distinction is in the language. Confucius might have missed the real implications of the concepts in his language, as any native speaker might. The Confucians who came after Mozi clearly had theoretical access to Mozi's distinction of morality and tradition and pursued the argument on Mozi's terms. I would resist characterising Chinese moral attitudes and norms of reasoning by the limitations of Confucius's own pre-philosophical level of understanding.

20. The Confucian interpretive tradition usually assumes Mozi wants "Heaven" to select the human ruler. The argument, however, is a rational choice argument directed at any audience (as is the Hobbesian parallel) to get us to see the wisdom of having leaders to avoid the state of Nature. If Heaven/Nature were going to set up a ruler, the argument would be pointless and its relevance to the act of selection would be lost. Two of the three versions of Mozi's teachings are silent on who does the selecting and the third explicitly says "the social world" makes the selection. Anti-Mohist commentary opines that this is a mistake for "Heaven" alone. I disagree.

21. This is partly for formal reasons concerning the focus on names rather than sententials, concentration on standards for the application of those names and absence of understanding or using universal sententials (rules) and of a distinct conception of "oughts" or duties and partly because of near absence of retributivism. The so-called Legalists are, like Mohists, essentially consequentialist or utilitarian in their arguments.

22. See Fingarette (1979), Ivanhoe (1990), and Hansen (1992, pp. 385–6) for further discussion of the issue of the "one thread" in *The Analects*.

23. The other mechanism explaining how one achieves the mandate (which effectively means defeating the enemy's army) is the natural loyalty and courage this innate preference instils for a moral/benevolent ruler. The moral ruler's soldiers will not defect or lose courage in battle as will those of the selfish ruler. Thus, even against overwhelming numerical odds, the moral ruler has a real advantage. Mencius's slogan of "winning the hearts and minds of the people" has even become part of the West's political vocabulary.

24. Mencius may be the only exception and he is not a clear one, as I argued above.

25. Of course, one may find such assumptions among a contemporary Chinese

moral community – given the influences on Chinese culture since 200 BC!

26. Mill's argument has notorious flaws – some of which would be less vicious in a Chinese context. For example, it was buttressed by Mill's faith that truth would win out in the marketplace of ideas. That has a more naive ring than would the classical Chinese version.

27. Remember that we are not talking here about behaviour, but about idealisations, attitudes and justifications that appeal to a moral community. The point is made if Chinese leaders feel a necessity to assert that they are democratic or to justify their rule by appeal to democratic principles.

Selected Bibliography

Ames, Roger, 1983, *The Art of Rulership: A Study in Ancient Chinese Political Thought*, Honolulu, University of Hawaii Press

— & David Hall, 1987, *Thinking Through Confucius*, Albany, State University of New York Press

— 1988, "Rites as Rights: The Confucian Alternative", pp. 199–214 in Leroy S. Rouner (ed.), *Human Rights and the World's Religions*, South Bend, University of Notre Dame Press

Blackburn, Simon, 1984, *Spreading the Word: Groundings in the Philosophy of Language*, Oxford, Clarendon Press, p. 368

Confucius, *The Analects* (Harvard Yenching Concordance Series, No. 16, 1972)

Cua, Anthony S., 1985, *Ethical Argumentation: A Study in Hsun Tzu's Moral Epistemology*, Honolulu, University of Hawaii Press

Dawson, Raymond, 1981, *Confucius*, New York, Hill and Wang

DeBary, W. Theodore, 1988, "Neo-Confucianism and Human Rights" pp. 183–98, in Leroy S. Rouner (ed.), *Human Rights and the World's Religions*, South Bend, University of Notre Dame Press

Donagan, Alan, 1977, *The Theory of Morality*, Chicago, University of Chicago Press

Dworkin, Ronald, 1977, *Taking Rights Seriously*, Cambridge, Harvard University Press

Eno, Robert, 1990, *The Confucian Creation of Heaven*, Buffalo, SUNY Series in Chinese Philosophy and Culture

Fingarette, Herbert, 1972, *Confucius: The Secular as Sacred*, New York, Harper and Row

— 1979, "Following the 'One Thread' of the Analects", *Studies in Classical Chinese Thought, Journal of the American Academy of Religion*, Thematic Issue vol. 47/3, 373–406

Gibbard, Allan, 1990, *Wise Choices, Apt Feelings: A Theory of Normative Judgment*, New York, Oxford University Press

Graham, Angus, 1964, "The Place of Reason in the Chinese Philosophical Tradition", pp. 28–56 in Raymond Dawson (ed.), *The Legacy of China*, London, Oxford University Press

— 1967, "The Background of the Mencian Theory of Human Nature", *Tsing Hua Journal of Chinese Studies*, 6/1–2, 215–74

— 1978, *Later Mohist Logic, Ethics and Science*, Hong Kong and London, Chinese University Press

Hansen, Chad, 1985a, "Individualism in Chinese Thought", pp. 35–56, in Donald Munro (ed.), *Individualism and Holism: Studies in Confucian and Taoist Values*, Ann Arbor, University of Michigan Press

— 1985b, "Punishment and Dignity in China", pp. 359–82, in Donald Munro (ed.), *Individualism and Holism: Studies in Confucian and Taoist Values*, Ann Arbor, University of Michigan Press

— 1992, *A Daoist Theory of Chinese Thought*, New York, Oxford University Press

— April 1972, "Freedom and Moral Responsibility in Confucian Ethics", *Philosophy East and West*, 22/2

— May 1993, "Chinese Ideographs and Western Ideas", *Journal of Asian Studies*

Harman, Gilbert, 1977, *The Nature of Morality*, New York, Oxford University Press

Hsiao, Kungchuan (trans. F.W. Mote), 1979, *A History of Chinese Political Thought, Volume I: From the Beginnings to the Sixth Century A.D.*, Princeton, Princeton University Press

Hughes, E.R., 1942, *Chinese Philosophy in Classical Times*, London, J.M. Dent & Sons Ltd

Ivanhoe, P.J., January 1990, "Reweaving the 'One Thread' of The Analects", *Philosophy East and West*, XL/1, 17–33

Kitcher, Philip, 1993, "The Evolution of Human Altruism", *The Journal of Philosophy*, 90/10, 497–516

Liang Qichao, 1930, *History of Chinese Political Thought*, London, Kegan Paul Trench Trubner & Co.

Lyons, David, 1965, *Forms and Limits of Utilitarianism*, Oxford, Clarendon Press

Mill, John Stuart, 1859, "On Liberty", London

Munro, Donald J., 1969, *The Concept of Man in Early China*, Stanford, Stanford University Press

— 1985, *Individualism and Holism: Studies in Confucian and Taoist Values*, Ann Arbor, MI, University of Michigan Center for Chinese Studies

Nathan, Andrew, 1985, *Chinese Democracy*, Berkeley, University of California Press

Parfit, Derek, 1984, *Reasons and Persons*, New York, Oxford University Press

Rawls, John, 1971, *A Theory of Justice*, Cambridge, Harvard University Press

— 1980, "Kantian Constructivism in Moral Theory", *The Journal of Philosophy*, Sept. 1980

— 1993, *Political Liberalism*, New York, Columbia University Press

Roetz, Heiner, 1992, *Confucian Ethics in the Axial Age*, Albany, NY, State University of New York Press

Rosemont, Henry Jr., 1988, "Why Take Rights Seriously? A Confucian Critique", pp. 167–82, in Leroy S. Rouner (ed.), *Human Rights and the World's Religions*, South Bend, University of Notre Dame Press

— 1991, *A Chinese Mirror: Moral Reflections on Political Economy and Society*, LaSalle, IL, Open Court

Rouner, Leroy S., 1988, *Human Rights and the World's Religions*, South Bend, University of Notre Dame Press, pp. xviii & 220

Chapter 7

Moral Orientation and Moral Judgment of Chinese Adolescents

MA HING-KEUNG

I. Introduction

This study investigates a person's orientation to perform altruistic, affective, law-abiding or self-actualising acts in hypothetical moral dilemmas. It also explores the relationships between these moral orientations and moral judgment.

Generally speaking, the altruistic, affective, law-abiding and self-actualising orientations are concerned with some important features of the affective and motivational aspects of moral development, and the moral judgment is regarded as the cognitive aspect of moral development. Current theories of moral development seldom investigate the cognitive and affective aspects as an integrated whole for a lifespan development. While the cognitive developmental approach established by Piaget (1932), Kohlberg (1969, 1976, 1981, 1984) and Rest (1979) deals intensively with the cognitive aspect, it does not account for the affective aspect directly or explicitly (see e.g., Peters, 1971). On the other hand, the psychoanalytic approach (e.g., Gilligan, 1976) lays strong emphasis on the feeling or affective aspect but neglects considerably the cognitive aspect. Other approaches are the behaviouristic theory (Eysenck, 1976) and social learning theory (Bandura, 1977; Mischel and Mischel, 1976), which are quite successful only in explaining overt behaviour. A description and criticism of the above theoretical perspectives is given in Lickona (1976) and Wright (1971).

Hoffman (1976, 1977, 1979) has established a theory for accounting for both the cognitive and affective aspects of empathy and altruism but he has not extended his theory to development beyond late childhood. Thompson and Hoffman (1980), using semi-projective stories in the study of the development of guilt in children, reported that their results provided modest support for Hoffman's theory. In short, M.L. Hoffman has taken a giant stride in developing a theory which integrates the cognitive and affective aspects of altruistic behaviour. On the other hand, Simpson (1976) has developed a holistic theory which attempts to account for the cognitive, affective and conative aspects of moral development in one setting, but unfortunately she has not presented any empirical evidence to support her model. Nevertheless, her insight in relating Maslow's (1970) hierarchy of basic needs to Kohlberg's (1969) stages of moral development is stimulating.

A description of different types of moral orientation is presented below.

II. Affective and Altruistic Orientation

According to Sharabany and Bar-Tal (1982, p. 50), there is no universally accepted definition of altruism, and the definition varies among theorists of different approaches. With reference to Berkowitz (1972) and Krebs (1970), Bar-Tal (1976, p. 5) defines altruistic behaviour as a voluntary act which must aim to benefit others and which must be carried out without expectation of a reward (see also Sharabany and Bar-Tal, 1982). A fairly similar definition of altruism is given in Leeds (1963, pp. 230–1), Schwartz and Howard (1984, p. 229), and Wispe (1972, p. 4). The above definition refers predominantly to self-sacrificial altruistic acts. Some psychologists also regard reciprocally altruistic acts as a type of altruism. Social exchange theorists (Blau, 1964; Homans, 1961, 1968; Thibaut and Kelley, 1959) argue that when people interact, they tend to reciprocate with one another in such a way as to maximise rewards and minimise costs. In other words, altruism is a means for future rewards or it is a type of social investment. Sociobiologists also argue that reciprocal altruism is naturally selected if the performance of altruistic behaviour results in "a return of altruistic behaviour towards the original altruist such that the ultimate benefit in units of inclusive fitness is greater than the cost" (Barash, 1977, p. 94). On the other hand, it may be argued that reciprocal altruism should not be regarded as a kind of altruism since it is basically selfish.

The following criteria for altruism based on Barash (1977), Bar-Tal (1976) and Leeds (1963) are proposed in this study:

1) Altruistic behaviour must be carried out voluntarily without expectation of a reward.

2) It must aim to benefit the recipient in at least one of the following ways: (a) it increases Darwinian fitness; (b) it facilitates the development of higher stages in cognition, morality, ego etc., and helps to attain new psychological abilities such as intellectual and social skills; (c) it increases the gratification of basic psychological needs such as physiological, safety, belongingness and love, esteem and self-actualisation needs (Maslow, 1970); and (d) it helps to restore and maintain emotional stability.

3) Overall, the donor is "doing good" as judged by the recipient.

III. The Hierarchy of Human Relationships

Based on the work of Barash (1977, p. 316), Carter (1980), and Hardin (1977, p. 13), the following "Hierarchy of Human Relationships" is hypothetically constructed in terms of altruism (Ma, 1982, 1985a, 1989).

130

A Hierarchy of Human Relationships

R_1 First kin, close relatives.

R_2 Best friends or intimates.

R_3 Strangers who are very weak, e.g., a blind person; or very young, e.g., a small child of six years; or who are elites of the society, e.g., a famous scientist who is a Nobel Prize winner.

R_4 Common strangers.

R_5 Someone you dislike or enemies.

The main features of the Hierarchy of Human Relationships are as follows:

1. Members in the R_1 group are usually genetically related. A term called coefficient of relationship (r) or genetic kinship used by sociobiologists (Hardin, 1977, p. 13; Wilson, 1975, pp. 74–5) is useful for elaboration of this genetic relatedness. Simply put, r between two persons A and B refers to the proportion of genes in A and B that are identical because of common descent. The r between a person (A) and one of his/her parents, son/daughter, or brother/sister is 1/2 and that between A and one of his/her grandparents, uncle, aunt, nephew, niece, and double first cousin is 1/4. In general, the larger (smaller) the r between an actor A and another person (B), the larger (smaller) is the probability that A will carry out an altruistic act regarding B.

2. Generally speaking, a person will value the importance of people in different categories in the following order: R_1, R_2, R_3, R_4, R_5. In other words, the probability that an actor A will carry out an altruistic act regarding a person B is highest if B belongs to the R_1 category and decreases consistently to the lowest when B belongs to the R_5 category in similar social situations.

3. The above division of the five groups of people is quite arbitrary but the order of the hierarchy – kin-friend-stranger-enemy – is invariant of the method of division.

Apart from the sociobiological basis mentioned above, there is also a social basis for the Hierarchy of Human Relationships. Genetically unrelated people who have developed deep affection and profound love for one another may also act altruistically towards one another. The tendency for an actor to perform an altruistic act towards a person with no genetic relatedness to the actor decreases in the following order of relationships: spouse/lover, best friend, acquaintance, stranger and enemy. Generally speaking, the interaction between an actor with his/her spouse, lover or best friend is often pleasant, approaching, affective and frequent. The actor is also familiar with these people and usually bears some essential similarities to them. The interaction between an actor and a stranger or an enemy is, however, less pleasant and less affective.

Ma (1989) used hypothetical moral dilemmas to study the proposed hierarchy and claimed that his findings supported the hierarchy of human relationships in Hong Kong, Mainland China and England. He also found that Chinese subjects from Hong Kong and Mainland China showed a stronger tendency to perform affective and altruistic acts towards others than did the English subjects. He argued that Chinese tend to emphasise *ch'ing* (human affection or sentiment) rather than *li* (reason, rational aspect) and value filial piety, group solidarity, collectivism and humanity (see e.g., Dien, 1982; Hsu, 1970; Yang, 1986). Such cultural influences may account for the stronger tendency in Chinese subjects to perform affective and altruistic acts towards others.

Three hypotheses were formulated based on the Hierarchy of Human Relationships. R_5 is not included in Hypothesis 3 because of the design of the test instrument.

Hypothesis H1: The tendency of an actor to sacrifice his/her life for a recipient decreases consistently from R_1 to R_5.

Hypothesis H2: The tendency of an actor to give up rescuing a stranger and turn to rescue a recipient in danger decreases consistently from R_1 to R_5.

Hypothesis H3: The tendency of an actor to help a recipient by covering up his/her crime decreases consistently from R_1 to R_4.

1. Law-abiding Orientation

According to Maslow's (1970) theory, basic needs are arranged in a hierarchy of pre-potency as follows: physiological, safety, belongingness and love, esteem, and self-actualisation. The relation between law-abiding orientation and psychological needs is formulated in Hypothesis H4.

Hypothesis H4: A person is less oriented to abide by the law if he or she is deficient in lower-order needs (e.g., physiological, safety or love needs) than in higher order needs (e.g., esteem, social or self-actualisation needs).

According to Hypothesis H4, if by chance a person picks up a lost bag which contains more than a thousand dollars, the tendency to keep the money is higher if the person needs money to cure a serious disease in an overseas hospital (to gratify physiological and safety needs, that is, survival needs) than if money is needed to study in a university abroad (to gratify esteem or social needs).

Hypothesis H3 is also concerned with law-abiding orientation. It states that the probability of an individual's (A) breaking the law to do something in favour of a person (B) decreases as the relatedness between A and B decreases from close relative to stranger. In other words, the probability of abiding by the law in this case is smallest for a close relative and the greatest for a stranger.

132

Ma (1985b, 1989) found that Chinese subjects from Hong Kong and Mainland China showed a stronger tendency to abide by the law than did the English subjects. He argued that Chinese children are usually brought up in a more authoritarian and less democratic way. They are usually taught to obey the authorities, to stick to the rigid norm and to abide by the law under any circumstances (see e.g., Liu, 1986, p. 78). In a critical review of Chinese patterns of socialisation, Ho (1986) also concludes that "traditionally, great emphasis was placed on obedience, proper conduct, moral training, and the acceptance of social obligations, in contrast to the lack of emphasis placed on independence, assertiveness, and creativity" (pp. 35–6). This kind of child-rearing method may account for the strong orientation in Chinese subjects to abide by the law.

2. Self-actualising Orientation

The concept of self-actualisation is one of the central themes of humanistic psychology. Maslow's (1970, p. 149–80) concept of self-actualisation will be employed here. Briefly speaking, self-actualising people tend to have deeper and more profound interpersonal relationships than other people. Self-actualising people are fair, democratic people who always know how to discriminate clearly between means and ends, and between good and evil. They also tend to show a deeper identification with the human species as a whole. In addition, they behave with a high degree of spontaneity, simplicity and naturalness.

Hypothesis H5: People are less oriented towards self-actualisation if they are in heavy deficiency of the lower-order needs such as belongingness needs than in heavy deficiency of the higher-order needs such as esteem and social needs.

3. Moral Orientations and Maslow's Hierarchy of Basic Needs

For convenience of discussion, Maslow's (1970) original hierarchy is slightly modified as follows: N_1 = Physiological and Safety Needs (i.e., Survival Needs); N_2 = Belongingness Needs; N_3 = Affective and Giving Needs; N_4 = Esteem Needs; and N_5 = Self-actualisation Needs. Two minor rearrangements of Maslow's original hierarchy were made: (1) The Physiological and Safety Needs were incorporated into one category which could be regarded as the survival needs of a person. Broadly speaking, survival needs are concerned with physical survival, for maintenance of life and for security or safety. (2) Maslow's Belongingness and Love Needs were subdivided into two levels: N_2

and N_3. The Belongingness Needs (N_2) deal with the need to love and to be loved by one's first kin, close relatives and best friends, and the Affective and Giving Needs (N_3) are concerned with a person's disposition to love or to show affection to the weak (e.g., a blind person), the good or the elite (e.g., a famous scientist) and the very young (e.g., a child of six years old).

The moral orientation of a person to perform affective and altruistic act towards others could well be regarded as one's tendency to gratify the Belongingness Needs (N_2) and Affective and Giving Needs (N_3) in the modified Hierarchy of Basic Needs. Similarly, the Law-abiding and self-actualising orientations mentioned above are related to the gratification of Esteem (N_4) and Self-actualisation (N_5) Needs. In addition, one's willingness to sacrifice one's life for others could also be related to one's tendency to gratify Survival Needs (N_1).

Hypothesis H6: One's tendency to gratify the psychological needs decreased consistently from N_2 (Belongingness Needs) to N_5 (Self-actualisation Needs).

4. Moral Judgment

Moral judgment or moral reasoning will be studied via Kohlberg's (1969, 1976, 1981, 1984) stages of moral judgment. Kohlberg's six stages of moral development are grouped into four levels (the corresponding Kohlberg stages are given in brackets): J_1 = Pre-conventional Level (Stages 1 and 2, that is, Heteronomous Morality and the stage of Individualism, Instrumental Purpose and Exchange); J_2 = the Stage of Mutual Interpersonal Expectations, Relationships, and Interpersonal Conformity (Stage 3); J_3 = the Social System and Conscience Stage (Stage 4); J_4 = Post-conventional and Principled Level (Stages 5 and 6). In an extensive review of 45 cross-cultural studies of moral development using Kohlberg's Moral Judgment Instrument, Snarey (1985) concludes that the data indicated Kohlberg's "Stage 1 to Stage 3/4 or 4 were in evidence virtually universally when one took into consideration the age range and sample size of the population under study" (p. 226). A similar conclusion was drawn in two earlier reviews by Bergling (1981) and Edwards (1981). Generally speaking, Kohlberg's pre-conventional and conventional stages are quite universal as far as cross-cultural data are concerned.

5. Relationship Between Moral Orientations and Moral Judgment

It is expected that people at a higher stage of moral judgment should in general show a stronger orientation towards sacrificing their lives for others in an emergency; that is, they should have a weaker tendency to gratify the N_1 needs in such situations (see also Rushton, 1981, p. 263). On the other hand, the N_2 and N_3 needs are concerned with the belongingness, affective and giving needs which involve altruistic orientations towards first kin, intimates and people who are very weak or very good. The gratification of these two lower-order needs are so basic and common to all people at different ages that people at different stages of moral judgment should show more or less similar gratification patterns of the N_2 and N_3 needs. As one grows up, one is more oriented towards seeking a higher degree of gratification of higher-order needs (e.g., N_4 or N_5 needs) as well as to develop higher stages of moral judgment. In other words, a person's behaviour becomes more pro-social and law-abiding as his/her structure of moral judgment develops to the conventional level. Those at the post-conventional level of moral judgment usually abide by the law except in extreme situations where there is a conflict of social law with the self-chosen ethical principles of universal justice (Kohlberg, 1976, 1981). Self-actualisers or people with a strong self-actualising orientation are fair, moral and democratic people (Maslow, 1970), and should be able to reason at the higher stage of moral judgment.

Hypothesis H7: The stage of moral judgment is negatively related to the orientation to gratify the N_1 needs, and positively related to the orientation to gratify the N_4 and N_5 needs. On the other hand, the relation between the stage of moral judgment and the orientation to gratify the N_2 and N_3 needs should be fairly weak.

In order to test these hypotheses more rigorously, we will combine several of the previous data sets in the following analyses. A total of 1,853 Grade 4 to 12 and university students were used for testing Hypotheses 1 to 6, and 961 Grade 10 to 12 and university students for testing Hypothesis 7.

IV. Method

1. Subjects

Subjects were divided into four sub-samples: Primary School (Grade 4 to 6), Junior Secondary School (Grade 7 to 9), Senior Secondary School (Grade

10 to 12), and University. There were 604 Primary School (307m, 297f), 288 Junior Secondary (143m, 145f), 670 Senior Secondary School (341m, 329f), and 291 University (162m, 129f) subjects in Hong Kong. The total was N = 1,853 (953m, 900f). All subjects were Chinese. The mean ages (standard deviation in parentheses) of Primary School, Junior Secondary School, Senior Secondary School, and University subjects were 11.46 (1.12), 14.22 (1.29), 17.39 (1.39), and 20.83 (1.56), respectively. There are six missing cases on the age variable. The Primary School and Secondary School subjects came from government-funded or private schools which admitted students of heterogeneous social background and mixed academic standard. The college subjects were recruited from one university and two tertiary institutes.

2. Instruments: Moral Development Test (MDT)

The Moral Development Test was constructed to study the development of moral orientations and moral judgment (Ma, 1982, 1988, 1989, 1992, 1993). It consisted of five dilemmas: (A) A Lost Bag, (B) The Sinking Boat, (C) A Doctor's Dilemma, (D) A Car Accident and (E) The Criminal. Each dilemma described a hypothetical situation and the subjects were asked to imagine themselves in the situation. The hypothetical dilemma was followed by sets of questions divided into two parts. Part I consisted of a set of persons or a set of specified conditions denoted by X_1, X_2, X_3 ... etc., constructed to study a person's orientation towards performing affective and altruistic acts or abiding by the law. Subjects were asked to rate each X_i on a seven-point scale (From "Definitely Yes" to "Definitely No"). The test format of the MDT Part II was based on Rest's (1979) Defining Issues Test and consisted of a set of nine Kohlbergian-type statements. Subjects were asked to rate on a five-point scale (from "Very Great Importance" to "No Importance") how important each of the statements would be in deciding their answers in Part I. A description of the five dilemmas is given below.

Dilemma (A): A lost bag
Suppose that one day, when walking by yourself along a road, you accidentally discover a bag. You open it and find that it contains a lot of money, almost 10,000 pounds, and some documents showing that the money belongs to a big company. It so happens that for a particular reason X, you need a great deal of money immediately and there is no other way for you to obtain such a large amount of money except by keeping the money in the bag. Would you do so if the reason X is __?

The Part I questions of this dilemma consisted of six X_js, two of which were: "You have been accepted by a world-famous university abroad for a two-year course which you earnestly desire to attend. However, there are no grants or scholarships available and the cost each year is about $50,000", and: "You are near death from a rare disease, which the doctors think may be cured only in a particular hospital in another country. The total expense will be about $100,000".

Two of the nine Part II statements in "A Lost Bag" were (the Js given in brackets are defined in the Introduction section): "Whether my chance of being caught by the police is high or not" (J_1), and: "Is it a citizen's responsibility to report the lost bag to the police?" (J_3).

Dilemma (B): The sinking boat

You and X are in a boat which is sinking, but only you or X can be rescued. Would you sacrifice yourself so that X could be rescued if X is __?

X: X_1 = a young stranger, 20 years old; X_2 = an old stranger, 70 years old; X_3 = a famous scientist who is also a Nobel Prize winner; X_4 = your brother or sister; X_5 = your best friend; X_6 = a postman; X_7 = someone you do not like or an enemy; X_8 = a child, six years old.

Three of the Part II statements in this dilemma were (the Js given in brackets are defined in the Introduction): "Am I willing to suffer the terrible and painful experience of being drowned so that X could be rescued?" (J_1) "Isn't it natural for a person to take care of his/her relatives or friends in case of emergency?" (J_2), and: "Is it my responsibility to sacrifice myself for X?" (J_3).

Dilemma (C): A doctor's dilemma

It described a young medical doctor called Susan who had overcome a lot of difficulties to work as a voluntary doctor in a remote village in a poor and underdeveloped country. After two years' work in the village, she is faced with a difficult problem X. The subjects were asked: "Suppose you were Susan, would you give up the present job in the village if the problem X is __?"

There were six X_js in this dilemma and two of them were: "Her fiancé Peter wrote to her and said that he could not wait any longer, if she is not going to return within a few months, he will not marry her", and: "Her mother suffers a stroke and is paralysed. She wants Susan to come back and look after her."

Dilemma (D): A car accident

Suppose that one day you are on a bus which is in an accident with a car and a heavy lorry carrying dangerous chemicals. Most of the passengers on the bus are injured and it looks as if some might be dead. Fortunately, you are uninjured. You see flames start to come from under the car and the lorry and you

137

must get away as quickly as possible. However, you feel that you are strong enough to help to move one person to safety and so you start to drag a stranger near you off the bus. Just as you leave the bus with the stranger, you hear someone (X) in the car crying out for help. But *you have only time to rescue one person* – would you rescue X instead of the stranger from the bus if you recognise X as __?

There are nine X_is in this dilemma and they are quite similar to those in "The Sinking Boat".

Dilemma (E): The criminal

In the following situation, you observed quite by chance a person X committing a crime. You also saw where X went afterwards and so you know where X has hidden himself or herself. *Would you report X to the police* if X is __?

Situation 1: X was robbing a bank at gunpoint for reasons unknown to you.

Situation 2: X was robbing a bank at gunpoint for reasons unknown to you, and suppose you were a police officer.

(In the following three situations, do *not* suppose you were a police officer.)

Situation 3: X was robbing a bank at gunpoint because his or her son has a rare disease and is near death. The doctors think the son may be cured only in a particular hospital in another country and the cost is about $100,000. There is no other way for X to get such a large amount of money except by robbery.

Situation 4: Suppose it is *you* who have the rare disease in Situation 3 and X was robbing the bank in order to get money so that you could be cured. There is no other way for you to get such a large amount of money.

Situation 5: There was an earthquake in the northern part of your country a few days ago. The government has been very inefficient in taking care of the people in the disaster area, and only a few rich people have offered financial help. X went to the area and found that thousands of people urgently needed food, medicine and social care. He/she felt so desperate about the situation that he/she went back and robbed a bank at gunpoint in the southern part in order to get money to buy food and medicine for the people in the disaster area.

The same list of four X_is is given in each of the above five situations, except in Situation 4 where there are only three X_is. The four X_is are: (1) someone you are acquainted with; (2) your best friend; (3) your brother or sister; (4) a stranger. In Situation 4, the stranger is excluded because it is supposed that a stranger may not know that the subject is very sick and it is also very rare for a person to rob a bank for a stranger.

Several sets of test indices are constructed as follows.

(1) Human Relationships indices: RB1–RB5; RD1–RD5; and RE1–RE4

The RB, RD and RE indices were formulated by averaging the subject's ratings of the group of people (X_is) concerned in the dilemmas B ("The Sinking Boat), D ("Car Accident") and E ("The Criminal"), respectively. For example, RB1 = your brother or sister; RB2 = your best friend; RB3 = a famous scientist who is also a Nobel Prize winner, and a child, six years old; RB4= a young stranger, 20 years old; an old stranger, 70 years old, and a postman; and RB5 = someone you don't like or an enemy.

The RD indices were similarly constructed. For Dilemma (E): The Criminal, the item responses in the five situations were grouped into four RE indices: RE1 to RE4 were concerned with (1) your brother or sister, (2) your best friend, (3) someone you are acquainted with, and (4) a stranger, respectively. For example, the RE1 index was concerned with one's orientation towards *not* reporting one's brother/sister who has committed a crime to police. A small (large) rating of the RBi, RDi or REi index means a low (high) tendency to carry out an altruistic act towards a person in the corresponding R_i category in the Hierarchy of Human Relationships. The R_3 category in the Hierarchy of Human Relationships was specifically extended to include one's acquaintance so that RE3 corresponded to the R_3 category in future discussion.

(2) A1–A6 (Law-abiding Orientation) indices

The A1 to A6 indices were defined by the subject's rating of the Part I questions (X_is) in Dilemma (A): A Lost Bag. The central theme of this dilemma was whether the social law that "one must not steal" should be obeyed or not in different situations. In short, A1 and A2 concerned the lower-order needs (survival and affection needs), and A3, A4, and A5 and A6 the higher-order needs (esteem and social needs). Generally speaking, a small (large) rating of the A indices means a smaller (greater) tendency to abide by the law.

(3) S1–S6 (Self-actualising Orientation) indices

This set of indices were explored by Dilemma (C): A doctor's dilemma. S1 was concerned with one's orientation towards taking care of one's sick mother, and S2 and S3 were concerned with financial and political problems which were difficult for ordinary adolescents to perceive or understand, hence the orientations to self-actualise in these three situations were expected to be small. In addition, the orientation to self-actualise when one's safety was in threat (S4) should also be quite small. On the other hand, in S5, concerned with one's responsibility to cure villagers suffering from plague, the tendency to self-actualise should be greater than S2, S3 or S4. Finally, in S6, Susan's fiancé Peter was supposed to be the very person who understood and loved her. That Peter forced Susan to give up her village job might be regarded as a selfish act

139

which would damage Susan's self-esteem, hence one's tendency to self-actualise in this case should be the highest. In general, it is argued that one is less oriented towards self-actualising if one is deficient in lower-order needs (e.g., safety or love needs) than in a deficiency of higher-order needs (e.g., esteem or social needs).

(4) N1–N5 (Moral Orientation) indices

The N1 to N5 indices expressed orientations towards gratifying the N_1 to N_5 needs; they were formed by averaging the subject's rating of the relevant Part I item responses in the MDT. In other words, the N2 and N3 indices represented an orientation towards gratifying the Belongingness (N_2) and Affective and Giving (N_3) needs; N2 was composed of R1 and R2, and N3 was simply the R3. The N4 index was composed of all the Law-abiding Orientation Indices (A1 to A6, E1 to E4) and it represented a tendency to gratify the Esteem and Social needs (N_4). In addition, the N5 index consisted of the Self-actualising Indices (S1 to S6) and one item response (X_7) in Dilemma (B): The sinking boat. It clearly represented the orientation towards self-actualising.

The N1 index was constructed in terms of mainly the eight item responses in Dilemma (B): The sinking boat, which was related to the tendency to perform self-sacrificing acts where different categories of people (R_1 to R_5) were involved. In this case, the index N1 reflected a choice between the orientation towards gratifying the Survival (N_1) needs and the Belongingness (N_2) and Affective and Giving (N_3) needs. The dilemma was a difficult one because the choice involved neighbouring psychological needs of close pre-potency in the Hierarchy of Basic Needs. Thus, the index N1 did not measure one's orientation towards gratifying solely or predominantly the Survival (N_1) needs. If, in the Sinking Boat dilemma, the situation was changed as follows: "Suppose you are in a boat which is sinking, would you try your best to rescue yourself?" Then the subjects' responses could be regarded as expressing their orientation towards surviving, that is an orientation towards gratifying predominantly the Survival needs (N_1). If such questions were set, it would be expected that the mean rating would be quite close to 7 and would naturally be on top of the other four N (N2 to N5) indices. However, the present N1 index was complicated by the orientation towards gratifying N2 and N3 needs, and the position of its mean rating had to be determined empirically. The reason N1 was retained in our study was purely for empirical exploration.

The Affective and Altruistic Orientation, Law-abiding Orientation, and Self-actualising Orientation indices were regarded as Specific Moral Orientation indices; and the N1 to N5 indices were called the General Moral Orientation Indices. The classification of the indices into two categories is quite arbitrary and is mainly for convenience of future discussion.

(5) Moral Judgment score: TJ

Each Part II statement represented a J_i stage of moral judgment. The J1 to J4 indices were the average ratings of the Part II statements representing the J_1 to J_4 stages of moral judgment. All the statements representing Kohlberg's Stages 5 and 6 were used to generate the index J4. Generation of these J1 to J4 indices is based on the same principle used by Rest (1979, p. 228) in computing the six stage scores of moral judgment from the rating data of his Defining Issues Test.

The overall moral judgment score, TJ, is defined as $TJ = (J3 + J4)/2 - (J1 + J2)/2$. Construction of the TJ index was based on a rationale similar to that used in the construction of the simple sum (SS) score in Rest's (1979, p. 236) Defining Issues Test. Generally, a small (large) value in the TJ index indicates a low (high) level of moral judgment.

(6) MDT indices

The MDT indices were constructed by a simple sum of relevant scores: (Higher Stage Scores – Lower Stage Scores). Generally speaking, a small (large) value in the MDT indices indicates a low (high) stage of moral development in the aspect studied. The MDT Part I and Part II indices, TN and TJ, were constructed according to the following formulas: $TN = (N4 + N5)/2 - (N2 + N3)/2$, and $TJ = (J3 + J4)/2 - (J1 + J2)/2$. The TN and TJ indices were simple sums of the relevant N or J scores. Construction of the two indices was based on a rationale similar to that used in the construction of the simple sum (SS) score in Rest's (1979, p. 236) Defining Issues Test. The psychometric properties of the MDT have been demonstrated to be acceptable in Ma (1982, 1988, 1989). For example, the test-retest reliabilities of the major MDT scores in a sample of 100 Hong Kong subjects were from .64 to .84 with an average in the .70s (Ma, 1988). The MDT scores correlated positively and significantly with moral judgment scores such as Rest's (1979) DIT scores and less significantly with cognitive, intelligence and personality scores (Ma, 1982, 1988). In addition, the correlation of the moral orientation indices in the MDT correlated positively and significantly with the moral judgment score in the MDT in a cross-cultural study in Hong Kong, Mainland China and England (Ma, 1989), which revealed some of the important features of the internal structure of the MDT.

A summary of the above indices is given in the Appendix.

3. Procedure

Subjects completed the test in their own schools. The test instruction was explained in detail by the experimenter at the beginning and then the subjects were given sufficient time to complete the tests. The average time for completing the MDT was about 45 minutes.

V. Results and Discussion

1. Human Relationships

The means and standard deviations of the Human Relationships Indices are presented in Table 1.

Table 1

Means and Standard Deviations of Human Relationships Indices

Index	Primary School (n=604)		Junior Secondary School (n=288)		Senior Secondary School (n=670)		University (n=291)	
	M	SD	M	SD	M	SD	M	SD
The Sinking Boat								
RB1	6.34	1.15	6.24	1.03	6.06	1.02	6.00	.96
RB2	5.32	1.43	5.52	1.26	5.38	1.25	5.75	.99
RB3	5.42	1.23	4.81	1.29	4.40	1.45	4.66	1.32
RB4	3.72	1.43	3.48	1.47	2.89	1.33	3.20	1.36
RB5	3.14	2.00	2.67	1.73	2.29	1.49	2.51	1.54
Car Accident								
RD1	6.58	.99	6.67	.81	6.65	.90	6.55	.81
RD2	5.81	1.19	5.77	.97	5.89	1.07	5.90	.98
RD3	4.91	1.06	4.61	.98	4.09	1.12	3.85	1.09
RD4	3.39	1.36	3.49	1.35	2.91	1.30	2.70	1.24
RD5	3.20	1.96	3.05	1.63	2.55	1.48	2.38	1.31

Index	Primary School (n=604)		Junior Secondary School (n=288)		Senior Secondary School (n=670)		University (n=291)	
	M	SD	M	SD	M	SD	M	SD
The Criminal								
RE1	4.42	1.45	4.15	1.44	5.30	1.27	4.86	1.37
RE2	4.03	1.25	3.94	1.21	4.95	1.21	4.66	1.33
RE3	3.38	1.02	3.63	1.03	4.18	1.05	3.83	1.16
RE4	2.41	.98	2.91	1.10	2.98	.93	2.67	.92

The mean rating of the R indices decreased consistently from: (i) RB1 to RB5; (ii) RD1 to RD5; and (iii) RE1 to RE4, in all sample groups, except with a minor reversal (RB2 and RB3) in the Primary School sample. The above findings provided clear support for the Hierarchy of Human Relationships. In addition, (a) the mean rating of the five RB indices clearly supported Hypothesis H1, which stated that the tendency of an actor to sacrifice his/her life for a recipient decreases consistently from R_1 to R_5; (b) the mean rating of the five RD indices clearly supported Hypothesis H2, which stated that the tendency of an actor to give up rescuing a stranger and turn to rescue a recipient in danger decreases consistently from R_1 to R_5; and (c) the mean rating of the four RE indices clearly supported Hypothesis H3, which stated that the tendency of an actor to help a recipient by covering up his/her crime decreases consistently from R_1 to R_4. In other words, the probability that an actor A would carry out an affective and altruistic act toward another person B was highest if B belonged to the R_1 (first kin or close relatives) category, and decreased consistently to the lowest when B belonged to the R_5 (enemies) category in similar social situations. The affective and altruistic act included sacrificing one's own life in Hypothesis H1, sacrificing another's life in Hypothesis H2, and breaking the law in Hypothesis 3.

2. Moral Orientation

The means and standard deviations of the Moral Orientation indices are presented in Table 2.

Table 2
Means and Standard Deviations of Moral Orientation Indices

Index	Primary School (n=604)		Junior Secondary School (n=288)		Senior Secondary School (n=670)		University (n=291)	
	M	SD	M	SD	M	SD	M	SD
			Law-abiding Orientation					
A1	2.94	1.68	2.67	1.48	2.38	1.43	3.05	1.81
A2	3.95	2.05	3.49	1.89	3.33	2.02	3.98	2.06
A3	4.18	1.95	3.69	1.78	3.62	1.74	4.63	1.84
A4	5.15	1.83	4.46	1.93	4.18	1.89	5.10	1.84
A5	3.91	1.81	4.22	1.71	4.54	1.70	5.43	1.56
A6	6.34	1.50	6.22	1.49	6.50	1.10	6.80	.67
			Self-actualising Orientation					
S1	2.15	1.40	2.21	1.28	2.16	1.25	2.45	1.24
S2	4.20	1.88	3.82	1.60	3.63	1.51	3.71	1.56
S3	4.33	1.99	4.00	1.86	3.72	1.76	4.02	1.68
S4	4.58	2.01	3.92	1.82	4.03	1.74	4.14	1.63
S5	4.52	1.93	3.96	1.92	4.28	1.89	4.37	1.69
S6	5.19	1.84	4.59	1.80	4.49	1.85	4.38	1.74
			Moral Orientation					
N1	3.47	1.00	3.78	1.03	4.17	1.05	3.87	1.06
N2	6.01	.73	6.05	.68	5.99	.70	6.05	.61
N3	5.08	.96	4.68	.91	4.19	1.02	4.12	.93
N4	4.39	.90	4.26	.84	3.70	.86	4.14	1.02
N5	4.02	.98	3.60	.92	3.51	.89	3.65	.96
			MDT Index					
TN	-1.34	.97	-1.44	.90	-1.49	.94	-1.19	.95
TJ	-	-	-	-	-.13	.51	.07	.50

3. Law-abiding Orientation

The mean rating of the A indices increased consistently from A1 to A6 in all sample groups except that (a) the mean rating of the A5 index was the second lowest in the Primary School sample, and (b) there was a minor reversal (A4, A5) in the Junior Secondary School sample. The findings supported Hypothesis H4 which states that a person is less oriented towards abiding by the law if he or she is deficient in lower-order needs (e.g., physiological and safety needs in A2 or love needs in A1) than in a deficiency of higher-order needs (e.g., esteem and social needs in A4 and A5) in three sample groups (Junior Secondary School, Senior Secondary School, and University) only. As for the Primary School subjects, it seems that they valued friendship much more strongly than the older subjects, and were therefore more willing to use the money in the lost bag to help their friends to pay back a loan. The rationale underlying this finding may be an interesting topic to explore in future studies. From Table 1, it was also found that the mean rating of the RE1 to RE4 indices decreased consistently in all the sample groups, which showed that the tendency to abide by the law was the least if the criminal was a close relative and the highest if the criminal was a stranger.

4. Self-actualising Orientation

The mean rating of the S indices increased consistently from S1 to S6 in all the sample groups except with a minor reversal (S4, S5) in the Primary School sample. The findings clearly supported Hypothesis H5 which states that one is less oriented towards self-actualising if one is in heavy deficiency of the lower-order needs such as Belongingness needs (S1) than of the higher-order needs such as Esteem and Social needs (S5 and S6).

5. General Moral Orientations

The findings in the General Moral Orientation indices (N1 to N5), defined in terms of the tendency to gratify Psychological needs, N_1 to N_5, showed that the mean rating decreased consistently from N2 to N5 in all the sample groups except for a minor reversal (N3, N4) in the University sample. The result clearly supported Hypothesis H6 which states that one's orientation towards gratifying Psychological needs decreased consistently from N_2 (Belongingness needs) to N_5 (Self-actualisation needs). As mentioned above, the meaning of the N1 index was quite complicated and its mean rating was not hypothesised to be the largest among the five N indices. The mean rating of N1 was found to be either between N3 and N4, or between N2 and N3 in the samples.

6. Relationship Between Moral Orientation and Moral Judgment

The correlation of the Moral Orientation (N1 – N5; TN) indices with the Moral Judgment (TJ) index are given in Table 3.

Table 3
Correlation of Moral Orientation (N) Indices with Moral Judgment (TJ) Index

	TJ Index	
Index	Senior Secondary School (n=670)	University (n=291)
N1	-.40**	-.44**
N2	.05	.03
N3	.21**	.18*
N4	.39**	.38**
N5	.31**	.44**
TN	.19**	.33**

* $p < .01$.** $p < .001$.

In general, it was found that the correlation (N1, TJ) was significant and negative, and the correlation (N2, TJ) was non-significant. On the other hand, the correlations of N3, N4 and N5 with TJ were positive and significant. If N1 was concerned with the lower needs, and N4 and N5 with the higher needs; then people of higher-level of moral judgment (i.e., larger TJ score) tended to have weaker orientation towards gratifying lower needs and stronger orientation towards gratifying higher needs. Generally, the result supported Hypothesis H7 which states that the stage of moral judgment is negatively related to the orientation towards gratifying the N_1 needs, and positively related to the orientation towards gratifying the N_4 and N_5 needs. On the other hand, the relationship of the stage of moral judgment with the orientation towards gratifying the N_2 and N_3 needs was relatively weaker than the relationship of moral judgment with the orientation towards gratifying the N_1, N_4, N_5 needs. The

146

TN index was a simple sum of N2 to N5 indices with the rating of the N2 and N3 indices being reversed. In general, a small (large) value of the TN index indicated a weaker (stronger) orientation towards gratifying N4 and N5 needs and a stronger (weaker) orientation towards gratifying N2 and N3 needs. From Table 3, the correlation of TN with TJ was positive and significant, which clearly supported the positive relationship of moral orientation to moral judgment.

VI. Concluding Remarks

The present findings clearly supported all the hypotheses in four sample groups of Chinese subjects (total N =1853), except Hypothesis H4 which was supported in Secondary School and University subjects only. The results widen our scope of understanding of moral development and lay down a foundation for further studies of the relation between moral orientation and moral judgment.

The finding that the relation between moral orientation and moral judgment was significant and positive appeared to be promising, and it provided some preliminary basis for integrating the affective and cognitive aspects of moral development into one single whole.

Some proposals for future research can be suggested. First, the present hierarchy of human relationships is a fairly limited one, covering only five types of people. A much more comprehensive hierarchy should be the next research target. Second, a wider range of hypothetical dilemmas should be constructed to enable an intensive study of the situational effects on moral orientation of different types of recipients. It is, of course, much more desirable to design studies to test the hierarchy of human relationships in real-life situations, which would serve as the ultimate test of the present theoretical hierarchy. Third, it would be interesting to test the above hypotheses in different cultures (see Ma, 1989).

VII. Appendix

Meaning of the indices

The Hierarchy of Human Relationships (Corresponding Human Relationship indices in parentheses)

R_1 First kin, close relatives (RB1, RD1, RE1).

R_2 Best friends or intimates (RB2, RD2, RE2).

R_3 Strangers who are very weak, or very young, or who are elites of the society (RB3, RD3).

       (RE3 = acquaintances).

R_4 Common strangers (RB4, RD4, RE4).

R_5 Someone you dislike or enemies (RB5, RD5)

Law-abiding Orientation

The tendency not to use the money in a lost bag when you need the money to:

A1   cure the serious disease of your brother/sister

A2   cure your serious disease

A3   pay back an overdue loan to a bank

A4   study at an overseas university

A5   help a friend to pay back a loan

A6   buy a luxury car

Self-actualising Orientation

The tendency to give up serving as a voluntary doctor in an underdeveloped country when:

S1   you needed to look after your sick mother

S2   you needed to borrow money to maintain the clinic

S3   you were forced to leave by the village headman because of a failure to rescue his son

S4   there was a civil war

S5   plague took place in both the village and your own country

S6   your fiancé forced you to return to marry him

Moral Orientation

N1   Survival orientation

N2   An orientation to gratify the Belongingness needs

N3   An orientation to gratify the Affective and Giving needs

N4   Law-abiding orientation

N5   Self-actualising orientation

MDT Index

$TN = (N4 + N5)/2 - (N2 + N3)/2$

$TJ = (J3 + J4)/2 - (J1 + J2)/2,$

where J1 to J4 are stage scores of moral judgment

References

Bandura, A., 1977, *Social Learning Theory*, New Jersey, Prentice Hall, 1977

Barash, D.P., 1977, *Sociobiology and Behaviour*, NY, Elsevier

Bar-Tal, D., 1976, *Prosocial Behavior: Theory and Research*, NY, John Wiley

Bergling, K., 1981, *Moral Development: The Validity of Kohlberg's Theory*, Stockholm, Almgvist & Wiksell International

Berkowitz, L., 1972, "Social Norms, Feelings, and Other Factors Affecting Helping and Altruism", in L. Berkowitz (ed.), *Advances in Experimental Social Psychology, Vol. 6*, pp. 63–108, NY, Academic Press

Blau, P.M., 1964, *Exchange and Power in Social Life*, NY, John Wiley

Carter, R.E., 1980, "What is Lawrence Kohlberg Doing?", *Journal of Moral Education*, 9, 88–102

Dien, D.S., 1982, "A Chinese Perspective on Kohlberg's Theory of Moral Development", *Developmental Review*, 2, 331–41

Edwards, C.P., 1981, "The Comparative Study of the Development of Moral Judgment and Reasoning", in R.L. Munroe, R.H. Munroe & B. Whiting (eds.), *Handbook of Cross-cultural Human Development*, NY, Garland Press

Eysenck, H.J., 1976, "The Biology of Morality", in T. Lickona (ed.), *Moral Development and Behavior*, New York, Holt, Rinehart & Winston

Gilligan, J., 1976, "Beyond Morality: Psychoanalytic Reflections on Shame, Guilt and Love", in T. Lickona (ed.), *Moral Development and Behavior*. NY, Holt, Rinehart & Winston

Hardin, G., 1977, *The Limits of Altruism: An Ecologist's View of Survival*, Bloomington, IN, Indiana University Press

Ho, D.Y.F., 1986, "Chinese Patterns of Socialization: A Critical Review", in M.H. Bond (ed.), *The Psychology of the Chinese People*, pp. 1–37, Hong Kong, Oxford University Press

Hoffman, M.L., 1976, "Empathy, Role Taking, Guilt, and Development of Altruistic Motives", in T. Lickona (ed.), *Moral Development and Behavior*, New York, Holt, Rinehart & Winston

— 1977, "Empathy, its Development and Prosocial Implications", *Nebraska Symposium on Motivation*, 25, 169–217

— 1979, "Development of Moral Thought, Feeling, and Behavior", *American Psychologist*, 34(10), 958–66

Homans, G.C., 1961, *Social Behavior: Its Elementary Forms*, London, Routledge & Kegan Paul

— 1968, *The Human Group*, Originally published in 1951, London, Routledge & Kegan Paul

Hsu, F.L.K., 1970, *Americans and Chinese: Reflections on Two Cultures and Their People*, New York, Doubleday

Kohlberg, L., 1969, "Stage and Sequence: The Cognitive-Developmental Approach to Socialization", in D.A. Goslin (ed.), *Handbook of Socialization: Theory and Research*, Chicago, IL, Rand-McNally, pp. 347–480

— 1976, "Moral Stage and Moralization: The Cognitive-Developmental Approach", in T. Lickona (ed.), *Moral Development and Behavior*, New York, Holt, Rinehart and Winston

— 1981, *Essays on Moral Development, Volume 1: The Philosophy of Moral Development*, San Francisco, Harper & Row

— 1984, *Essays on Moral Development, Volume 2: The Philosophy of Moral Development*, San Francisco, Harper & Row

Krebs, D.L., 1970, "Altruism – An Examination of the Concept and a Review of the Literature", *Psychological Bulletin*, *73*, 258–302

Leeds, R., 1963, "Altruism and the Norm of Giving", *Merrill-Palmer Quarterly of Behavior and Development, 9*, 229–40

Lickona, T., 1976, *Moral Development and Behavior: Theory, Research, and Social Issues*, NY, Holt, Rinehart and Winston

Liu, I.M., 1986, "Chinese Cognition", in M.H. Bond (ed.), *The Psychology of the Chinese People*, pp. 73–105, Hong Kong, Oxford University Press

Ma H.K., 1982, *A Study of Moral Development with Special Reference to Psychological Needs, Human Relationships and Structures of Moral Judgment*, unpublished Ph.D. dissertation, University of London

— 1985a, "Cross-Cultural Study of the Hierarchical Structure of Human Relationships", *Psychological Reports*, 57, 1079–83

— 1985b, "Cross-Cultural Study of the Development of Law-abiding Orientation", *Psychological Reports*, 57, 967–74

— 1988, *Construction and Validation of an Objective Measure of the Affective and Cognitive Aspects of Moral Development in Hong Kong*, paper presented at the 46th Annual Convention of the International Council of Psychologists, Singapore, August 21–25, 1988

— 1989, "Moral Orientation and Moral Judgment in Adolescents in Hong Kong, Mainland China and England", *Journal of Cross-cultural Psychology*, 20, 152–77

— 1992, "The Relation of Altruistic Orientation to Human Relationships and Moral Judgment in Chinese People", *International Journal of Psychology, 27*, 377–400

— 1993, "The Relation of Altruistic Orientation to Human Relationships and Situational Factors in Chinese Children", *Journal of Genetic Psychology, 154*, 85–96

Maslow, A.H., 1970, *Motivation and Personality* (2nd ed.), New York, Harper & Row

Mischel, W., & H.N. Mischel, 1976, "A Cognitive Social-Learning Approach to Morality and Self-Regulation", in T. Lickona (ed.), *Moral Development and Behavior*, New York, Holt, Rinehart & Winston

Peters, R.S., 1971, "Moral Development: A Plea for Pluralism", in T. Mischel (ed.), *Cognitive Development and Epistemology*, N.Y., Academic Press

Piaget, J., 1932, *The Moral Judgment of the Child*, trans. M. Gabain, London, Routledge & Kegan Paul

Rest, J.R., 1979, *Development in Judging Moral Issues*, Minneapolis, University of Minnesota Press

Rushton, J.P., 1981, "The Altruistic Personality", in J.P. Rushton & R.M. Sorrentino (eds.), *Altruism and Helping Behavior*, Hillsdale, N.J., Erlbaum

Schwartz, S.H., & J.A. Howard, 1984, "Internalized Values as Motivators of Altruism", in E. Staub, D. Bar-Tal, J. Karylowski & J. Reykowski (eds.), *Development and Maintenance of Prosocial Behavior: International Perspectives on Positive Morality*, pp. 229–55. NY, Plenum

Sharabany, R., & D. Bar-Tal, 1982, "Theories of the Development of Altruism: Review, Comparison and Integration", *International Journal of Behavioral Development*, *5*, 49–80

Simpson, E.L., 1976, "A Holistic Approach to Moral Development and Behavior", in T. Lickona (ed.), *Moral Development and Behavior*, New York, Holt, Rinehart & Winston

Snarey, J.R., 1985, "Cross-cultural Universality of Social-Moral Development: A Critical Review of Kohlbergian Research", *Psychological Bulletin*, 97, 202–32

Thibaut, J.W., & H.H. Kelley, 1959, *The Social Psychology of Groups*, NY, John Wiley

Thompson, R.A., & M.L. Hoffman, 1980, "Empathy and the Development of Guilt in Children", *Developmental Psychology*, 16(2), 155–6

Wilson, E.O., 1975, *Sociobiology: The New Synthesis*, Cambridge, MA, Belknap Press

Wispe, L.G., 1972, "Positive Forms of Social Behavior: An Overview", *Journal of Social Issues, 28*, 1–19

Wright, D., 1971, *The Psychology of Moral Behavior*, Middlesex, Penguin

Yang, K.S., 1986, "Chinese Personality and its Change", in M.H. Bond (ed.), *The Psychology of the Chinese People*, pp. 106–70, Hong Kong, Oxford University Press

Chapter 8

Is the Dissemination of Pornography Harmful to Women?

LAURENCE GOLDSTEIN

I. Introduction

Unlike Singapore and in most other countries in this part of Asia, pornographic material is widely available in Hong Kong. There is a big market in X-rated videos, a large proportion of films on the commercial circuit are softly pornographic, and dirty magazines are freely available, and circulate around schoolrooms. Some members of the public, leaders of the community and social workers see this as cause for concern but, so it might be argued, it is not one of the most important things for moral philosophers to worry about.

This is wrong for at least two reasons. First, even if the question of access to pornography may not seem particularly weighty when compared with some moral issues, it does serve to bring into focus central and fundamental theoretical questions. For example, there is the question of *liberty* – should there be limits set on what we are free to read and to distribute; if not, what should be censored and by whom and for what purpose? Then there is the question of *equality* – how highly should we value the ideal of everyone being treated equally, and to what extent are women being treated *unequally* if they are the principal victims of pornographic representations in which humans are portrayed in degraded states? Second, the conclusions of our theoretical deliberations may have practical outcomes which could have far-reaching effects both on the general treatment of women and on our policies concerning various kinds of freedom.

In answer to my title question of whether the dissemination of pornography is harmful to women, I shall immediately give the answer "Yes". If someone asks you whether you are in pain, and you answer sincerely that you are, then you are in pain; your state is one about the existence of which you have first-person authority. Similarly, if a woman says that she is hurt by seeing a pornographic depiction or by seeing men enjoying pornography, or even by knowing that pornography is there to be seen, then, so long as she is speaking truthfully, she is hurt. And, of course, many women do honestly claim to be hurt in these ways. So it may appear that the question raised in the title has been answered, leaving nothing left to debate.

Not quite. Hurt feelings or even the feeling of revulsion are certainly harms that we can well do without, but there is another sense of the word "harm" in which it is intelligible to say: "Despite being hurt, you are not really *harmed*." For example, some medical procedures, such as injections, hurt but are not harmful – quite the reverse. So there is space for asking what harm pornography really does to women, and what degree of harm is done, and whether harm of that degree outbalances certain competing goods that pornography supplies.

The "goods" associated with pornography are basically of two kinds. First is the good of pornography itself, as a source of titillation and sexual pleasure, a form of entertainment. Advocates of pornography have also spoken of its value as sexual aid and educational aid, its contribution to the advancement of the arts, and its use as a means of exposing and debunking. The second kind of good is more abstract. The easy availability of pornography in a society can be regarded as a celebration of some of the freedoms that that society is privileged to enjoy – freedoms that are not granted in tyrannical or totalitarian regimes – and as an endorsement of values held dear in a liberal democracy, values which would be threatened by official moves to censor or ban offensive material.

Both of these alleged goods associated with pornography will surface in this paper, but they will not be its main focus. I shall first try to say, in a rough-and-ready way, what pornography is. Then I shall look at a debate which centres on the issue of censorship versus liberty. Although many people who have debated this issue have concluded that the harm done by pornography is not sufficient to justify the sort of remedial action that involves encroachment on liberty, it seems to me important to inquire just how we can assess the *degree* of harm. My problem does not concern how we can possibly take into account all the ramifying effects of exposure to pornography, although that would make another very good subject for investigation. Rather, I shall be asking whether there is a privileged moral perspective which is simply unavailable to a large proportion of the population. If there is, then ethics, or at least ethical questions in the vicinity of the one we are presently discussing, are not susceptible to observer-independent answers – there is no "view from no-where" in Thomas Nagel's phrase – and we should accord more weight to the views of those with the privileged vantage point. Some recent feminist writing has embraced this latter position, and authors have argued for a distinctive "female ethic".

While not wishing to subscribe to the relativity of moral values and of moral argument, I shall conclude by attempting to show that men are generally in a weak position, and women are generally in a strong one in confronting certain aspects of the question of whether pornography ought to be censored. For comparison: a hearing-impaired person may not be the best to consult on whether a certain chord is A minor, but whether it is A minor is an objective matter, and the best people from whom to seek an opinion are those with perfect pitch.

II. On (not) Defining Pornography

A lot of effort has been spent by writers who see it as important to define pornography, for it has been thought that we need some sharp criterion for distinguishing the pornographic from the artistically erotic. Yet searching for an exact definition of pornography is likely to be a fruitless exercise. Certainly, no short definition seems adequate. We could try "The obscene depictions of sexual organs or behaviour" (cf. the introductory essay to Copp and Wendell, 1983, p. 17). But this is entirely inadequate, as we still have all the work to do to define "obscene" and the definition does not really get to the heart of the issue. For example, would we regard a film of two rhinoceroses copulating in mud as obscene? Suppose the film were shot entirely in close-up, so that what one mostly saw was the thrusting of a rhinoceros's penis?

What about longer definitions? One such was contained in a feminist anti-pornography ordinance passed in 1984 by the Indianapolis City Council. It runs as follows:

> We define pornography as the graphic sexually explicit subordination of women through pictures or words that also includes women dehu-manised as sexual objects, things or commodities; enjoying pain or humiliation or rape; being tied up, cut up, mutilated, bruised or physi-cally hurt; in postures of sexual submission or servility or display; re-duced to body parts, penetrated by objects or animals, or presented in

scenarios of degradation, injury, torture; shown as filthy or inferior; bleeding, bruised or hurt in a context which makes these conditions sexual. (Quoted in Langton, 1990, p. 332.)

What is good about this definition is that it is not really a definition. It does not try for some slick form of words which, at a highly abstract level, attempts to capture the "essence" of pornography, leaving itself open to some clever counter-example, but rather gives a series of paradigm cases of the sort of material that many people find disgusting. It is useful to have such an account before us, since many people, including many women, do not feel particularly strongly about pornography and this may be because they have not seen enough pornography (or not enough pornography of the right kind). (I hasten to add, though, that the drafters of this ordinance are not soft on soft porn either.)

Where the definition is unsatisfactory, however, is in the first line, where it tries to be definitional, where it says that pornography is the graphic sexually explicit subordination of women. The women posing for the photos are often highly paid, and are known to be highly paid, so they could be said to be exploiting men's lusts rather than being themselves exploited. Certainly the models are often *depicted* as subordinate, but that doesn't mean they are actually subordinated – to think otherwise is to confuse fiction with fact. Since we are normally able to observe this distinction, when reading a novel or when watching a non-pornographic film, it would be a mistake to think that we can't similarly suspend belief when we are viewing pornographic material.

However, I take the drafters of the ordinance to be saying not just that the models are subordinated, but that women *in general* are subordinated by sexually arousing depictions of women in provocative poses. The difficulty here is that we now are left with little guidance as to how to classify particular specimens: we see a picture in a magazine of a naked woman spread-eagled on a bed, with her head dangling lasciviously over the side. This may be sexually arousing, but does it relegate women in general to an inferior position? Does it even dehumanise the subject, making of her a sex object? The magazine may have made an effort to *humanise* the subject. There may be a description of her personality and background, of her beliefs, likes and dislikes. There may be a peep into her sex life. The purpose of this text may be precisely to go beyond two-dimensional image, and make the girl appear a more flesh-and-blood individual, a real, self-composed, non-subordinated person who, if you are extremely lucky, you could bump into on the street. Supplying this supplementary information may, of course, be done with the intention of increasing the degree of sexual arousal. But here, as in much softly pornographic material, the effect is achieved by portraying the model as self-assured and in control, making the choice to use her body to excite male fantasies. Never does the text describe her as a wretched waif forced by economic hardship to debase and degrade herself.

It is a familiar point that an image is not in itself pornographic – a close-up photograph of a vagina would be pornographic in a pornographic magazine, but the same photograph would not be so regarded if it featured in a medical text. It is natural, then, to suppose that whether an image or a text is porno-graphic must depend not on the depiction itself but on the intentions of the person doing the depicting. And indeed, *intention* often features in definitions of pornography. Thus, in its report, the British Committee on Obscenity and Pornography (chaired by the distinguished philosopher Bernard Williams) says that a pornographic representation "has a certain function or intention, to arouse its audience sexually, and also a certain content, explicit representations of sexual material (organs, postures, activities etc.). A work has to have both this function and this content to be a piece of pornography".

It is a mistake, however, to thus define pornography in terms of intentions. For it is quite conceivable, for example, that a woman author, in describing a scene of sexual violence, may arouse male readers even though she has no intention whatsoever of doing so. If, unbeknown to the author, her text far exceeds ambient standards of public decency, then we should rightly term the material pornographic. Pornographic but unintentionally so.

It may be true to say that what is pornographic violates certain standards of decency, but this hardly constitutes a definition. If we require a definition to be a formula by means of which we can isolate exactly the set of pornographic things, then it is unlikely that the requirement can be satisfied. No form of words will precisely delimit the set – how could it when that set is vague and in a state of flux? The best we can do is to advert to paradigm cases. Paradigm cases are easy enough to locate: simply think of examples that clearly fit one or other of the descriptions mentioned in the McKinnon/Dworkin ordinance. All we need, in order to pursue the discussion, is to have in mind examples like that.

III. Are Women Subordinated by Pornography? Ronald Dworkin vs. Rae Langton

We have seen that the attempt to *define* pornography is likely to fail. But that does not prevent us from raising the substantive question of whether women are subordinated by pornography. The Indianapolis City Council produced an unequivocal answer to this question. After reviewing research on the issue, it announced the following conclusion:

> Pornography is a discriminatory practice based on sex which denies women equal opportunities in society. Pornography is central in creating and maintaining sex as a basis for discrimination. Pornography is a systematic practice of exploitation and subordination based on sex which differentially harms women. The bigotry and contempt it promotes, with the acts of aggression it fosters, harm women's opportunities for equality of rights in employment, education, access to and use of public accommodations, and acquisition of real property; promote rape, battery, child abuse, kidnapping and prostitution and inhibit just enforcement of laws against such acts; and contribute significantly to restricting women in particular from full exercise of citizenship and participation in public life. (Quoted in Langton, 1990, p. 336.)

If indeed, pornography does in some way contribute to the unequal treatment of women, then a tension will arise in the value systems of liberal thinkers who, on the one hand, favour equality of concern and respect for all and, on the other, advocate freedom of expression, including the freedom to publish hard-core pornography.

It could be argued that John Stuart Mill, the father of modern liberalism, would, on the basis of the position argued for in his essay "The Subjection of Women", be in favour of the censorship of pornography. While it is true that, in his famous work "On Liberty", Mill advocates freedom of expression, and regards coercion by the state as legitimate only to prevent one citizen doing harm to another, it is likely that he would have regarded the apparently consensual participation by women in the production of pornography as the result of a particularly insidious kind of coercion by men. I shall not argue the case here, since that job has been done (in Dyzenhaus, 1992). What I shall do is to consider the approach taken by a modern liberal, Ronald Dworkin, who very clearly comes out against censorship.

In 1981, Dworkin published an article called "Do We Have a Right to Pornography?" (Dworkin, 1981). His answer was that we do have such a right and, in his book *A Matter of Principle* (Dworkin, 1985), he reiterates that view. Dworkin considers a variety of the harms that pornography is alleged to do and shows that such harms are comparable to others which we are prepared to sustain rather than to forbid their perpetration. He also offers a positive argument for the freedom to manufacture and distribute pornography. What is crucial, as he sees it, is that we each have the "right to moral independence". This right is enshrined in the principle that an individual should not be deprived of his or her share of social goods just because many, or most, people don't like the way that that individual thinks is the best way of conducting his or her life.

LAURENCE GOLDSTEIN

Here we seem to have a clear, liberal principle of non-interference, and adherence to this principle would seem to enjoin us to allow people access to pornography, if that's what they enjoy. And, arguably, their enjoyment of it is private and does not harm anyone. However, Rae Langton (Langton, 1990) employs the interesting *ad hominem* strategy of showing that, by following exactly the same pattern of argument that Dworkin himself used in an essay called "Reverse Discrimination" when discussing a civil rights case (in Dworkin, 1977), one would arrive at a pro-censorship position on pornography.

In that essay on civil rights, Dworkin argued that *equality of treatment* is of more fundamental importance than enactment of a policy that satisfies the desires of the majority. So, says Langton, he is bound by the requirements of consistency to accept (what he does not accept) that society does not have the right to pornography, since the promulgation of pornography denies equality of treatment to women. A permissive policy towards pornography differentially *harms* women.

What is Langton's evidence for this last claim and what sort of harm is she talking about? Well, as we have already mentioned, some women feel upset and insulted by pornography, but Langton seems to agree with Dworkin that this kind of subjective feeling is not an adequate foundation on which to rest an argument. Quoting Dworkin, she says: "Everything depends upon whether the feeling of insult is produced by some more objective feature that would disqualify the policy [of permitting pornography] even if the insult were not felt" (Langton, 1990, p. 340). And Langton thinks that there is such a feature. She thinks that pornography acts as a kind of propaganda for what Joel Feinberg (1985, pp. 150–1) calls "the cult of macho", an ideology that supports and reinforces men's violence towards women, and serves to perpetuate women's subordination (Langton, 1990, p. 341). Heta and Matti Häyry put this claim even more forcefully; they surmise that the effect of hard-core pornographic movies on young males is to inculcate "ideals of violent masculine supremacy" so that the censorship of such films could be justified "by an appeal to the harm that the cult of the macho inflicts on women by embodying and supporting oppressive and violent sociocultural structures" (Häyry and Häyry, 1992, p. 7). Langton agrees that real harm is done to women (even if only indirectly) by the dissemination of this kind of pornography and she concludes that a permissive policy is a violation of women's rights. Langton, then, suggests a resolution of the conflict between the protection of women's rights and the freedom of expression that purveyors of pornography seek to enjoy: restrict that latter freedom. However, if pornography is propaganda, as Langton and others suggest, then it is the advocacy of a certain view, an expression of opinion. And surely liberals will view with alarm the idea that we should prevent people expressing their opinions. Mill pointed out that when opinions are suppressed, truth is the victim.

Dworkin's most recent contribution to the debate occurs, in summary form, in Dworkin, 1991. He points out that the Indianapolis Ordinance is not just a mild restraint on negative liberty, consistent with free speech. It prohibits any "production, sale, exhibition or distribution" of the material it defined as pornographic, so clearly the ordinance offends the principle that nobody must be prevented from publishing or reading what he or she wishes on the ground that its content is immoral or offensive.

Both a federal district court and a Circuit Court held that the ordinance was unconstitutional because it violated the First Amendment to the U.S. Constitution, which guarantees the negative liberty of free speech. One of the judges made the point that the First Amendment is precisely designed to forbid the banning of speech on account of the message it contained. The ordinance sought to ban pornography on the grounds that it conveyed the quite specific message that women are submissive and enjoy being dominated. That message may be false or insulting but, according to the American Constitution, that is not grounds for banning it. "The essence of negative liberty," writes Dworkin, "is freedom to offend."

Some lawyers have argued that pornography should be banned because it causes harm to women by increasing the likelihood that women will be raped. If such a causal link could be established, then there might indeed be grounds for banning pornography. But, so far, there has been no persuasive evidence that exposure to pornography causes more actual incidents of assault (it may increase the desire to rape, without this desire leading to actual incidents). Dworkin cites a report of some recent research: "The evidence does not point to pornography as a cause of deviant sexual orientation in offenders. Rather, it seems to be used as part of that deviant sexual orientation" (Dworkin, 1991). Although Dworkin does not cite it, there is even a body of research which indicates a *negative* correlation between the availability of pornography and one particularly nasty form of sexual aggression, namely child molestation (Kutchinsky, 1973).

Some feminists, as we have seen, argue that pornography should be banned because it encourages views which lead to the subordination of women and unequal and unfair treatment of them. Dworkin has an intelligent response to that: it would be unconstitutional to ban speech *directly advocating* the subordination of women and advocating unequal treatment for them. So clearly we cannot ban something which might indirectly be promoting the same end (Dworkin, 1991).

159

Another argument Dworkin considers is that pornography, by subordinating women, causes them to be taken less seriously than men, and so to have less political power because of the way they are perceived. This would amount to depriving women of a positive liberty. Dworkin is sceptical of this causal claim, and he makes the point that the way women are depicted in television advertisements (one could think of some of the advertisements for brandy that appear on Hong Kong television) does far more to instil an image of women as inferior and subordinate. Does that mean that all these things should be banned? Many feminists would reply "Yes", but that reply again disregards the First Amendment, which allows for free speech even though the ideas disseminated by such speech have consequences undesirable for positive liberty.

Let me summarise, in a few words, the position that our somewhat meandering review has now reached. We raised the question of whether women are subordinated (in some sense of the word) by the dissemination of pornography. It seems clear that the consumption by impressionable men of certain kinds of pornographic material may result in the fostering or strengthening of attitudes detrimental to women, although evidence of a direct causal link between pornography and rape or deviant behaviour has not been conclusively established. But if pornography does not amount to incitement to violent behaviour, but is construed as propaganda – the expression of opinions that many of us find repulsive – then, if we endorse the values of a free, liberal society, we should put up with it if for no other reason than that we wouldn't like non-standard opinions of our own to be officially stifled.

This conclusion seems to me unsatisfying, and I think that a different result can be obtained, first, by pointing out flaws in both Langton's argument and Dworkin's. I think that Langton is too ready to agree with Dworkin that, if women feel insulted by pornography, that feeling "must be based on a misperception" if no "objective feature" underwriting it can be found. She says "... the fact that a policy causes some insult and distress is not sufficient reason for thinking that there is something wrong with the policy, when that policy is otherwise justified". My response to that is that surely everything depends on the nature and degree of the insult and distress. Are these things open to objective measure? And is it really essential that pornography have some "objective feature", i.e. some feature accessible to all sufficiently diligent observers, the presence of which is uniquely able to justify (the abolition of) a policy? This relates to my second problem with Langton: expressions of opinion are intelligible to all sufficiently diligent observers. But is it clear that pornography is expression of opinion? Could it be that pornography is much closer to the illocutionary act of treating women as moral inferiors, thereby not just harming, but wronging them? (Altman, 1993). If pornography is not just expression of opinion, then its unfettered promulgation is not guaranteed by legislation such as the First Amendment. The Williams Committee is clear on this point:

> It is important for the rationale for restricting pornographic publications that it is not for advocating any opinion that the restriction is proposed, and that the upset that they cause to the public is not a reaction to opinions which are found unacceptable. (Cited in Copp and Wendell, 1983, p. 30.)

Against Dworkin, I would question whether his commitment to toleration does not, in certain circumstances, amount to an abnegation of one's responsibilities. He is, in effect, *prescribing* for women that they be tolerant to the dissemination of pornography without displaying any sensitivity to the question of how much toleration women can reasonably tolerate. Nobody advocates unlimited toleration. It would be foolhardy to argue, in a utilitarian way, that if you are tolerant of others then they, when they acquire power, will be tolerant of you. And, while one may have *a priori* grounds for believing that there may be non-consequentialist arguments for universal principles, it is not so easy to hold that there could be such arguments for defeasible principles, such as the Principle of Toleration.

IV. The Privileged Perspective of Women

I want to return to these points after breaking off for what will seem a comic interlude. That is provided by a section from Thomas Nagel's book *The View from Nowhere* (Nagel, 1986, pp. 208-9) at the beginning of a chapter called "Birth, Death and the Meaning of Life". Nagel here recounts the true story of how he liberated a large spider which, for several months, he had observed languishing in a urinal in the Philosophy Department at Princeton University. After rescuing the spider from a life which seemed to Nagel "miserable and exhausting" and releasing him on the floor adjoining his porcelain prison, Nagel returned the next day only to find the spider, its legs all shrivelled up, dead. Obviously Nagel's perception of the good life, which includes the freedom to roam and not to be urinated upon, was not shared by the spider. Nagel says of his story that "it illustrates the hazards of combining perspectives that are radically distinct".

How is this story connected with morality? The connection can be made through a principle of universalisability – do to others as you would be done by *if you were them*. For example, I am not a masochist so, in trying to determine morally how to treat a masochist (e.g., should I inflict pain on him if he asked me to), I need to consider whether I should treat him in the same way as I would want to be treated. I don't want people to inflict pain on me, so I should refuse the masochist his request. Pretty clearly, that reasoning is unsound, for it neglects the clause "if you were them". I should give the masochist what he wants. For if he wants pain, then, although I can't really understand his wanting it, if that is what he wants, and nobody else is harmed or disadvantaged, then his wish should be granted. The principle of universalisability is preserved, since we are merely following the maxim to grant people their reasonable requests. I want my reasonable requests granted, so the principle of universalisability enjoins me to grant the reasonable requests of other people, including masochists. Although I can't understand his liking for pain, I can ascertain that he's making a genuine request for it, since we speak the same language.

This raises obvious problems in the case of animals – Descartes argued, famously, that they were insufficiently like us to merit the same moral treatment. In the case of vivisection, Descartes was either stupid or dissembling, for pain is a clear case, where, whatever the dissimilarities, the similarities between certain species and ourselves are so striking as to make consideration of their sensations imperative. (It does not follow that we should treat them the same – if we gain from their pain, we may still argue that they are less important and so can be put to use for testing the potential harmfulness to humans of new products such as foods and drugs (but not cosmetics)). In the case of emotional distress, the question of how to treat animals becomes less problematic – after all, we can't mock a turtle. But, in the case of humans, this is precisely the moral issue raised by Nagel's discussion. In his classic paper "What is it like to be a bat?", Nagel had argued that it is impossible for humans to imagine what it is like for a bat to be a bat. We cannot "extrapolate to the inner life of the bat from our own case" (Nagel, 1973, pp. 168–9). Nagel insists that he is not talking about an individual's perspective but the perspective of a *type*. So, from our point of view, the question that Nagel's discussion raises is: in terms of psychological/emotional makeup, are *women* a distinguishable perspectival type? That is to say, do women have certain kinds of emotional reaction or certain ways of seeing things morally that are unavailable to men?

Rosalind Hursthouse calls one of the chapters in her book *Ending Lives* "The Special Position of Women" (Hursthouse, 1986). She thinks that women's views on abortion need to be given particular weight, not because women are most closely involved, nor because it is their bodies over which they have special rights, but because they have relevant perceptions that are inaccessible to men – or, as Nagel might say, men don't know what it's like for a woman to be a woman. A similar point might be made in the context of a discussion about whether pornography is sufficiently harmful to women that it ought to be censored. One form of harm is the consequences, alluded to by Feinberg and the Häyrys, of damage done to the male psyche; but that's not the kind of thing about which women have any special insight. But they may have special non-transmittable knowledge of harm in the form of the hurt felt at observing men lusting after female bodies or of men gorging themselves on representations of violence to women.

It might be objected that we are being needlessly mysterious about the inaccessibility of perspective. After all, increasingly these days, women themselves are becoming consumers of pornography in the shape of naked men and of films and live performances designed to provoke arousal. So, one might say, women have access to what it's like for a man to be a man enjoying pornography; correlatively, if a man wants to understand the disgust with which some women view men enjoying pornography, all he has to do is to reflect on how he would feel about observing women drooling over pictures of well-hung men. But such a response rests on an inadequate grasp of Nagel's point, for it contains an unwarranted assumption that can be highlighted by transposing to the bat case. If someone claims that they don't know what it's like for a bat reacting to a human's fear of bats, it would be singularly unhelpful to reply that all he has to do is to reflect how he would react to a bat's fearing him!

If a man cannot know what it is like for a woman to be a woman, and, in particular, cannot get inside the skin of a woman when it comes to understanding her moral indignation about pornography, then this will have serious consequences, first among which is a challenge to the objectivity of ethics. So the obvious question to be asked at this point is: is the hypothesis that there is such a psychological/emotional perspective which is in principle foreclosed to men a plausible one? Nagel himself (in conversation) is inclined to answer "No", because he thinks that a common language and similar forms of life make for a common perspective (cf. Wittgenstein, 1953: "to imagine a language means to imagine a form of life"). Yet two different sorts of evidence, biological and sociological, point to the answer "Yes".

It is now well established that men and women tend to perform differently in different mental tasks. For example, women tend to be better at identifying matching items and to have greater verbal fluency; men perform better on spatial tasks, e.g., the mental rotation of objects. In research reported in *Scientific American*, Doreen Kimura points out that this shows up at a very early age. She says "the effects of sex hormones on brain organisation occur so early in life that from the start the environment is acting on differently wired brains in girls and boys" (Kimura, 1992, p. 81). Later in life, fluctuations in hormonal levels (e.g., during the menstrual cycle) produce corresponding fluctuations in ability to perform mental tasks. At the end of her article, she says: "The finding of ... quite substantial sex differences suggests that men and women may have different occupational interests and capabilities, independent of societal influences" (p. 87).

The type of work done by Kimura does not address the specific question of whether men and women tend to have different attitudes towards pornography, but studying her results does have the salutary effect of opening our minds to the possibility that, over a whole range of attitudes, men and women differ in significant ways. Evidence from applied linguistics seems to point to the same conclusion (Tannen, 1990). Work much more closely related to the specific issue of difference of attitudes between men and women towards sex has been carried out by Randy Thornhill and Nancy Wilmsen Thornhill. Their research indicates that sexual coerciveness in males is a psychological adaptation in the biological sense – the product of thousands of years of evolutionary history. Psychological adaptation to sexuality is, they say, sexually dimorphic, and includes many highly specialised adaptations (Thornhill and Thornhill, 1992, p. 364). In short, men are selected for rape. The effect of the social environment is only to inhibit (in most cases) this natural tendency. Men who *think* they've been drinking alcohol (even when they haven't) become more excited by depictions of rape, since being somewhat "under the influence" is accepted as the occasion for dropping one's guard (see the Thornhills' report of Briddell's experiment, p. 370). These differences between the mindscapes of men and women make the differences between human visual perception and bat sonar echo-location seem tiny by comparison! If men have become sexually coercive by nature, then how they regard pornography is inevitably going to be vastly different from the way that women regard it. Men have less chance of gaining a woman's sexual perspective than of getting a bat's view of the world.

Let's suppose that the above conclusion is correct. Does it follow that men and women do not share a common morality? Jean Grimshaw considers two suggestions. The first is that "there are in fact common or typical differences in the ways in which women and men think or reason about moral issues". The second suggestion starts from the assumption that specific social practices generate their own vision of what is "good" or what is especially to be valued, their own concerns and practices, and their own criteria for what is to be seen as a "virtue". It may be possible, then, to argue that the social practices which have traditionally been regarded as female, in particular the practices associated with mothering and with the more general care and nurturing of others, can be seen as generating ethical priorities and conceptions of virtue which should not only not be devalued but which can also provide a corrective to the

164

more destructive values and priorities of those spheres of activity which have been dominated by men (Grimshaw, 1992, p. 225).

Grimshaw makes the point that both of these suggestions have sometimes been anchored in a view that there are systematic differences between male and female personalities, differences in structure between male and female psyches. She cites Olive Schreiner who in her essay "Women and War" (in her *Women and Labour*, 1915) suggested that women "are too aware of the cost of human life in giving birth, too aware of the labour involved in giving life to children and sustaining it, ever to be able to view the waste of lives in war with calm or equanimity". Modern feminist authors including Carol Gilligan, Nel Noddins and Moira Gatens have similarly claimed that there are aspects of women's experience denied to men which are the source of a "female ethic".

Grimshaw expresses well-justified doubts about this claim. She mentions problems – for example, the lack of any supporting historical evidence – with the idea that there are a set of alternative "core" values shared by all women. Increasingly in the West, child-care and medicalisation of childbirth have come to be regarded as not belonging exclusively in the domain of women. Further, as Grimshaw points out, women themselves have appropriated these alleged values associated with motherhood "in the service of such things as devotion to Hitler's 'Fatherland' or the bitter opposition to feminism and equal rights in the U.S.A." (Grimshaw, 1992, p. 232).

Grimshaw's point here is not that the alleged gender-specific values exist but have been misunderstood or distorted by the unscrupulous few. I think her real message is that we should be sceptical of so nebulous a notion as these distinctive values associated with mothering; it's doubtful whether they are tangible enough to form the cornerstone of a "female ethic". Grimshaw believes that it is useless to try "appealing to any completely general set of differences between women and men, or any autonomous realm of female values which can provide a simple corrective or alternative to the values of male-dominated spheres of activity". Yet she also thinks that we shouldn't totally disregard the difference that gender makes. As she says, "the influence of feminism on social and on intellectual life has derived, after all, from its recognition that gender *is* a central analytic category both in understanding social structures and in envisaging social arrangements in which women might be less oppressed or marginalised than they are now". Also, along with Kate Soper, she thinks that "in some contexts, such as that of walking alone late at night, there is likely to be a structured difference between male and female experience and feelings which it may often be difficult to ascribe to anything other than the fact that one is, simply, a woman or a man" (Grimshaw, 1992, p. 233).

It seems to me that, although this example of Grimshaw's is not a particularly good one (I guess that a small white man would also feel a bit uncomfortable walking through a black area of Detroit late at night), what she is suggesting must be right. As a man, I can have none but the remotest idea of the kind of pain that is sometimes experienced at childbirth. Severe constipation is the closest thing I can imagine, but I'm sure that that's well wide of the mark. Jane Mary Trau has a better example which brings us back to our main theme: "This fear of association with the women represented in pornography is very real for many women, and is very difficult for the most enlightened and liberated men to comprehend. It is not a fear, necessarily, of physical harm, viz., rape, but a fear of devaluation, of subordination; a fear of being perceived as *porneia* [Greek: lowest-grade whore], and of suffering the loss of rights and privileges which accompanies that devaluation" (Trau, 1991). What can *I*, as a man, say about this? It's a fear that I can't comprehend, except in a remote and abstract way. And Trau says it's a fear that is real for "many" women. Again, hear Andrea Dworkin in response to an article of John Irving's: "Maybe Mr. Irving and others do not know that in the world of women, pornography is the real geography of how men use us and torment us and hate us" (Andrea Dworkin, 1992). Clearly not all women feel things quite like that but, if it is a view that accurately reflects the experiences of many women, then this is an important dimension of the pornography issue that men may not be able to grasp.

V. The Practicalities of Censorship

Pornography is a billion-dollar industry ($10 billion a year turnover in the U.S.A. alone – see Langton, 1990, fn. 76) with a huge market, accounting, for example, for 20 per cent of the sales of videocassettes in that country (see Linsley, 1991, p. 138). If there were a ban on a wide range of pornographic material, what would become of the purveyors and consumers of such material? Fox-hunting is still a popular sport in some countries. What happens, basically is that men on horses accompanied by a pack of dogs chase a fox across country. If the uneatable fox is caught, the huntsmen can enjoy the pleasure of seeing it torn to pieces by the hounds. Lovers of animals would like to see this sport outlawed, but what if it were? One possibility is that the huntsmen might take up chess or charity work. But it is far more likely that these "unspeakable" people would find other ways to satisfy their bloodlust. It could be argued, with some plausibility, that one fox's life every couple of weeks is a small price to pay for keeping these dangerous people off the streets where they might do a lot more harm.

We can speculate in a similar way about what regular consumers of pornography would do if deprived of their material. One possibility is that they would devote themselves to amiable pursuits such as gardening, helping the needy or chatting with friends. But there are darker possibilities. If, as before, one could argue that the pornography satisfies some primitive need, then finding alternative channels for the gratification of those needs might lead to behaviour far more odious and harmful than the private consumption of pornographic images.

Needless to say, the matter is not as simple as this. Some will say that the assumption that a significant proportion of the human population will always have the lust for blood or a taste for the degradation of women is pessimistic and unwarranted. They will say, for example, that, rather than answering to a basic need, pornography helps to *create* a certain unhealthy sexual climate, a climate that the banning of pornography could help dissipate. Various empirical studies have addressed these questions. A study (Russell, in Copp and Wendell, 1983) shows a diversity of aggressive behaviour by men towards women apparently resulting from ideas imparted to the men by pornographic pictures, movies or books. The research has thrown up highly conflicting results and, as Geoffrey Blowers has convincingly argued, such research is, in the present state of the art, highly suspect (Blowers, 1986).

VI. Conclusion

The design of good research methodologies and the practical implications of different censorship policies are matters that cannot be resolved in this paper. My previous argument commits me to the view that there are other issues concerning pornography my qualifications for the discussion of which are severely limited by my sex. Since one important dimension of the problem is outside the grasp of myself and other males, all I would advocate is that, when it comes to policy-making, the views of women be accorded special weight.

References

Altman, Andrew, 1993, "Liberalism and Campus Hate Speech: A Philosophical Examination", *Ethics* 103, pp. 302–17

Blowers, Geoffrey, 1986, "Pornography: Some Points for Consideration in the Continuing Debate", *Hong Kong Psychological Society Bulletin* 16/17, pp. 7–24

Copp, David, and Susan Wendell (eds.), 1983, *Pornography and Censorship*, Buffalo, Prometheus

Dworkin, Andrea, 1992, letter to *New York Times Book Review*, May 3, p. 15 in response to John Irving's "Pornography and the New Puritans", *New York Times Book Review*, March 29, 1992

Dworkin, Ronald, 1977, *Taking Rights Seriously*, Cambridge MA, Harvard University Press

— 1981, "Do We Have a Right to Pornography?", *Oxford Journal of Legal Studies* 1, pp. 177–212

— 1985, *A Matter of Principle*, Cambridge MA, Harvard University Press.

— 1991, "Liberty and Pornography", *The New York Review of Books*, August 15, pp. 12–15

Dyzenhaus, David, 1992, "John Stuart Mill and the Harm of Pornography", *Ethics* 102, pp. 534–51

Feinberg, Joel, 1985, *The Moral Limits of Criminal Law III: Offense to Others*, Oxford, Oxford University Press

Grimshaw, Jean, 1992, "The Idea of a Female Ethic." Philosophy East and West 42:221-238

Häyry, Heta, and Matti Häyry, 1992, "Feinberg, Obscenity and the Harmfulness of Artistic Pornography", (unpublished TS p. 7)

Hursthouse, Rosalind, 1987, *Beginning Lives*, Oxford, Blackwell

Kimura, Doreen, 1992, "Sex Differences in the Brain", *Scientific American* (September), pp. 81–7

Kutchinsky, B., 1973, "The Effect of Easy Availability of Pornography on the Incidence of Sex Crimes: the Danish Experience", *Journal of Social Issues* 29, pp. 163–81; reprinted in *Pornography and Censorship*, David Copp and Susan Wendell (eds.), Buffalo, Prometheus

Langton, Rae, 1990, "Whose Right? Ronald Dworkin, Women, and Pornographers", *Philosophy and Public Affairs* 19, pp. 311–59

Linsley, William, 1991, "The Case Against Censorship of Pornography", in *Pornography: Private Right or Public Menace?*, R.M. Baird and S.E. Rosenbaum (eds.), Buffalo, Prometheus Books

Nagel, Thomas, 1973, *Mortal Questions*, Cambridge, Cambridge University Press

— 1986, *The View from Nowhere*, Oxford, Oxford University Press

Tannen, Deborah, 1990, *You Just Don't Understand: Women and Men in Conversa-*

tion, New York, Ballantine Books

Thornhill, Randy, and Nancy Wilmsen Thornhill, 1992, "The Evolutionary Psychology of Men's Co-ercive Sexuality", *Behavioral and Brain Sciences* 15, pp. 363–421

Trau, Jane Mary, 1991, "Limitation of Artistic Expression and Public Funding of the Arts", *The International Journal of Applied Philosophy* 6, pp. 57–63

Wittgenstein, Ludwig, 1953, *Philosophical Investigations*, Oxford, Blackwell

Chapter 9

Abortion and Uncertainty[1]

Li Hon-lam

Thomas Nagel has said that the morality of abortion poses the most intractable of all moral problems.[2] And it is hard to disagree with him. Nevertheless, it is possible to be confident about the morality of abortion in three exceptional cases. The first case involves a grossly deformed foetus.[3] In the second case, the mother's life will be seriously endangered unless the foetus is aborted.[4] The third case is one in which the foetus is the result of rape.[5] These three cases aside, a credible solution is difficult to arrive at in the more usual cases. In this paper, I attempt a strategy of reasoning under uncertainty, namely, Pascal's Wager.

I. Introduction

Whether or not abortion is immoral is crucially dependent on whether a foetus is a person. Not every philosopher would agree with this statement. In Section I of this paper, I shall review three famous arguments according to which, even if a foetus is a person, abortion is justified. The conclusion I reach is that all three arguments fail. On this basis, there seems no reason to believe that the problem of abortion can be solved without tackling the question as to a foetus's personhood. Of course, I cannot rule out there being other good arguments for or against abortion which avoid the question of whether a foetus is a person.

In Section II, I examine six criteria which purport to determine when a foetus is a person. My conclusion is that none of these are credible.

In Section III, I apply the method of Pascal's Wager to arrive at the conclusion that abortion is, in the usual cases, unjustified. Here I assume that a foetus is either a person or a non-person, and that we are simply ignorant of when a foetus becomes a person.

II. Attempts that Avoid the Issue as to Personhood

Judith Thomson makes the now-classic argument that the mother has the sole right to her body, even if another person is dependent on it for survival (Thomson, 1973). Suppose one day you wake up, finding yourself tied in bed to a world-famous violinist who, due to an urgent operation, now needs to be hooked to you for nine months and ten days, because only you have the right blood type to save him. Must you help? According to Thomson's view, though it would be sweet of you to help, you may refuse. This argument appeals to feminists. In my view, this argument can *at most* show that the pregnant woman has the right to abortion only if her pregnancy was due to rape.[6] For only in the case of rape is it clear that the victim is not responsible for the pregnancy. Even the case of accidental contraceptive failure is unlike the case of rape, because in the former case the couple should know that contraceptives are not 100 per cent safe.[7]

Another famous feminist argument aims at a wider scope of application, and is supposed to apply to cases where a foetus is due to accidental failure of contraceptives. This argument by Jane English (English, 1975) is based on the notion of self-defence, and claims that in a case where the couple have used a contraceptive which accidentally fails, the mother would have the right to defend herself against the pregnancy (and the foetus).

Imagine that you live in a town, in which there are innocent children hypnotised by a mad scientist. These children come out only in the evening to attack people. If you are attacked, you will have to lie in bed for nine months and 10 days (that is how long pregnancies take on the average). You can equip your-

171

self with one or two electronic robots, which usually can fend off attacks. But, being electronic appliances, they are not always reliable. Hence, you cannot totally avoid the attacks unless you completely avoid going out in the evening. However, not going out in the evening at all is highly "inconvenient" for you. So suppose one evening, you go out, equipped with a robot. As expected, you are attacked by a hypnotised child. Unfortunately, your robot is not working. So what can you do when the hypnotised child tries to attack you?

You know that if attacked, you will have to lie down for nine months. You know that your only effective defence is to shoot the child with your pistol, thus probably killing him. You also know that, though the mad scientist is wicked, the child is innocent. Jane English argues that just as we may shoot to death attacking robbers on the grounds of self-defence, so you may also shoot to death the innocent child on the same grounds. It should now be clear in English's example that the hypnotised child is analogous to the foetus, that the electronic robot is analogous to contraceptives, and that going out in the evening is analogous to having sex. So if English's argument is successful, then she could justify abortion in the case of accidental contraceptive failure.

One possible objection to her argument is that it uses a false analogy between being attacked by robbers and being attacked by innocent children. For the innocent children, unlike the robbers, are not life-endangering. Since the notion of self-defence has to depend on imminent life-endangerment, this argument for abortion cannot stand. English could reply that the above objection is based on a legal understanding of "self-defence" requiring imminent life-endangerment. But why should morality follow law in this instance? In my view, though this reply is a good one, English still has to justify the extent to which the self-defence argument applies. Surely, if (instead of attacking you) the hypnotised child only hit you on the hand, you could not possibly justify killing the child on the grounds of self-defence. The question for English becomes: Where to draw the line? English needs to show that the hypnotised child's attack is a sufficiently grave act to invoke the self-defence argument. But this has not been shown.

The third argument which avoids the question as to a foetus's personhood is the view of Jonathan Glover (Glover, 1977, chapter 11). This argument applies to any case of unwanted pregnancy. The argument is: We should do what maximises good consequences and minimises bad consequences. Permitting abortion of any unwanted pregnancy will maximise good consequences and minimise bad consequences, because major social evils are often caused by those people born as unwanted babies. Therefore we ought to permit abortion of any unwanted pregnancy. In my view, the problem with this argument lies in what should count as a good consequence involving foetuses. In particular, in maximising good consequences and minimising bad consequences for every person, should a foetus count as a person? Will a family with two happy parents and two happy children with an aborted foetus be a better consequence than one with five less happy people (because the unwanted fifth child has overburdened the family)? The answer depends on whether a foetus is a person, and whether abortion is murder. So Glover begs the question by arguing as if foetuses don't count in the consequentialist calculus.

The lesson can be generalised. The problem of abortion is resistant to consequentialism in general, and utilitarianism in particular, unless the question as to a foetus's personhood is answered.

III. Six Criteria of Personhood

Refuting the flawed arguments in Section I cannot establish that there are no plausible arguments concerning abortion which do not depend on whether a foetus is a person or not. Nevertheless there seems no reason to believe that the issue can be resolved without dealing with the question of whether or not a foetus is a person.

I now shall examine six important criteria put forward by various philosophers for determining the beginning of personhood: birth, conception, quickening, viability, presence of brain waves, possession of self-awareness and self-motivation.[8]

1. Birth

Birth is more a folk criterion for determining the beginning of personhood. Few philosophers support this criterion. Why should the answer to the question of whether a foetus is a person depend on whether it is inside or outside its mother's body? Why should a baby prematurely born in the seventh month be a person, whereas a nine-month-old foetus not be a person?

2. Conception

One argument is that a fertilised egg is a person, since it has the genetic code of a human being. However, if each of our body cells (except brain cells) can be cloned to a person, is each of our cells a person? It seems not.

Another argument is that a fertilised egg is a person, because it has the potential to become an adult person. But this argument is flawed, since the same can be said of an egg and a sperm just about to merge (i.e. immediately prior to fertilisation). For they also possess almost the same potential to become an adult. No one would say that an egg and a sperm are a person; if you separate them, making it impossible for them to merge, no one would charge you with abortion or murder.

3. Quickening

According to folk belief, a foetus receives its soul when it first moves in the womb. Quickening, like birth, was a folk criterion which few philosophers or physicians would recognise as reasonable today. We now know that, prior to the point of quickening, a foetus has already had different kinds of reflexive movements. Further, why should the first movement of the foetus indicate its reception of the soul? The view that we have souls is also questionable.

4. Viability

Whether a foetus can survive outside the mother used to be considered the correct criterion. The problem with this criterion is that the viability of a foetus would depend on whether the foetus happened to be in a country of advanced medical technology, like the United States, or in a country with few medical facilities, like New Guinea. But how can the important question of whether a foetus is a person depend crucially on whether it be in the United States, or New Guinea?

5. Possession of Brain Waves

Some people argue that since total cessation of brain waves is now generally agreed to be the end of a person's life, by mirror symmetry, the beginning of brain waves should indicate the beginning of a person's life (Veatch, 1983). I believe, however, that we are not justified in concluding from this "mirror symmetry" that both a corpse and a foetus are non-persons. For the two are not similar. There exists superficial similarity between a corpse and a foetus prior to the eighth week in that both have no brain waves. However, whereas a corpse has no further potential to have brain waves, a foetus prior to the eighth week has great potential to develop brain waves. Further, cessation of brain waves is an indicator of death only because it reliably indicates the cessation of other vital bodily functions. Thus, death is the cessation of all vital bodily functions. A foetus prior to the eighth week, therefore, is very dissimilar to a corpse, because it is growing whereas a corpse is decomposing.

6. Possession of Self-awareness and Self-motivation

Warren's argument starts from the belief that the concept of personhood should not only apply to human beings, but also to outerspace-persons (Warren, 1973). Imagine a space traveller who lands on an unknown planet and encounters a race of beings utterly unlike anything he has encountered before. How can he decide whether they are outerspace-persons, or rather the sort of thing which he need not feel guilty about treating as, say, a source of food? Warren argues that, obviously, if these beings possess rational features such as self-awareness, self-motivation and the ability to reason and communicate – or even a suitable subset of them – then they are persons; conversely, if they do not possess *any* of these features, then they are definitely not persons. It follows that infants up to 18 months old and foetuses are not persons, since they lack any of these features.

This argument relies much on intuition.[9] In particular, it crucially relies on the intuition that the space traveller is morally permitted to feed on beings which do not possess any of the rational features on the grounds that they are thereby not persons. But this intuition can be denied. For surely the space traveller may not feed on outerspace-persons' live foetuses and infants (let us assume that they too lack the rational features), just as he may not feed on live human foetuses and infants. In Warren's view, even a fully developed foetus is considerably less personlike than is the average mammal, indeed the average fish, and thus cannot be said to have any more right to life than a newborn guppy (Warren, 1973, p. 167). This seems absurd, however. For we believe it morally justifiable to feed on fish, but not on human foetuses, let alone fully developed ones. This suggests that Warren's criterion is flawed, since we would not consider a fully developed human foetus to be morally on a par with a newborn guppy. Moreover, critics disagree with Warren's view that infants up to 18 months old are not persons; in response, she argues that they may not be killed as long as there are people willing to take care of them. This reply is, however, unconvincing, since the same could be said of goldfish: as long as there are people willing to take care of goldfish, they may not be killed. Equating infanticide with the killing of goldfish here seems absurd. Further, a man who was irrational would not thereby fail to be a person (English, 1975). Further, would those in coma and those dreamlessly sleeping be counted as (temporarily?) non-persons? The answer should be no. All of these arguments show that Warren's criterion is too restrictive. But it is also too broad. Mammals possess self-awareness, if not self-motivation, and also the ability to communicate and perhaps reason. The same might be said of birds, reptiles, and perhaps even fish, though to a lesser extent. Do we wish to regard all of these as persons, even to some extent? Probably not.

I conclude that none of these six important criteria can withstand criticism, and they must therefore be discarded.

IV. The Relevance of Pascal's Wager

The results established in Section II show that at present we have no credible criterion for determining when a foetus begins to be a person. This Section will outline a fresh approach to tackling the problem of abortion.

In this Section, I assume that the principle of bivalence is applicable to the concept of personhood.[10] More specifically, I assume that a foetus at any stage either is a person, or it is a non-person. If (as I believe) we do not know whether a foetus is a person or not, we can make use of a certain strategy of reasoning under uncertainty. I have in mind Pascal's Wager. The argument contained in Pascal's Wager teaches us how to take reasonable risks in the face of uncertainty. So if we are faced with two alternatives, about which we have no sense as to which is true, but from each of which consequence of different gravity follows, then it is unreasonable to assume the risk of the graver consequence, and hence reasonable to assume the risk of the less grave consequence. Pascal famously applies this argument to the conclusion that we should believe in God. For if I believe in God, and God does not exist, I lose nothing, whereas if you don't believe in God, and God does not exist, you win nothing. On the other hand, if I believe in God, and God exists, I win everything, whereas if you don't believe in God, and God exists, you lose everything. So I am taking a very reasonable risk, whereas you are taking a very unreasonable risk. Thus, to take reasonable risk, we must consider the consequences of various risks.[11]

I believe that Pascal's Wager, when applied to the question of whether we should believe in God, seems to produce a false conclusion. For one thing, to believe is to believe involuntarily; advising or even forcing yourself to believe in something (e.g., God) may not lead to your believing in God. But more important, since God is omniscient, He knows the motive with which you force yourself to believe Him. And He might not appreciate that. He might even send you to hell, not heaven. But the problem here is not so much Pascal's Wager, as the nature of God and the nature of belief. Pascal's Wager can still be used in other situations.

Suppose you are in a limousine going to the airport for an important international conference in philosophy. Suddenly, it dawns on you that you might not have your passport with you. Upon reflection, you can't decide whether your passport is somewhere in your luggage, or left at home. And you don't even have any sense as to which possibility is more likely. Suppose, furthermore, that you can verify whether your passport is somewhere in your luggage by unlocking your suitcases and searching for it. It would require the limousine to stop for you to get your luggage, and it will take up to 15 minutes for you to confirm one way or another. But should you confirm that you don't have the passport with you, you still would have enough time to go back home and get it. An alternative is to wait till you arrive at the airport. Then you don't have to incur the trouble of stopping the limousine, and it would be easier for you to search for your passport in the airport. But if your passport is not in your luggage, then you won't have enough time to go back home to get it. What should you do? I think any reasonable person should take the risk of the less grave consequence; in this case, one should stop the limousine, confirm the whereabouts of one's passport, and if one doesn't have it, go home to get it. This is exactly what Pascal's Wager would recommend.[12]

If we apply Pascal's Wager to the problem of abortion, the conclusion will be roughly as follows. Except in the cases of rape, gross deformation of foetus, and foetus endangering the life of the mother, abortion should not be allowed, because reasoning under uncertainty, coupled with a broad consequentialism, would generate conclusions against abortion. By assumption, either a foetus is a person, or it is a non-person. Should a foetus be a non-person, a policy which prohibits abortion would at most burden some families; but should a foetus be a person, a policy which permits abortion would be permitting murder, which is much worse. Thus, to permit abortion would be to risk the graver consequence. If we accept Pascal's Wager, then we should prohibit abortion. Of course, I am assuming that we are in a society in which having one (more) unwanted child would not make the whole family so badly-off as to cause one or more members to die of starvation. I am also assuming that by bearing the (unwanted) child, the mother will not suffer so much pain as to want to commit suicide, that her life is not endangered by the pregnancy, and that her life will not be ruined by bearing a child, etc. Thus I have only considered the simple case in which Pascal's Wager applies. But what if some of the above assumptions are relaxed? What if by having the baby the physical and psychological pain that the mother has to go through is such that her life will likely be ruined (as in the case of a rape victim)? The answer is that Pascal's Wager would not apply. Pascal's Wager applies only if one of the possible outcomes under consideration is clearly worse than the others.[13] But in these above cases, this condition is not fulfilled.

So far I have assumed that the principle of bivalence applies to the concept of personhood; that is, a foetus is either a person or a non-person. What if this assumption is given up or shown to be false? What if a foetus can be neither fully a person, nor fully a non-person, but somewhere in between? In other words, what if a foetus can be a person to some degree? The simple answer is that if a foetus is a person to some degree, then Pascal's Wager would seem inapplicable to the abortion problem. A full-scale analysis, however, will be the subject for another occasion.

Notes

1. I am especially grateful to John Bennett, Allen Wood, Mark Fisher, Dave Archard and Joseph C.W. Chan for very helpful written comments on earlier drafts of this paper. I am also grateful to Kai-yee Wong, Jonathan K.L. Chan and Yuan-kang Shih for helpful discussion.

2. Nagel made this point in a talk at Cornell in the Fall of 1986.

3. The justification for abortion in this case is that the life of the person whom a *grossly* deformed foetus becomes would not be worth living. (By "the person whom a … foetus becomes", I do not presuppose one way or the other as to the personhood of a foetus.)

4. Between saving the mother and the foetus, we should save the mother because the intrinsic value of her life is greater than that of the foetus. I hope to offer a fuller account for this claim on another occasion. But the usual justification of self-defence does not always work. If the source of endangerment of the mother's life does not come from the foetus, e.g., when during pregnancy the mother discovers cervical cancer, the cure of which would kill the foetus, then self-defence would not provide any justification for abortion. On the latter point, see Davis, 1984.

5. While many people would agree that abortion is justified in the case of rape, its justification is more elusive than is commonly assumed. For one who believes that a foetus is a person might have difficulty in endorsing abortion as a way to relieve pain

for the victim. I believe that our sympathy for the victim has to do with her being free from any responsibility in her forced conception. A fuller justification has to be deferred to another occasion. Another justification is provided by Judith J. Thomson. See below.

6. In Noonan, 1973, p. 150, John T. Noonan, Jr. cites a court rule of Minnesota and argues that we owe a duty of humanity to save the life of strangers. This argument seems to cast some doubt on Thomson's view.

7. Thomson further argues that (1) abortion is permitted in cases of endangerment of the mother (on the ground of self-defence) and (2) also in cases of accidental contraceptive failure. I believe that Thomson is successful to some extent in (1), but unsuccessful in (2).

8. Regarding the first, third, and fourth criteria, I have benefited from the discussion in Singer, 1979, chapter 6.

9. "[A]ny being which satisfies none of [the conditions of rationality] is certainly not a person. I consider this claim to be *so obvious* that I think anyone who denied it ... would thereby demonstrate that he had no notion at all of what a person is" (Warren, 1973, p. 165; emphasis added).

10. According to the principle of bivalence, every proposition is determinately either true or false. See Dummett, 1991, pp. 9-10.

11. In Pascal, 1662, 418, Pascal argues for Pascal's Wager on the footing that the chance of God's existence and that of God's non-existence are equal. But this footing seems to me both questionable and unnecessary.

12. Theoretical justification can be offered for Pascal's Wager. In what follows, Case 1 and Case 2 do not involve Pascal's Wager, but they help us to see why Case 3 (Pascal's Wager) is justifiable.

Case 1: One seeks an outcome achievable via means *a* and means *b* with different probabilities of success. Which course of action should one take? It is self-evident that the correct course is whichever means has the higher probability of success.

Case 2: Two means *c* and *d* lead to outcomes *C* and *D* respectively. One has no sense as to their probabilities of success. Which course should one take? In the absence of probabilities, one should seek the means leading to the outcome that is more desirable.

Case 3 (The justification for Pascal's Wager): Means *e* leads to either outcome *E1* or *E2*, but not both, with unknown probabilities. Means *f* leads to either outcome *F1* or *F2*, but not both, with unknown probabilities. Which course should one take? Since one does not know of the respective probabilities in question, the correct course to take is the course leading to better consequences, all things considered. That is, is the combination of outcomes "either *E1* or *E2*" better than the combination "either *F1* or *F2*"? Pascal's Wager claims that comparisons can be made between these two combination of outcomes, with unknown probabilities, if one of these outcomes (say *E1*) is much worse than the other three outcomes. If *F1* is much better than the rest, then one should take the combination "either *F1* or *F2*". On the other hand, if one of the four outcomes (say *F1*) is much better than the other three, then one should take the combination "either *F1* or *F2*". There are of course difficult cases in which Pascal's Wager is not applicable. For instance, if *E1* and *F1* are both much worse than *E2* and *F2*, then Pascal's Wager is not of much help. Or if *E1* is much worse, and *E2* is much better, than the other outcomes, again it is not clear what one should choose.

13. See Note 12.

References

Davis, Nancy, 1984, "Abortion and Self-Defense", in *Philosophy and Public Affairs*, Vol. 13, No. 3, Summer 1984

Dummett, Michael, 1991, *The Logical Basis of Metaphysics*, London, Ducksworth

English, Jane, 1975, "Abortion and the Concept of a Person", pp. 233–43 in *Canadian Journal of Philosophy*, Vol. 5, No. 2 (October 1975); also reprinted as pp. 170–6 in *Morality in Practice*, 2nd Edition, James P. Sterba (ed.), Belmont, California, Wadsworth Publishing Company

Glover, Jonathan, 1977, *Causing Death and Saving Lives*, chapter 11, Harmondsworth, England, Penguin Books Ltd

Noonan, John T., Jr., 1973, "How to Argue About Abortion", pp. 149–59 in *Morality in Practice*, 2nd Edition, James P. Sterba (ed.), Belmont, California, Wadsworth Publishing Company

Pascal, Blaise, 1662, *Pensees*, 418

Singer, Peter, 1979, *Practical Ethics*, Cambridge, Cambridge University Press

Thomson, Judith Jarvis, 1973, "A Defence of Abortion", *Philosophy and Public Affairs*, Vol. 1, No. 1 (1971), pp. 47–66

Veatch, Robert M., 1983, "Definitions of Life and Death: Should There Be Consistency?", in *Contemporary Issues in Bioethics*, 3rd Edition, Tom L. Beauchamp & LeRoy Walter (eds.), Belmont, California, Wadsworth Publishing Company

Warren, Mary Anne, 1973, "On the Moral and Legal Status of Abortion", in *The Monist*, Vol. 57, No. 1 (January 1973); also reprinted as pp. 159–69, in *Morality in Practice*, 2nd Edition, James P. Sterba (ed.), Belmont, California, Wadsworth Publishing Company

Chapter 10

Ethical Reflections on Artificial Reproduction Policies in Hong Kong

LO PING-CHEUNG

I. Preliminary Remarks

Artificial reproduction, or "Scientifically Assisted Human Reproduction", as the Hong Kong government prefers to call it, has been practised in Hong Kong for some time. Artificial insemination was first introduced in 1981, *in-vitro* fertilisation in 1985, and gamete intra-fallopian transfer in 1986.[1] All along, however, the Hong Kong government has had no regulation of these practices. Foreseeing the emergence of complicated social and legal problems that will come with these practices, in November 1987 the Secretary for Health and Welfare appointed a Committee on Scientifically Assisted Human Reproduction to look into the issues involved. An *Interim Report* was presented by the Committee in July 1989 for public consultation, which evoked some responses and public discussion. Quite a number of scholars and social workers objected to some of the recommendations therein.[2] In May 1992, however, the Committee presented its *Final Report* to the Secretary of Health and Welfare, affirming all the recommendations made in the *Interim Report*, with no replies to the public objections. Once again, the Secretary for Health and Welfare conducted a public consultation in March 1993, though in a very low-key manner. More objections were voiced by scholars and concerned citizen groups,[3] and the government has remained silent since then. The public has not been not told when the government will start the legislative process to incorporate the *Final Report*'s recommendations into law. When that moment comes, intense debate in the Legislative Council is expected. This paper is intended to facilitate informed public debate on the issues involved.

I think the government should regulate and monitor all SAHR (Scientifically Assisted Human Reproduction) activities in Hong Kong. The stakes are too high to leave them alone. To set up a controlling body for this purpose (*Final Report* 3.2) is a correct move, and the recommendation that an ethics committee should be set up as part of this controlling body should especially be applauded. The *Final Report* rightly observes that "SAHR involves social, *moral, ethical*, legal, as well as medical and technological considerations" (*Final Report* 3.5, italics mine). Accordingly, the composition of the proposed ethics committee should be an improvement on the composition of the SAHR Committee which produced the *Final Report*, by including at least one ethics scholar. The members of the SAHR Committee were drawn from the background and professions *only* of "medicine, law, social work, psychology and family planning" (*Final Report* 1.4); ethics was conspicuously and mysteriously absent. How can one talk about ethics seriously without consulting the opinion of those who devote full-time study to this subject? No wonder both the *Interim Report* and the *Final Report* were criticised for containing obvious ethical inconsistencies and blunders in moral reasoning.[4]

Before going into details, I want to point out a fundamental issue behind SAHR procedures, lest we mistake the trees for the forest. The *Consultation Paper* says: "On the other hand, medical technology has developed considerably since the late 1970s to make unconventional therapy, SAHR procedures, a real alternative to alleviate infertility" (para. 4). First of all, I am not sure that all kinds of SAHR procedures can be regarded as "therapy", as the quoted sentence calls it. I am not going to elaborate this view here, but shall come back to this point in the last two paragraphs of Section B below. What I want to pick up from this quoted sentence is that SAHR procedures are *not only* about the alleviation of infertility. They are also about the morally responsible use of technology. SAHR procedures, when they become more common, should be looked at not only as isolated incidents, but as a new social phenomenon. SAHR has to do with human procreation, child-rearing, family structure and social changes. The thoughtless use of reproductive technology will be fraught with many problems more serious than infertility. Technology can bring us not only promises, but also unanticipated threats (Blank, 1990, pp. 20–2). I shall elaborate this idea in the detailed discussions below.

182

Substantively speaking, I share some Western scholars' deep ethical reservations concerning the employment of reproductive technology that makes use of gametes from someone outside marriage or that somehow enlists the procreative contribution of an extra-marital party. In other words, while I do not see anything wrong with AIH (Artificial Insemination by Husband) and IVF (*In Vitro* Fertilisation) by means of a couple's own gametes, I have serious doubts concerning the appropriateness of AID (Artificial Insemination by Donor, or DI, Donor Insemination, as the Hong Kong government prefers to call it), surrogate motherhood, egg donation, embryo donation, etc.

II. Donor Insemination

1. Ethical Considerations

The first thing that needs to be said about the *Final Report*'s recommendation of Donor Insemination (DI) is that *the recommendation is based on bad reasoning*. The *Final Report* says: "Since DI has been practised in Hong Kong for over 15 years and seems to be acceptable, it should also be allowed to continue" (2.3 [a]). First, let us examine the premise of this reasoning. How can one know that there *seems* to be social acceptance of DI? The government has not conducted any extensive opinion poll on this issue. Hence the answer is probably that social *resistance* to DI has not been felt. In other words, the above premise ("Since DI has been practised in Hong Kong for over 15 years and seems to be acceptable") most probably comes from another inference whose argument form is "since social resistance to x is not felt, x is socially acceptable". This inference, however, is fallacious: unawareness of social resistance to x (which is negative) does not necessarily mean that the majority of citizens like or endorse x (which is positive). Consider this counter-example: a despotic dictator claims that his regime is well-liked because he rules unopposed. What an *argument from silence*! We should understand that unawareness of social resistance to x can be due to a number of reasons. For example, when x is little known or not well understood in society, it is quite understandable that there will be hardly any social resistance to it. In fact, the alleged social non-resistance to DI can indeed be explained in such terms. Many people in Hong Kong are not aware of the existing practice of DI because the whole procedure is shrouded in secrecy and mystery. The medical profession excluded, hardly anyone knows a friend or neighbour who is a recipient of or born of DI. The media cannot find anybody to be interviewed because the couples involved always want to keep it a well-guarded matrimonial secret. Except for the rearing parents, nobody knows the fate of a child born of DI. With the public so ignorant of the consequences of DI, how can one expect anybody to raise a fact-substantiated objection? Social silence, all by itself, is not solid evidence of social approval.

The second reason that renders the aforementioned recommendation in 2.3(a) fallacious is that the reasoning has committed what philosophers call "*naturalistic fallacy*". Even if the majority of people in Hong Kong understand the nature and consequences of DI and positively welcome the practice, this does not imply that DI is morally legitimate. In other words, the argument form of "since x is socially accepted, x is morally legitimate" is fallacious ethical reasoning – one can never directly infer from "x *is the* case" to "x *should be* the case". (To infer from "x *seems to be* case" to "x should be the case", as in *Final Report* 2.3[a], is an even bigger intellectual disaster.) "Is" does not imply "ought", and "fact" is different from "value". As the English philosopher G.E. Moore explains, we cannot infer from the fact that x is desired to the moral judgment that x is desirable. Desirability has to do with what *ought* to be desired or *deserves* to be desired, rather than with what currently is desired (Moore, 1903, sect. 40). Whether DI is ethically legitimate is to be judged on the basis of in-depth ethical reflection, not on the basis of opinion polls. What is trendy is not necessarily ethical. If the Committee thinks that DI should be allowed in Hong Kong, it should come up with a proper ethical reason. (Once again, the absence of an ethics scholar in the SAHR Committee is to be lamented.)

How should one go about such ethical reflection? We need to examine the very nature of procreation by DI and the short-term and long-term consequences that this practice will probably bring about for the parties involved and for society. As an ethics scholar, I have much ethical reservation about procreation by DI, for two reasons.

First, *DI divorces family from marriage.* Unlike AIH (Artificial Insemination by Husband), DI requires the procreative contribution of an extra-marital party (and in the case of single persons and homosexuals, DI is employed in a non-marital context). This signifies a monumental departure from the well-established family structure of humankind, viz., to procreate within marriage, or to build a family on the basis of matrimony, monogamous or polygamous. DI makes it possible to intentionally create a baby whose genetic father will never be the rearing or social father, i.e. a member of the baby's family. The establishment of such a family is not the outgrowth of a marriage, but the hybridisation of two marriages. (In all likelihood, the sperm donor either is married or will eventually get married.) DI marks the *first intentional revolution of human family structure*. (I am not saying that human family structure cannot be changed. In fact, the increase in the divorce rate and the consequent one-parent family or step-parent family are already eroding the traditional family structure. But these are unfortunate accidents, rather than social paradigms, that are never planned for.) Since family is the basic unit of society, and DI brings about an epoch-making transformation of family structure, what is at stake with DI is more than infertility and is nothing less than the future of human society. Are we ready for this? Have we given much thought to the wellbeing of children raised in these new families and the far-reaching, rampant social problems that might follow? We certainly have procreative liberty, but we also have procreative responsibility, especially responsibility to future generations. We should not be afraid of social change *per se*, but it is irresponsible to initiate a social revolution with little advance calculation. Since the divorce of family-building from matrimony will lead us into such an ocean of unknowns and uncharted territories, prudence dictates that we should exercise caution (which is not equivalent to absolute prohibition) by halting all DI activities. We should await the results of more in-depth, multi-disciplinary scholarly studies of this issue before recklessly embarking on such a journey of no return (Bouma, *et al.*, 1989).

Second, *DI invites technological tampering with human procreation*. We live in a "hi-tech" society which cultivates the misconception that those who do not make use of the latest technology are losers. Hence we invite technology to invade every part of our lives. We are not mindful, however, that technocratisation of human life can change the very nature of our lives. When procreation is no longer the exclusive endeavour of a couple, but also the business of an extra-marital third party and even of society, thanks to technology, we are in fact altering the nature of procreation. Babies are no longer *begotten*, but *made* (O'Donovan, 1984); they are not human *offspring*, but technological *products*. They are scientific miracles and another trophy of the human conquest of nature. The end-result of social engineering they are, the gift of Mother Nature they are not. What a distorted vision of life is this! In short, we certainly should not despise technology; there is hardly any person on earth whose life cannot be improved by technology. However, neither should we worship technology. To procreate or not to procreate? That is *not* the issue. The issue is, rather, should we allow the latest technology to dictate what we should do with our families? What kind of persons do we want to be? Is there any sacred space in life that is off-limits to technological intrusion (Bouma, *et al.*, 1989, pp. 189–95)?

Let me resume the discussion of SAHR as therapy initiated in my Prelimi-

185

nary Remarks. Unlike AIH, DI is not "unconventional therapy", as the *Consultation Paper* (para. 4) claims. Unconventional it truly is; medical therapy, in the ordinary sense of language, it is not. Medicine has to do with the maintenance of health and the prevention, alleviation or cure of disease, whereas therapy aims for the restoration of bodily disorder. DI, however, neither cures a disease nor relieves a biological malfunction. It only satisfies a desire, the desire to bear a child in spite of the fact that the couple is unable to do so. DI is not SAHR in the proper sense, as AIH is, because it does not *assist the couple* to have *their own* children, in the ordinary sense of the phrase. It only provides an alternative, viz., to ask another man to father the woman's child without sexual contact. DI is not therapy, because it does not make the infertile fertile or assist the infertile to conceive, which is the case with AIH. DI does not assist the human procreative nature in taking its usual course, as AIH does; it only satisfies human desires by recommending another course. DI is only the genie of Aladdin's lamp; it satisfies our desire without changing the way we are, just like the genie makes Aladdin appear like a prince without turning him into a real prince. It provides a service, but it does not offer therapy. (DI is medical therapy only in the sense that plastic surgery is medical therapy. When a woman has her breasts enlarged by inserting silicon pads, has she received therapy?)

I take pains to argue the point that DI is not therapy because therapy, in our common conception, is unambiguously good. DI, however, in virtue of the two worrisome features mentioned above, is not unambiguously good. Hence to call DI therapy is an act of "persuasive definition", as philosophers call it; it gives DI an unwarranted favourable overtone that will blunt our ethical sensitivity. It misleads us into thinking that DI is unambiguously good. Therefore, whether or not DI is therapy is not just a quarrel over words. It has to do with whether or not we have *begged the ethical question*.

2. Public Policy Concerns

In the event that the Hong Kong government does not heed the call for ethical caution and soon proceeds to offer legal protection to DI, I also have a few suggestions to make regarding the regulation and monitoring of this practice.

1. I agree with the *Final Report* recommendations that only banked semen should be used so that diseases can be checked and chances of incest reduced (3.7). I also agree that semen from any one donor should not be used to produce more than three pregnancies (3.10).

2. I support the SAHR Committee's guiding principle of providing "maximum protection to *all parties* involved in SAHR" (*Final Report*, 3.11, italics mine; cf. 4.2). However, I do not think the *Final Report* recommendations have applied this principle adequately. The interests and rights of the children born of DI, in particular, received no attention.

First, the *Final Report* recommends that "a child born by DI should be given the right of verification on reaching the age of majority, but that the identity of the semen donor should remain confidential" (3.12). I think the DI child's right to know should exceed the information of the circumstances of his or her conception. The DI child also has *the right to know the non-identifying information about his or her genetic father which is essential to his or her basic wellbeing*. This should include at least, as the U.K. *Warnock Report* (4.21) suggests, the ethnic origin and the genetic health of the donor. If the genetic health of the donor remains a mystery, the DI child's life can be endangered. If the donor's ethnic cannot be determined, the DI child can experience identity confusion and even crisis. We would have done the DI child gross injustice if we were to withhold these two pieces of information from the child. (Again, the fact that DI caters to the desires of infertile couples troubles me. The basic wellbeing of the DI child matters more than the desires of the couple.) Besides, the concern to maintain a steady supply of donated sperm should not have a higher moral priority than the fundamental interests of the DI child. Hence the steady supply of sperm donations should not be purchased at the price of withholding the aforementioned information.

Second, it should also be recognised that a DI child has *the right not to be emotionally harmed by the accidental disclosure of the circumstances of his or her conception*. As studies abroad reveal, most legal parents of DI children want to keep the circumstances of the child's conception a dark secret. They deceive the child, relatives and family friends, maintaining that the rearing father is indeed the genetic father. Part of the reason for such secrecy and deceit is to prevent the husband from being embarrassed by public knowledge of his infertility. (Again, the focus of concern is on the couple, not on the child!) However, a DI child may accidentally learn of the circumstances of his or her conception, for example, by overhearing a conversation. Such a shock will subject the child to tremendous emotional distress. In order to protect the child from such emotional harm, the government should encourage openness and discourage deceit by, for example, forbidding the rearing father to register his name as the genetic father on the child's birth certificate.

3. Besides the DI child's rights, the barren couple seeking DI also has the right to choose. On the one hand, it is unreasonable that the couple does not have the slightest room for choice in the kind of man from whom they receive the sperm donation. For example, they should have the right to choose the ethnic race of the donor. It would be a nightmare for a Chinese couple if their DI child had all the physical characteristics of a Caucasian child, simply because they had received the sperm, unbeknown to them, of a Caucasian. On the other hand, the right to choose certainly cannot be unlimited. For example, the couple cannot be allowed to shop around in the sperm bank until they find the sperm of the donor with the highest IQ, highest academic achievement, or most artistic talent. The government needs to regulate on *the scope of the infertile couple's right to choose*. For example, can they request the sperm of a donor whose physical appearance resembles the husband so as to avoid possible future embarrassment? If this is allowed, can they also request the sperm of a donor whose intellectual capacity resembles that of the husband?

4. Even if the government prohibits DI from being used as a eugenics scheme, given the fact that the *Final Report* dismisses the idea of a central sperm bank (2.3 [g]), how can we prevent private clinics from setting up a "genius sperm bank" and reaping huge profits from this "innovative" entrepreneurship? It is a widely known fact that such genius sperm banks already exist in some Western countries.[5] Human nature is as such that our desires can never be fully satisfied. The satisfaction of one desire, thanks to technology, will only stimulate another desire. *Just as human beings are not content with cars replacing horses and want faster cars, human beings will not be content with simply making babies and will want to make a particular kind of baby* (Bouma, *et al.*, 1989, p. 191). Once the genie of Aladdin's lamp promises to provide cross-fertilisation, people will ask him to look for better breeds. One thing the government can do to prevent eugenics from entering the door opened by DI is to *set up a central sperm bank and prohibit the practice of DI in private clinics.* (The activities of this central sperm bank should also be closely monitored, lest the government becomes the eugenics mastermind.)

III. Surrogacy

1. Ethical Considerations

The ethical concerns that demand caution regarding DI also apply here. Like DI, to procreate through surrogate mothers, socially speaking, is to divorce family from marriage and to invite technological tampering with human procreation. Furthermore, the very nature of surrogacy will create more problems than it solves. Unlike DI, in which the donor disappears after leaving his semen behind in a test-tube, a surrogate mother is extensively involved in the procreative process. Her participation is visible and lasts for some time. She takes up the sacred and eye-catching task of falling pregnant and carrying the child to term. Such extensive participation of an extra-marital third party in the procreative process raises a number of new ethical concerns.

1. Fragmentation of motherhood. The surrogate mother is more than a "donor", a person who discards the orgasmic emission which he does not want to keep anyway. She is at least the gestational *mother* of the child so born. Unlike sperm donors, the surrogate mother physically experiences parenthood; for nine months her bodily process compels her to feel that she is mothering a child. Hence the surrogate arrangement in procreation intentionally creates two self-aware mothers for one baby (three mothers if the egg comes from neither the commissioning wife nor from the surrogate mother). Again, what is at stake here is the structure of the human family and the adjudication of parental responsibilities.

A by-product of such fragmentation of motherhood is the possible confusion of family relationships. We all know about the infamous 1987 case in South Africa in which the mother bore a child for her daughter. Should the resulting child call this generous woman "grandma" or "mommy"? There are other similar cases in Western countries, e.g., a woman bears a child for her sister, etc. Should we welcome the intentional creation of such families which will bring about not only confusing family relationships but also, as a result, a novel set of destabilising family problems?

2. Harm to the child. The *Final Report* is sensitive to the unpleasant possibility that a DI child might be stigmatised as illegitimate (3.8). Similar moral sensitivity, however, is not shown in regard to the child born of surrogacy. As I explained above, unlike DI, which can be hidden as a family secret, to have a child through surrogacy is bound to become public knowledge, especially in a gossiping society such as Hong Kong's. Neighbours and family friends all know that this child has been begotten by another mother. (An average Hong Kong citizen is not a scientist. He or she does not distinguish between the genetic mother and the gestational mother. Even if the rearing mother contributes genetically to the procreation, the child born of surrogacy will still be known as "begotten by another woman".) In all likelihood, this child will be ridiculed and stigmatised as "illegitimate" by the neighbours' children and at school. In promoting procreative liberty, have we also exercised procreative responsibility?

Another possibility that should worry us is the chance that the child born of surrogacy turns out to be handicapped or biologically defective in some way. It is quite probable that this child will be rejected and abandoned. When there is

189

no single couple to be "full parents" to a child, there is always the risk that the child will be rejected as foreign. Such a risk is intensified when "the product" delivered is defective. Again, should society recommend an innovative mode of procreation which offers fewer safeguards for the interests of the child than that of an ordinary procreation?

3. Surrogate mother used as an instrument. Even though the *Final Report* stipulates that the surrogate mother plays only a gestational role, with the egg contributed by the commissioning wife (4.1 [14]), the stipulation accentuates, rather than alleviates, a moral problem. When a surrogate mother's role is limited only to gestation, she becomes more like an incubator. She is used as the human equivalent of an artificial womb. It does not promote the interests of women when surrogate mothers are used only as instruments (New York, 1988).

4. Availability to singles and homosexuals. Though the *Final Report* stipulates that surrogacy should only be allowed for infertile married couples (4.1 [16]), there is no way to ensure that surrogacy, and DI as well, will not be used by others. Once the technology is made available there will be a lucrative underground market for it. Furthermore, if DI and surrogacy are legally available to some adults but not to singles and homosexuals, it can be charged that this is discrimination against these two groups of people. Singles and homosexuals, like infertile heterosexual couples, cannot procreate. It is legally unfair, as it is argued, that the latest reproductive technology is made available to infertile heterosexual couples, but not to them. They have the same *parental desire* to have their own children, and the genie of Aladdin's lamp should serve them as well. (In fact, *The Glover Report* [1989] recommends that it should not be illegal for homosexual couples to take advantage of the new technologies.) Setting legal issues aside, in reality many lesbians in the U.S.A. are known to be beneficiaries of DI. For example, since 1982 the Feminist Health Centre for Women in Oakland, California has had a sperm bank offering service to lesbians (Glover, 1989). It was also reported that at least 1,500 unmarried women a year in the U.S.A. are artificially inseminated (Blank, 1990, p. 110). Thus, either we should ban all extra-marital procreative contributions in the use of reproductive technology, or we should accept that singles and homosexuals should also be allowed to make use of such technology.

Is there anything wrong with making available the latest reproductive technology to singles and homosexuals? It is happening in some Western countries anyway. Well, two things should worry us. First, is it in the best interests of children to have them intentionally born into a fatherless or motherless family? Once again, freedom is not the same as licence, and procreative liberty is to be exercised within the bounds of procreative responsibility – responsibility to the children so born. Second, by intentionally creating single-parent families and homosexual-parents families we are on our way to dismantling the traditional structure of the human family. Are we sure that such a social revolution will bring society more benefits than harm? Have we done enough research on this issue before we embark on this journey of no return? In the light of the monumental social changes that can be brought about, can we afford to be reckless? The only way to prevent intentional single-parenting and homosexual double-parenting is to ban all extra-marital procreative contribution.

2. Public Policy Concerns

Again, in the event that the government determines to go ahead with legalising surrogacy, I urge it to take heed to the following comments.

1. I applaud the SAHR Committee's recommendation that commercial surrogacy be banned. The evils of commercial surrogacy, as has emerged in Western countries, are too numerous to be listed here. Stiff penalties have to be given to commissioning couples and agents who employ women as paid surrogate mothers. Given the fact that in Hong Kong many illegal activities are alive and well "underground" (e.g., prostitution, organised gambling, abortion), it is unrealistic not to expect the emergence of a *black market* of "womb renting" and "babies for sale".

2. Again, in the spirit of ensuring maximum protection of the interests of all parties involved (*Final Report*, 3.11, 4.2), our focus of attention should not be exclusively on the infertile couple. The surrogate mother, because of her vulnerability to exploitation, especially deserves our attention. The government should give legal recognition that surrogate mothers enjoy the following two rights. First, *a surrogate mother has the right to have continuing contact* (e.g., through periodic visitation) *with the child she gives birth to.* This would recognise that she is indeed the child's gestational *mother*, not just an incubator that can be disposed of after use. She is a human being who has been intimately related to the child, not an instrument of the commissioning couple. Second, she has *the right to change her mind and keep the new-born baby.* In other words, there should be a specified reasonable period of time in which she can decide to retain the baby, as is the case in regular adoption procedure, which is noted in the *Final Report* (3.26).

3. In light of the experience of Western countries, we should expect that there will be legal *disputes between the surrogate mother and the commissioning couple* (e.g., the famous "Baby M" case in the U.S.A.). Even though the *Final Report* is not entirely unaware of this possibility (3.17, 3.26–7), it is surprising that there is no recommendation in this regard. Such disputes can arise either before or after the birth of the baby. In the former case the surrogate mother changes her mind and decides to terminate the contract by having an abortion. ("It is procreative choice," says the surrogate mother. "She kills our baby!" cries the commissioning couple.) In the latter case, the surrogate mother decides to keep the baby she gave birth to. We should think of a way of resolving such disputes ahead of time, lest the gossip magazines and newspaper columns play King Solomon.

IV. Embryo Research

The *Final Report* recommends that leftover IVF-use embryos can be used for research in the first two weeks after fertilisation. Even though there is no public consensus on whether or not an embryo in this early stage is a human being, we do know that the issue of embryo research has aroused emotional controversy abroad. Does a human embryo have the right not to be used for research without the embryo's own consent? Should there be a limit on the kind of research that can be done on embryos so obtained (e.g., only in relation to finding a therapy for infertility)? At any rate, the seriousness of this issue is totally out of proportion to the tininess and passivity of the human embryo. *The* Final Report *has not shown any sign of serious thought on the moral dimension of this issue*. I therefore urge the government to seek wider consultation on this issue before taking any action.

V. Concluding Comments

1. I do not find any ethical objection to using reproductive technology to assist a husband and a wife to overcome reproductive obstacles. I have deep ethical reservation, however, regarding enlisting the procreative contribution of an extra-marital party (cf. Bouma, *et al.*, 1989, p. 194).

2. We certainly should not be nonchalant about the sense of incompletion and unfulfilment of barren couples. We need to share their pain and sorrows and more medical research needs to be done to find both more effective prevention of and therapy for infertility (cf. Blank, 1990, pp. 227–9).

192

3. We, as mortals and creatures, should accept our inadequacies, inabilities and limitations. There is a boundary beyond which perhaps we should never trespass. We indeed have freedom, but freedom is not an excuse for licence. Our freedom to have a family is to be exercised in the context of two kinds of responsibility – procreative responsibility (toward our children born by means of reproductive technology) and responsible use of technology (toward human society).[6]

4. Undoubtedly, artificial reproduction is an important scientific and technological breakthrough. But the fact that technology is available for use does not imply that it should be used. We should think ahead and first consider its long-term moral and social implications. From a wider perspective reproductive technology is not just about infertility; it has far-reaching implications for the human family and society. The social revolution that reproductive technology can bring about is fraught with many problems more serious than infertility. Accordingly, the scientific and technological breakthrough should be matched with greater moral sensitivity and ethical caution (cf. Arditti, *et al.*, 1984; Corea, 1985).

5. The global ecological crisis has taught us expensive lessons that we cannot afford to ignore: (i) our unbridled use of technology leads to widespread pollution and depletion of natural resources; (ii) to live only for ourselves, regardless of the future generations, leads to severe damage to the environment; (iii) the mentality of conquering and manipulating nature is a false religion. Once again, we are at a crossroads. We might duplicate our folly and create a social disaster, in addition to the present ecological disasters.

We should therefore encourage a *"green" use of reproductive technology*, which has the following characteristics, in correspondence with the three aforementioned lessons. (i) Our use of reproductive technology should be cautious rather than unbridled. Extra-marital and non-marital applications of this technology, in particular, deserve second thought. (ii) We should not only live for ourselves by satisfying our desire to have children by any means, but should also live for our children and the future of human society (cf. Blank, 1990, pp. 208–15, 231; Jonas, 1984). The pillar that supports the stability of society, viz., the stable family, should not be pulled down with nothing to replace it. (iii) We should not use reproductive technology to manipulate biological nature in any way we want. We should live in harmony with nature; the natural procreative process is neither a god to which we must submit nor an object of conquest and subjection (cf. Bouma, *et al.*, 1989).

6. Robert H. Blank, Associate Director of the Program for Bio-social Research at Northern Illinois University, notes in his comprehensive study (Blank, 1990, p. 215) that for most governments, unfortunately, "fragmented, piecemeal, and simplistic attempts to deal with the complex problems concerning the reproductive technologies are the norm. The resulting policies continue to fall far short of what is needed as we grapple with continually more difficult decisions". I hope the Hong Kong government will have the courage to look for a more morally sensible reproductive policy.

Notes

1. This information is from the *Consultation Paper on the Final Report of the Committee on Scientifically Assisted Human Reproduction*, Appendix C.

2. For a good sample of these objections, see the *Sheh Luen Quarterly* (1990), published by the Hong Kong Social Service Association.

3. A group of City Polytechnic Institute lecturers, and the present writer, published criticisms of the *Final Report* in the *Hong Kong Economic Journal*, July and August 1993.

4. It is noteworthy that the British committee on the same subject matter and the resulting report were chaired and written not by a physician or scientist, but by a moral philosopher, Mary Warnock; hence the abbreviated title *The Warnock Report*. The same is true of *The Glover Report*, a report of a similar nature for the European Community. In contrast, the Hong Kong government has not paid serious attention to the moral dimensions of the issues involved.

5. As of 1987, the Repository for Germinal Choice in Escondido, California, U.S.A., had semen samples of five Nobel laureates and of other men of note, and 37 children had been born from such sperm (Blank, 1990, pp. 60–1).

6. Even in the liberal society of the U.S.A., the call to curb some individual liberties for the sake of social responsibility is gaining ascendancy, especially in the Communitarian Movement; see, for example, their journal *The Responsive Community: Rights and Responsibilities*.

References

Arditti, Rita, Renate Duelli Klein and Shelly Minden, 1984, *Test-tube Women: What Future of Motherhood?*, London, Pandora Press

Blank, Robert H., 1990, *Regulating Reproduction*, New York, Columbia University Press

Bouma III, Hessel, Douglas Diekema, Edward Langerak, Theodore Rottman and Allen Verhey, 1989, *Christian Faith, Health, and Medical Practice*, Grand Rapids, Michigan, Eerdmans

Corea, Gena, 1985, *The Mother Machine: Reproductive Technologies from Artificial Insemination to Artificial Wombs*, New York, Harper & Row

Glover, Jonathan *et al.*, 1989, *Fertility & the Family: The Glover Report on Reproductive Technologies to the European Commission*, London, Fourth Estate

Hong Kong Government, Health and Welfare Branch, 1993, *Consultation Paper on Final Report of the Committee on Scientifically Assisted Human Reproduction*, Hong Kong

Jonas, Hans, 1984, *The Imperative of Responsibility: In Search of an Ethics for the Technological Age,* Chicago, University of Chicago Press

Jones, D. Gareth, 1987, *Manufacturing Humans: The Challenge of the New Reproductive Technologies*, Leicester, England, Inter-Varsity Press

Moore, G.E., 1903, *Principia Ethica*, Cambridge, Cambridge University Press

Naisbitt, John, and Patricia Aburdene, 1990, *Megatrends 2000: Ten New Directions for the 1990s*, New York, William Morrow and Company

New York State Task Force on Life and the Law, 1988, *Surrogate Parenting: Analysis and Recommendations for Public Policy*, New York, The New York State Task Force on Life and the law

O'Donovan, Oliver, 1984, *Begotten or Made?*, Oxford, Clarendon Press

Ramsey, Paul, 1970, *Fabricated Man*, New Haven, Yale University Press

Warnock, Mary, 1985, *A Question of Life: The Warnock Report on Human Fertilisation and Embryology*, Oxford, Basil Blackwell

Chapter 11

Testing for HIV in Hong Kong: Challenge to Ethics and Public Policy

JOEL ZIMBELMAN

I. Introduction

AIDS has arrived in Hong Kong, and demographic trends suggest that the epidemic will grow in the territory in the coming decade. What should be the response of government and health-care authorities to this situation, particularly with respect to HIV testing and notifying as part of a larger programme of infection control? In light of its growing commitment to both efficacious programmes of public health and to civil rights, public health officials and legislators will need to give increasing attention to balancing these competing commitments. This will be complicated by the political uncertainty of the coming decade; the pressures to sacrifice some civil rights when these are thought to conflict with public health interests; and the call by some groups to assure an HIV testing policy that protects the "innocent".

Part I of this paper reviews the demographics of and social attitudes towards HIV and AIDS in Hong Kong and explores the moral values that are affirmed by this society. I introduce a number of criteria by which we might assess available options for HIV testing, screening, and the disclosure of test results. In Part II I assess several testing and screening options. I argue that Hong Kong ought to implement a programme that emphasises voluntary selective testing of certain high-risk populations. In Part III I evaluate a range of options with respect to the disclosure of test results. I argue for a policy that emphasises voluntary selective disclosure. In Part IV I conclude by suggesting that such policies have the best chance of protecting both the hard-won public health standards and the growing commitment to civil rights evidenced in Hong Kong.

II. The Present Situation in Hong Kong

1. The Epidemiology of HIV and AIDS in Hong Kong

HIV (Human Immunosuppressive Virus) is characterised by its relatively low infection rate among humans and, following infection, a long asymptomatic (though still infective) period which proceeds full-blown AIDS (Acquired Immune Deficiency Syndrome) (Harris, 1993, p. 6, 7). HIV infection, when manifested as AIDS, is nearly always fatal. Still, survival rates among seropositive (HIV+) individuals who have not developed AIDS after nearly 10 years suggests that the inevitable progression of HIV to AIDS for all persons may have some exceptions (Hoffman, 1990, pp. 63–74, 95–120; Department of Health, 1992; 1993, pp. 4–15, 54–58; Stine, 1993, p. 105).

HIV infection continues to expand rapidly through the populations of Asia, with no sign that the epidemic has yet reached a mature state (World Health Organisation, 1993; U.S. Bureau of the Census, 1994, pp. 12–13). In Hong Kong, where the first AIDS case was diagnosed in 1985, the rate of growth of HIV and AIDS cases is steady but slower than that of many Asian nations. With around 450 known cases of HIV and approximately 100 confirmed cases of AIDS (though actual numbers are probably many times this), Hong Kong has probably not yet felt the brunt of the epidemic (Wiseman, 1994b; 1994d). The groups most at risk of contracting HIV in Hong Kong are similar to those in other parts of the world: homosexual, bisexual, and with increasing frequency heterosexual populations (including women); and intravenous drug users (Stine, 1993, 156–94; Wiseman, 1994a; 1994b; 1994d).[1] Worldwide, rates of HIV transmission between patients and health-care workers (HCWs) are quite low and approach zero with respect to nosocomial transmissions between HCWs and patients (Pauker, 1990; Danila, 1991; Elder, 1991; Ciesielski, 1992; Stine, 1993, pp. 168–9).

It is often assumed that the spread of HIV involves consensual, voluntary, intimate contact rather than non-consensual, involuntary contact (Childress, 1987, p. 28). Short of rape, perinatal transmission, unknown transmission via blood or blood products, or cases where a person's drug addiction renders them unable to give full and voluntary consent to risky activities, HIV is the result of consensual activity. Many people know what types of actions and behaviour can lead to HIV infection. But the vast majority of persons engaging in high-risk activities do not appreciate (due to ignorance, an inability to process calculations of risk probability, or because of self-deception) that they are personally at risk. Many, perhaps the majority of persons who are seropositive have no idea of their status. Even in situations where seropositive individuals have that knowledge, partner notification rates are low and many cases go unreported to public health officials, exacerbating the problem of uninformed risk (Landis, 1992; U.S. Bureau of the Census, 1994, p. 3).

In spite of these observations, there is evidence that interventions can lower the prevalence of HIV. Early testing, detection of seropositivity, lifestyle changes, and (in some limited cases) therapeutic intervention for seropositive individuals has the potential to improve the quality of life and/or life expectancy.

2. Social Values and Attitudes in Hong Kong

"Public reaction to [HIV] has been a mixture of fear, anger, fascination, aversion, dread, and denial – all in good measure at different times" (Fineberg, 1990, p. 30). Hong Kong is no exception to such reactions, and the attitudes of its citizens provide some insight into the background considerations and challenges that will need to be faced in the establishment of an efficacious HIV testing and notification policy.

Public health experts in Hong Kong recognise that HIV is a serious threat to the society's wellbeing. Among the population at large, however, there is a pervasive ignorance (though perhaps no more than in most developed countries) of the causes, epidemiology, clinical manifestations, and means of controlling the disease. The attitude among many in Hong Kong seems to be: "It's not a problem here." Also present, but more prevalent across the border in the People's Republic of China (PRC), is the belief that HIV/AIDS is a Western or "*gweilo*" disease. Further, ignorance of the HIV risk to heterosexuals and women is great in the territory.

In addition to ignorance, HIV/AIDS discrimination exists across Hong Kong society. Public knowledge of a person's HIV status results almost uniformly in varying degrees of discrimination. This means that the costs of testing and knowing one's HIV status are quite high; perhaps higher than a reasonable, self-interested person would care to risk. In light of the social costs and the questionable efficacy of nearly all drug therapies at the present time, it has been argued by some that purely self-interested individuals in Hong Kong would be advised not to be tested. The result of this logic, of course, is that such a decision increases the rate of transmission and prevalence of HIV in the population.

Most Hong Kong people fail to fully appreciate the nature or risk of HIV infection and AIDS in part because of the relationship that they believe holds between HIV and homosexuality. Strong feelings against homosexuality are prevalent in Hong Kong: feelings that have their roots in both traditional Chinese culture and in 19th- and 20th-century Christian and Western influences. Until recently, the spread of HIV in Western industrial societies was more rapid among the gay population.[2] These sentiments and demographics have shaped the beliefs among Hong Kong people that (1) HIV/AIDS is a disease that predominantly affects gays; and (2) one acquires HIV/AIDS by being gay. By extension, many people believe that the danger of HIV transmission by and among other population groups is less of a threat because of who they are (heterosexual men and women) and because they do not engage in the types of behaviour and sexual activities that transmit the disease (Langone, 1991, p. 85). Unfortunately, these beliefs fail to account for the fact that HIV is a growing threat to the heterosexual populations of most developing nations, and that HIV has always been predominantly (though not exclusively) a heterosexual disease in Africa and Asia (World Health Organisation, 1993).

Also complicating the development and implementation of an effective HIV policy is the fact that double standards of acceptable or tolerable male and female sexual activity exist in Hong Kong. Sexual promiscuity is greater among Hong Kong men than women. And the power of women within and outside marriage to demand monogamy, sexual fidelity and condom use of their sexual partners (including their husbands) is lower than in some other societies. Since women in heterosexual encounters are always more at risk than men for contracting all types of venereal disease and other infections, this means that women are greatly at risk of contracting HIV.

199

3. Moral Values in Hong Kong

Moral values are general imperatives and guidelines that define good and bad, right and wrong, and virtuous and vicious character and conduct. All societies affirm and embody certain moral values and principles. We can delineate the moral values central to much of Hong Kong society.

The people and institutions of the territory, beyond a commitment to their own self-interest, evidence a fairly strong commitment to the common good and to public health. This is clearly seen in the territory's policy priorities, funding choices, laws and social organisation. This commitment is grounded in and derived from several moral values. Hong Kong is committed to a general moral imperative of respect for persons as beings worthy of consideration by others. Respect for persons also obligates persons and societies to recognise and give weight to the interests of other persons, to avoid harm to others (non-maleficence) and to seek their good (beneficence).

Often respect for persons is reflected in and expressed through the moral principle of utility. Respect for persons in the public health arena will often require that society "seek the greatest good for the greatest number of persons" through specific health-care policies that promote not just the interests of some, but the public interest and welfare (Munson, 1992, pp. 35–7).

At the same time, Hong Kong is a territory in which the rule of law exists and which affirms the moral principle of justice. Justice is reflected in specific commitments to fair (though not necessarily equal) distribution schemes concerning goods and benefits as well as costs and risks (Munson, 1992, pp. 37–40). Such a commitment to distributive justice may be reflected in different arrangements for the distribution of certain goods and services (e.g., housing, access to primary education, vaccination programmes, a comprehensive programme of public health) that might differ from acceptable and morally justifiable arrangements for the distribution of other goods (e.g., access to apartments on the Peak, ownership of BMWs, access to higher education, concert tickets).

At the same time, justice also embodies a respect for procedural concerns largely codified in the rule of law and the establishment of regulations, procedures, and guidelines. Justice is rarely perfect or comprehensive, both because our societies are not utopias, and because the goods of justice must be balanced against the demands of other moral and non-moral values. Still, the ideal of justice remains central to the conduct of Hong Kong society.

In addition to its broad commitment to the social good, Hong Kong society evidences a growing commitment to rights of various kinds. The society is developing broader and deeper commitments to respect for personal autonomy and an individual's right to self-determination (Munson, 1992, p. 40). The modern instantiation of the moral value of respect for autonomy is a product both of the common law notion of the right to bodily integrity as well as the 18th-century Enlightenment's commitment to respect for persons and the moral standing of individuals. These traditions have argued that individuals possess rights by dint of their status as persons or members of an identified community. These rights obligate other persons to act in a specific manner toward the holders of such rights. First, respect for persons and their autonomy suggests that, when seeking to advance a person's interests, we "balance the good and harm to an individual that may follow [from our action] so that there is a net effect of the good" on that person (Fineberg, 1990, p. 30). Second, respect for persons and for their autonomy and right to self-determination requires that a person's wishes and desires (not just their interests) inform decisions involving that person. Finally, combining the above formulations, respect for autonomy suggests that society and other persons have an obligation to respect both certain rights and interests of persons in a way that prohibits those rights and interests from being sacrificed for the perceived or actual good of others.

This commitment to respect for autonomy can also be viewed as one grounding for the flourishing of changing cultural values that recognise and respect persons' rights to freedom of movement; the power accorded personal decision-making; respect for privacy, confidentiality, and liberty rights; and the emerging respect given to democratic institutions by Hong Kong people. Such conventions are emerging in common law and judicial provinces and, with more frequency, in the legal codes, ordinances and bills affirmed by the government of Hong Kong.[3] Under such legislation, individuals who are members of the community (including HIV-negative and HIV-positive individuals) have moral and civil rights, though such rights are certainly not absolute.

Respecting these rights is required in the face of the moral values and the terms of the moral convention to which Hong Kong has committed itself. Indeed, the HIV crisis is distinct, in that it is Hong Kong's first public health crisis in an era of broadly recognised, legislatively protected civil rights and liberties. At the same time there exist good practical and politically expedient reasons for respecting these values. By distinguishing rights from goods, I am not suggesting that respecting individual rights is not a social good. Rather, respecting autonomy rights as one broad value among many may be seen as a good that accrues to individuals and the society as a whole.

There is widespread agreement that the moral principles just outlined are binding and have probative force in the larger Hong Kong community; that they hold at least *prima facie* or presumptive status. If this assessment is correct, then the people and government of Hong Kong have an obligation to fulfil the demands of all of these moral principles to the greatest degree possible, with greater attention to fulfilling the most important ones. Still, there is little agreement in Hong Kong over what these principles imply, how they should be specified, what weight they should carry in moral reasoning, and how exactly they ought to inform the shape and substance of law and public policy (cf. Childress, 1987, p. 28). Certainly in some situations some moral principles can be overridden by others (Munson, 1992, pp. 42–5). For example, respect for autonomy might be justifiably overridden in some situations because of the particular demands of beneficence or utility. Indeed, the human experience of moral conflicts and dilemmas implies that all general moral obligations cannot simultaneously be respected and/or instantiated in every particular context or situation of life. For the ethical pluralist – one who affirms that persons are bound by more than a single moral value or imperative – life is complicated, messy, and tragic. Still, such may be the price to be paid for affirming the many moral values to which we feel we must be committed. And it means that we must recognise the inevitability of difficult moral choices in public policy decisions.

Resolving moral dilemmas, however, means that this process, while sensitive to contextual demands, is not a purely situational undertaking. To affirm the *prima facie* status of moral principles means that we are morally bound to make a significant attempt to respect the integrity and status of all of our competing moral values and principles. These moral principles may be infringed, but only with explanation and public justification; and only when such infringement is the least necessary to accomplish our goal (Childress, 1987, p. 29; 1991, pp. 53–5). Respect for autonomy and for rights to self-determination does not mean that those values must always be respected at the expense of public health or what is good for other persons. It does require, however, that reasonable (and sometimes even costly) options to infringing a person's rights be considered and perhaps adopted. In addition, infringement of a given moral principle needs to be shown to be effective and necessary to realising the important obligations of some other moral principle(s). In other words, we must be able to show that "the probable benefits of a policy infringing [some principles] … outweigh both the moral rule(s) infringed and any negative consequences" (Childress, 1991, p. 54). Thus, a utilitarian or consequentialist calculation of what policy will result in the greatest respect for the public good may not in and of itself be a strong enough moral argument to infringe on other moral values, such as respect for autonomy.

4. Moral Principles and the Shape of an Ethically Justifiable Screening Programme

If Hong Kong is committed to the moral values and the process of moral adjudication just discussed, then those values and that process ought to inform the territory's decision about whether or not to undertake an HIV screening programme and the shape of that programme. Both Childress and Bayer have suggested a number of formal criteria, justified with respect to the moral principles just outlined, that must be met by any ethically justifiable screening programme (Bayer, 1989, pp. 634–40).

1. The purpose of the screening must be ethically acceptable and the knowledge discovered from screening must be efficacious. Why do we want the information that we are seeking? The primary purpose of HIV screening and testing, which is based on beneficence, is threefold. First, the medical purpose is "to benefit the individual being tested" by providing the information needed to make informed and realistic treatment decisions and life plans. The second ethically justifiable reason for screening, the public health or preventative purpose, "is to reduce the likelihood of the spread of infection to others". A third justification for screening, the surveillance justification, "is to track the spread of the epidemic", as part of a larger commitment to public health and prevention (Fineberg, 1990, p. 29).

However, it is not enough simply to have good motives, reasons, or justifications for engaging in a testing and/or screening programme. In addition to passing the formal test of acceptability, it must be demonstrated, based on empirical and factual considerations, that a testing or screening programme can be effective: that it has a good chance of accomplishing its goal. The benefits of such goals will need to outweigh the burdens inflicted on individuals and society.

2. The means to be used in testing and/or screening and the intended use of the information must be appropriate to our purpose. How do we plan to get the information that we require? How will that information be used once it is acquired? If public health (grounded in beneficence) is our primary goal, then certain types of information about a person's HIV status, or the statistical incidence of HIV in a population, may be required. At the same time, the *prima facie* moral principles of respect for persons and respect for autonomy (and the derivative values of privacy and confidentiality) need to be honoured. If we are going to infringe on people's rights, we need to show that we are infringing on those rights to the least degree possible consistent with our other aims (Childress, 1991, p. 55).

Hong Kong must also explore questions about the intended use to which information of HIV status is to be put, and the potential (unintended and/or probable) uses that might be made of such information. It is one thing to say that society needs to know a person's HIV status in order to "protect the public". But a commitment to the moral principles and process of moral justification discussed earlier means that proponents of screening programmes must be able to specify how having that knowledge will protect that person, their intimates and associates, and the public.

3. High-quality laboratory services must be used, and funding for such services and their confirmation and interpretation must be assured before any screening programme begins. Based on the principles of respect for persons, beneficence, and utility, testing is not justified if tests aren't accurate; if they aren't sensitive enough; if their predictive value is unacceptably low; or if the cost of the tests precludes them from being used in a way that will result in useful information. This suggests as well that there is a moral imperative for the provision of research on improving the quality of tests (including confirmatory testing) and funding for qualified technicians and test interpreters. Acquiring useful information in an ethical manner about HIV status will cost a lot of money regardless of whether such screening is voluntary or involuntary.

4. Individuals must be notified that screening or testing will take place. This is morally required under our respect for the principle of autonomy. Even when we can justify testing and screening either with permission or coercively, we have a duty, based on respect for persons and for their autonomy, to disclose the fact of such testing and to give reasons and justification for that infringement (Childress, 1991, p. 54, 55).

5. Individuals who are screened have a right to be informed of the results of their tests. Based on principles of beneficence and public welfare, those conducting screening programmes have an obligation to reveal test results to those tested whether or not the results of such tests are desired or not. Not providing such information opposes the principle of respect for persons and undercuts the responsibility that individuals have in light of the demands of other moral principles. Failure to provide individuals with this information also undercuts the effectiveness of empowering persons when possible to take responsibility for altering their own behaviour.

6. The confidentiality of screened individuals must be protected. This maxim is readily derived from the principles of respect for persons, respect for autonomy, beneficence, utility, confidentiality, and privacy. Here, pragmatic arguments are particularly compelling. Because of the fear (whether reasonable or not) that the loss of confidentiality in testing and disseminating test results could destroy a person's career and/or personal life, the consequences of not respecting confidentiality can undercut any broad public health benefits that might result from a voluntary screening programme.

7. Medical and counselling support must be available before and after screening to interpret and deal with HIV test results. Modern medicine and public health give little regard to whether truly informed (which also means educated) consent for such tests has been given; to how such testing is perceived by its target population; or to how the information from such screening will most likely be interpreted and used. Greater attention and resources need to be given to establishing a justification for testing and screening that is understood by target audiences, that develops a public support system for communicating important information effectively and accurately, and that addresses the devastating fallout from acquiring such knowledge.

Attention to these seven "threshold requirements" is morally required in all public health programmes concerning HIV testing and notification. These criteria are lexically ordered. We are morally required to meet each of these criteria in the order that they are presented before we are permitted to move on to the next stage of establishing a testing and screening programme. If any one of these criteria are not significantly met at each stage of a policy for which they are relevant and applicable, then serious questions exist about the moral permissibility of embarking on that particular testing or screening programme.

While these criteria provide a point of departure, they are insufficient in themselves for assuring an effective and ethically legitimate HIV screening programme. Greater attention needs to be directed to the analysis of contextual considerations that accurately assesses the probable success of specific programmes, and that gives proper attention to the particular social, cultural, psychological and historical situation that exists in Hong Kong.

III. HIV Testing

1. Testing and Screening Options

James Childress has suggested that the dual commitment to public health (reflected in the extent to which screening for HIV is undertaken) and respect for persons and their autonomy (reflected in consideration of the degree of voluntariness affirmed by a given screening programme) provides us with a helpful matrix for describing and assessing various screening options (Childress, 1987, pp. 29–30; 1991, pp. 56–70).

Table 1

| | | degree of voluntariness | |
		compulsory	consensual
extent of screening	universal	1	2
	selective	3	4

Option 1. Universal-compulsory testing: "Everyone must be tested."

While certain benefits could result from society's knowledge of everyone's HIV status (individuals might alter their behaviour; society might better be able to mandate policy changes that would slow the spread of the disease), affirming Option 1 as a testing option has costs and problems.

First, the question remains about the use to which the information gained from such screening might be put. Screening can be morally justified as a means to protect the public's health. But it is not immediately apparent how the possession of such information by public health officials would accomplish that goal. Because the prevalence of HIV is greatest in (though certainly not entirely restricted to) high-risk populations, a programme of universal screening that would screen individuals outside these groups is not a necessary prerequisite to protecting the public health. Even if the only purpose of such testing is to provide persons with knowledge of their HIV status so that they can make informed choices about lifestyle changes or (voluntary) notification of other persons concerning HIV status, such knowledge – if gained coercively – probably will not result in these desired outcomes (Childress, 1991, p. 57). Indeed, the prevalence of false positive results among low-risk populations (see below) might generate panic and fear, and thus undermine both an accurate public health assessment and a realistic sense of personal risk.

Second, it is not clear that screening for HIV in the population as a whole could give us the information that we seek – a determination of who is seropositive and who is seronegative. Ordinary screening among populations where the prevalence of HIV is very low will not provide accurate information concerning the prevalence of the disease (Bayer, 1989, pp. 634-5; Pauker, 1990, pp. 34–7). If the narrow goal of a screening programme is to uncover only true positives (that is, people who test positive and are in fact positive for HIV), then such a programme must eliminate false positives (persons who test positive but are in fact HIV-) and false negatives (persons who test negative but are in fact HIV+) from screening results. The primary test now used to test for HIV (the ELISA test) is very sensitive – it gives very low rates of false negative results. But the price of sensitivity is loss of specificity – ELISA gives many false positive values. These false positive rates are particularly high when the populations tested are those in which the prevalence of HIV is very low (in some low-risk populations, 90 per cent of initial positive ELISA tests can be false positives) Public health officials are thus advised to run the ELISA and a second, corroborating test (the Western blot) on all seropositive ELISA test results (Rhame, 1989, pp. 1251–2; Stine, 1993, pp. 283–302). Screening is further complicated by the fact that HIV exhibits a fairly lengthy latency period (the period between actual infection and the development of antibodies to the virus, the presence of which serve as the indirect means of determining if the virus is present). This means that, theoretically, retesting of all seronegative subjects every few months is necessary to identify newly occurring seropositive individuals – an expensive and logistically daunting task.

Third, the cost of universal screening and testing would be prohibitive (particularly in light of the need for continual and periodic testing of the whole population). At the same time, such screening is not cost-effective when compared to other interventions available to public health officials (for example voluntary testing, education, perhaps even needle exchange programmes and condom distribution programmes; though such programmes have their own complications and limitations).

A final argument against universal-compulsory testing is that such a policy appears to abrogate important moral principles (such as respect for persons and for their autonomy, freedom and privacy) and certain civil rights, since any such policy would be highly coercive. Such abrogation of moral principles and civil rights is certainly permissible if it is adequately justified and if it infringes on moral principles to the least extent possible in light of the requirements of other moral values (for example, beneficence, utility and public health). But the compensating benefit from such a serious abrogation of fundamental moral principles cannot presently be shown, and so appears to be morally unjustifiable (Childress, 1987, p. 29).

Option 2: Universal-consensual testing: "Test everyone who wants to be tested."

As with Option 1, Option 2 provides important information to test subjects, and so meets the moral requirements of individual beneficence. Option 2 has two advantages over Option 1. First, it is less costly, since only a fraction of the population will be tested (though other costs associated with classifying the population and then targeting segments for testing will be incurred). Second,

Option 2 is not coercive: it appears to respect autonomy and freedom, since only those who consent to testing will be tested.

However, as with Option 1, Option 2 fails the tests of social beneficence, public health, cost-effectiveness, and utility. Consensual testing, without psychological or material inducement, will not uncover that many seropositive individuals, particularly when the disease for which one is screening is not prevalent among the population that is being tested. The fewer the number of persons in the society exercising their option for testing, the less efficacious for public health such testing will be. And as a result, the cost-effectiveness of such a screening programme remains low. However, as a greater proportion of persons in the general population begin to request testing, the costs rise, but the cost-effectiveness of testing will get no better, and in fact might deteriorate. Some studies suggest that universal-consensual testing may be even less cost-effective and beneficial in terms of social welfare than a universal-compulsory programme, precisely because it allows for the self-selecting of test recipients. Various studies suggest that those most at risk of HIV will not submit to testing in the absence of accompanying incentives or education. But if such targeting is essential to cost-effective and beneficial screening, then the argument for universal testing, whether consensual or compulsory, is rendered impotent.

Option 3: Selective-compulsory testing: "Test the groups of people or individuals that we determine should be tested, whether or not they want to be tested."

The arguments for selective-compulsory testing overcome a number of the limitations of Option 1 by targeting high-risk populations. Not only will the knowledge gained from such testing have a high predictive value (it will be more accurate) than other options; it will be less costly and more cost-effective as well. But Option 3 introduces new problems that do not arise in either Option 1 or Option 2. For instance, public health officials must decide who should be tested – what groups of high-risk persons should be targeted for testing and screening. Who should make the decision about who to test, and how should the decision be made? Such determinations will need to be based in part on calculations of utility and public health, as well as on pragmatic concerns such as technical feasibility and political viability.

Other concerns accompany Option 3. Respect for some moral principles appears to be jeopardised by this option. We need to ask whether or not such testing results in a deterioration of respect for the moral values that we take as important to society, particularly respect for autonomy, freedom, certain moral and civil rights, and justice. Because certain classes of persons are subjected to mandatory testing, Option 3 fails to meet the criticism of those who feel that it runs roughshod over the principles of respect for autonomy and freedom. But if great social benefit might result from such a programme, and if it could be shown that compulsory-selective screening were the only or even the best way of accomplishing our goal, such dismissal of certain moral principles might be justified.

In addition, Option 3 raises questions concerning distributive justice – about the fairness of how the benefits and burdens of HIV testing are distributed among members of the society. All screening programmes, but in particular selective-compulsory programmes, may unfairly distribute the benefits and burdens of testing. Most persons who are tested in any screening scheme may benefit personally in a number of ways from that knowledge. But, as noted earlier, there are impressive costs associated with being tested as well. The debate about the moral propriety of saddling certain individuals with those costs has not been seriously evaluated and discussed. As a result, it seems premature to commit the society and particular classes of individuals in society to this screening option.

There is some debate about how to label most extant selective screening schemes. Most appear to be voluntary or consensual, since "individuals often can choose whether to enter certain situations where screening is mandatory" (Childress, 1987, p. 30). Under such an interpretation, testing of some classes of individuals (for example, immigrants from high-risk groups who apply for visas, or individuals seeking employment with a firm that makes public the fact that all employees will be tested as part of the application process or before being offered a job) might be ethically problematic. But assuring that such testing was consensual rather than compulsory would not be the major concern.

Still, there are two problems with defining such testing as consensual. First, it suggests that if such testing is truly consensual, then it is permissible. But in the ethical framework developed earlier, the consensual nature of a test is not the only, nor the most important, consideration in determining the moral justifiability of a screening option.

Second, by defining such situations as consensual, we can easily underestimate the degree of coercion, pressure, or compulsion attached to such testing. As Childress notes:

> Voluntariness may be compromised in various ways. We tend to think of coercion as the major compromise of voluntariness – for example, forcing someone to undergo a test for HIV antibody. However, conditional requirements – if you want X, then you have to do Y – may also be morally problematic ... requiring HIV antibody testing as a condition for obtaining some strongly desired benefit ... may constitute an undue incentive, even if it is not, strictly speaking, coercive because the person can choose to decline the benefit ... One important question

209

then is whether it is fair to impose the condition, even if the person is free to take it or leave it. This question expresses the important general point that selection of targets for mandatory screening – or even for voluntary screening – is in part a matter of justice in the distribution of benefits and burdens (Childress, 1991, p. 59).

In many cases, HIV testing is being established in settings where the need for employment, travel, certain types of medical care, hospitalisation, or to adopt renders the language of voluntary consent for HIV testing problematic.

It is easiest to justifying selective-compulsory screening on classes of persons or individuals who impose significant risk to others. Here, the clearest and least controversial loci for class-based testing are to those who donate sperm, blood, and tissue and organs.[4] Adoption agencies might also be justified in asking for HIV tests of prospective parents (and do in Hong Kong), though questions remain about the need for such information.[5]

Pre-marital testing at the time of marriage application and the testing of immigrants or those applying for residence or legitimate alien status raise difficult issues concerning efficacy, cost, cost-effectiveness, and questions about the interpretation and use of test results from low-risk and low-incidence populations (Childress, 1991, pp. 63–4, 68–9). The choice of the start of marriage as one loci for testing is somewhat odd, given the fact that, in nearly all societies where HIV is a concern, marriage does not mark the start of sexual activity. And in many societies marriage does not signify an ultimate commitment to monogamy. Where such mandatory screening legislation has been enacted, there has been a precipitous drop in the application of marriage licenses in that general locale (persons simply get married elsewhere). Even if screening were to uncover a fair number of seropositive individuals, society would still need to grapple with the problem of what to do with that information. Would the information be given to the person tested, or would the prospective spouse be given that information as well? Would we prohibit seropositive persons from getting married, simply require counselling, or isolate them from the society?

While testing immigrants might be easier to justify for Hong Kong than, for example, the United States (Hong Kong's actual per capita incidence of seropositivity is probably less than in the United States and the territory is probably not a net exporter of HIV), its feasibility can be questioned, given that 70 million persons enter the territory each year. Once seropositive individuals were identified, Hong Kong would have the added burden of deciding what to do with that knowledge and those persons. It might require refusing admission to certain persons, or limiting their movements and activities.

Premarital and immigrant testing raise two other concerns. First, testing these individuals and labelling them universally as "dangers to public health and safety" might suggest that the same is true of anyone and everyone who is seropositive. Yet public health studies suggest that this is far from true, since not everyone who is seropositive engages in risky behaviour or passively puts others at risk. Second, instituting mandatory screening policies for travellers – but more significantly for those desiring marriage or individuals applying for residence or legitimate alien status – could force seropositive individuals underground, further endangering the public health (Childress, 1991, p. 69).

The case for mandatory testing of prostitutes and intravenous (IV) drug users is non-controversial in the public mind. Both engage in morally unsavoury activities and break the law by plying their trade. IV drug users and possibly prostitutes are significant vectors for the transmission of HIV to the heterosexual population where the number of new seropositive cases is growing. But there are several problems with mandating HIV screening of these groups. First, most IV drug users and prostitutes are never arrested in Hong Kong. Since arrest is most often a prerequisite to testing under Option 3, the effectiveness of simply mandating such screening is not clear. Second, even if a given IV drug user or prostitute is found to be seropositive, it is unclear what should now be done with that information or that person. Prisons full of seropositive drug users and prostitutes (by no means the majority of those infected) might quell some public fears but would not significantly reduce the risk to public health. Recommending that these individuals practise safe sex might be good advice, but then public health officials would be moving from a mandatory screening to an educational programme, thus abandoning Option 3, at least with respect to these groups (and serious questions remain about the efficacy of present education programmes among these groups). Some prostitutes already practise safe sex (perhaps even some who are seropositive). But if a client requests unprotected sex with a seropositive prostitute, what is the prostitute's advantage to declining the financial exchange? Besides, Hong Kong operates under the maxim "let the buyer beware" in every other area of commercial exchange in the territory. Why should it eschew that general cultural tendency in this case and make prostitutes carry a disproportionate social and economic burden for the spread of this disease? We might certainly justify "confin[ing] a recalcitrant prostitute [or IV drug user] who puts others at serious risk" (Childress, 1991, p. 67). But here authorities would be saddled with the hope of serial arrest, and of proving that there was knowledge of and intent to put others at risk.

Mandatory selective screening policies on military recruits, prisoners, individuals in resident institutional settings, and in private business have been discussed at length (Childress, 1991, pp. 66–8; Committee on Education and Publicity on AIDS, 1992; Bayer, 1989, p. 637). From a public health perspective, targeted testing on these populations may be less efficacious than on other groups, and so its ethical justification in terms of many moral principles is questionable.

Of growing interest to Hong Kong is the debate over whether and how to test individuals in the health-care setting (both patients and HCWs). The standard arguments against mandatory selective patient testing, grounded in respect for autonomy, consent, and patients rights, are familiar (Childress, 1991, p. 60). Practical, medically-based arguments can be mustered as well. Some persons argue that, in light of recent evidence that suggests that there exist no efficacious therapies for HIV and AIDS, there is no patient-centred argument for HIV testing. And if the primary purpose for testing is to provide information to persons so that they can effect voluntary changes in behaviour, compulsory testing is not the best way to effect such outcomes. Behavioural changes are always low in persons tested against their will.

A second argument suggests that if HCWs just follow normal infection control procedures, they are fairly safe from infection (Stine, 1993, pp. 252–3). The reality, of course, is that knowing with a high degree of accuracy the seropositive status of your patient improves the vigilance of HCWs at infection control. Others argue that part of what it means to be a HCW is to take on certain risks in the line of duty. If a person is unwilling to take on such risks, they should perhaps consider another profession (Daniels, 1991).[6]

Finally it is argued that mandatory testing of patients would keep out of the health-care system those patients that are most in need of at least palliative care.

Others offer counter-arguments (including those grounded in public health and "the health-care worker's right to know") for a policy of mandatory testing on hospital and clinic patients in general, or at least some sub-classes of such patients (for example, patients who conform to specific clinical profiles, those with open wounds, or those undergoing surgery).

Different sorts of problems arise with respect to the testing of HCWs. Some persons argue that HCWs should not routinely be screened because "careful investigation of the potential of HIV transmission from infected workers and professionals to patients indicates no evidence of such transmission when standard infection control precautions are taken" (Bayer, 1989, p. 637; Pauker, 1990, p. 35; Hilts, 1991a; 1991b; Stine, 1993, pp. 168–9, 253–4). Further, because patients are not at great risk of contracting HIV from HCWs, society ought to hold HCWs to the same standards as other members of the society. If society affirms voluntary testing in general for the society, then it ought to extend the same requirements to HCWs.

Others counter that if society believes that respect for autonomy is important, then even patients who request knowledge of HCWs' HIV status based on irrational risk-benefit calculations have some right to such information (Daniels, 1992). In any event, patients have a right to know what added risks, beyond the usual and reasonable, they take by being treated by a (potentially seropositive) physician. The fiduciary relationship that exists between doctor and patient, but increasingly between patient and other HCWs (particularly nurses, who view themselves as "patient advocates"), requires that such information be disclosed (Bird, 1991).

Whatever policy is ultimately adopted, the benefits of knowledge gained from the mandatory testing of patients and/or HCWs needs to be balanced against the costs (ethical, financial, social, political) incurred in adopting such a policy.

Option 4: Selective-consensual testing: "Test everyone that we determine should be tested who will let us test them."

Most recent calls for wider testing advance this option (Childress, 1991; Rhame, 1989; Janssen, 1992). Option 4 appears to meet many of the demands of the most vigorous civil libertarians because, through its voluntary approach, it avoids infringing on individual rights and autonomy. From a public health perspective, Option 4 may also meet many basic requirements of a good testing programme. As long as strict confidentiality is assured, Option 4, in conjunction with targeted education programmes, will encourage more at-risk persons to be tested than any other option. Recent studies suggest that a voluntary testing option is the choice most likely to effect behavioural changes in at-risk individuals (where there is a desire for knowledge on the part of the test target for personal knowledge of seropositivity) (Rhame, 1989). Studies also suggest that voluntary targeted testing also increases the likelihood of notification of at-risk sex partners (Landis, 1992). Option 4 is less costly and more cost-effective than either Options 2 or 3. And unlike the universal testing Options 1 and 2, Option 4 allows knowledge generated from studies of demographics and infection patterns to inform decisions about how to allocate public health resources.

But problems exist with Option 4. First, Option 4 is less helpful from a statistical, and therefore a surveillance perspective, than the universal Options 1 and 2. While Option 4 might strengthen testing of at-risk populations, it fails to provide broader epidemiological data about the spread of the disease across the society; and does not facilitate the identification of emerging high-risk groups.

A second problem with Option 4 involves what Robert Wennberg has termed the phenomenon of "negative fallout". Members of an identified high-risk class who fail to be tested may feel undue pressure to "test out", thus rendering the consensual nature of their test suspect (Wennberg, 1989, pp. 187–8).

A third argument against even encouraging voluntary testing focuses on the use made of and the ability to guard the confidentiality of test results. Since the reasons for HIV testing are often suspect in the minds of those targeted for testing, and since it is virtually impossible to guarantee the confidentiality of an HIV test in a hospital setting (it might be better protected in medical office or public health clinic settings, particularly where such testing is done anonymously), critics question whether such tests should be encouraged, given the high cost to individuals of public knowledge of such test results and the poor treatment options available presently.

Finally, debate rages about who should be targeted for voluntary testing. Certain high-risk groups come to mind: homosexual and bisexual men; intravenous drug users; prostitutes; individuals receiving certain blood or blood-product transfusions. But questions remain about whether and how to target members of these groups; and whether other populations (for example, hospital patients and certain HCWs) ought to be targeted.[7]

2. Present Screening Policies in Hong Kong and Recommendations

By law, HIV/AIDS is not a notifiable disease in Hong Kong. Only voluntary screening and reporting programmes are in place in the territory and there exist no mandatory screening programmes targeted at specific groups.[8] However, a number of recommendations regarding HIV screening policies can be advanced.

1. Increase knowledge of HIV in Asia. While there is a growing awareness among health officials and the public at large of the general potential risk to communities from HIV, Hong Kong and other regions of Asia need to expand their knowledge of the epidemic as it applies to their particular geographic region. For example, who are the high-risk groups in Hong Kong? What is the cost of screening programmes of various types? Of running ELISA and corroborating Western blot tests? Of allowing the epidemic to expand unchecked? Of instituting educational programmes? How will the spread of HIV in Thailand, the PRC, and the Philippines effect Hong Kong? To its credit, Hong Kong has planned, is now seeking funding for, and is undertaking several surveys that will provide information on the sexual practices of its population (as background to establishing a more comprehensive, targeted, and vigorous education programme) and better data for HIV/AIDS surveillance (Wiseman,

1994c; Lee, 1994a). The results of these surveys will benefit not only the territory, but the region as a whole.

2. Pursue policies that seek to improve overall public health; that prevent the epidemic from going "underground"; that are cost-effective; and that respect autonomy, freedom, rights to self-determination, and justice and fairness to the greatest degree possible. To this end, public health departments ought to strengthen their public education programmes, targeting both established and newly at-risk groups. Hong Kong appears well on its way to effecting such a coordinated policy (Wiseman, 1994c).

3. Support consensual selective testing, especially of identified high-risk populations, optimally instituted through volunteer community groups and non-government organisations (NGOs) (but with government support, oversight, and coordination) in non-hospital and non-government clinic settings; encourage anonymous testing as a way of assuring confidentiality of test results. Such testing might be done either at direct public expense or made a mandatory service in all basic health insurance packages. Short of testing without patients' permission, the best option would be to implement broad testing and screening programmes through physicians who would encourage HIV testing of patients who meet specific profiles. The advantage of testing in physicians' offices rather than through NGO or state-sponsored clinics is that the chances of recruiting test subjects who might not self-select, of meaningful interpretation of test results, and of various types of counselling may be increased.

To opt for voluntary testing is not to let seropositive individuals "off the hook" in a way that they are then able to avoid responsibility for initiating testing, lifestyle changes following testing, or management of their disease. Such a programme implicitly affirms a presumptive moral obligation to certain action on the part of seropositive individuals or those that engage in high-risk behaviour or activities. At the same time it suggests that the experience of screening in other settings and a realistic assessment of the fears driving persons underground need to be soberly incorporated into screening programmes.

4. In particular, avoid mandatory testing of the following groups: general hospital patients, general surgery patients, health-care workers, dentists, pregnant women, premarital screening, immigrants, and those engaging in international travel. At this time, there is no evidence that the mandatory testing of these classes of individuals is either in the public interest or cost-beneficial to Hong Kong.

In hospitals, staff ought to encourage patients who conform to specific patient profiles or present corroborating physical manifestations to be tested. Still, I would not encourage routine screening of all hospital patients since I do not believe that the public health arguments for such a programme are compelling (Danila, 1991; cf. Janssen, 1992).

In concurrence with Hong Kong public health practice, I would not recommend mandatory, let alone optional/voluntary, testing of any HCWs. There are no good reasons to engage in compulsory or even universal voluntary testing of HCWs at this time. The fact that few if any cases of documented or confirmed HCW-patient nosocomial HIV infection exist, the implications of false-positive tests, the establishment of a reverse expectation that all patients should also be tested, the standard cost-benefit arguments of implementing such a programme, and arguments (justified in terms both of duty and utility) from privacy and confidentiality, all mitigate against establishing such a policy (Gostin, 1990; Daniels, 1992; Furrow, 1989; Lo, 1992; McNeill, 1990; Fleck, 1991; but cf. Bird, 1991). Further, arguments for HCW testing argued in terms of justice or reciprocity are not compelling. Physicians always put themselves at greater risk for infection from a patient than *vice versa.*

Prohibit businesses and government agencies from routine testing for HIV of prospective or current employees as a condition of new or continuing employment when no compelling public health arguments for such testing can be given. This recommendation extends to individuals involved in all aspects of health-care delivery, food preparation, and education (residential special educational schools might be an exception). Studies reveal that using HIV tests as "gatekeepers" to job admission does little to protect a company from incurring the costs associated with HIV infection and AIDS. In fact, such screening diverts funds from education and does nothing to address the larger societal problem of HIV infection (Weldon, 1994). Again, it should be emphasised that Hong Kong has in principle affirmed all of these recommendations and appears to have no plans to alter its present policies on these issues.

Prohibit health insurance companies from requiring HIV tests or from making decisions about the acceptability of health coverage on the basis of test results. This recommendation is justified in light of an appreciation of the overriding importance of the need for and provision of health care in industrialised and post-industrialised societies, and the justice of burden-sharing for the HIV epidemic. In equitable health-care programmes, pre-existing medical conditions should rarely be a reason not to accept anyone into any health-care plan. Since all health insurance companies in a given locale would be prohibited from such discrimination, equity among insurance companies is maintained with respect to the marginal cost of adsorbing the treatment of HIV and AIDS patients. The argument of health insurance companies that HIV patient-care is expensive is not without merit, but that should be an issue dealt with in terms of overall premium rates and decisions about reasonable and expected treatment for such patients, not by refusing to provide any health care or medical treatment to such patients. Prohibiting HIV testing by health insurers is not incompatible with a decision, based on other moral principles, not to provide comprehensive or unlimited treatment to those who suffer from HIV or AIDS.

Finally, prohibit life insurance companies from requiring HIV tests as a condition of insurability, but allow for retrospective access to all health-care records after death to ensure that knowledge of actual or a high probability of seropositivity did not serve as the motive for purchasing insurance.

5. Require that all laboratories that run HIV tests be required to anonymously and statistically report the results of those tests to the Department of Health as one source of information in a coordinated programme of surveillance. The sex and age of the person being tested should be reported as well as a way of strengthening the usefulness of such data in the development of public health policies.

6. There may be exceptions to the generally voluntary-consensual policy elaborated above. Certainly these would include the compulsory and universal testing of blood, solid organ, and tissue donors, and of individuals found guilty of forcible or statutory rape (including prisoners). Compulsory testing of some patients in clinical settings, hospitals, or other institutional-care settings might be justified in such cases where, for example, a HCW receives a needle stick injury or is exposed to a patient's blood or body fluids in some other fashion. Still, justifying such exceptions needs to be balanced against calculations of actual risk probabilities, commitments to public health, and the obligations and rights established by other moral values and principles.

IV. Disclosure and Notification Options

1. Notification and Disclosure Options

As with screening, several options exist with respect to policies governing the notification and disclosure of HIV status gained from testing or screening. These options vary in the degree to which they accord with beneficence and public welfare, on the one hand, and respect for patient autonomy, privacy, confidentiality, and the maintenance of special and fiduciary relationships, on the other. For the purpose of analysis, we can distinguish four notification and disclosure options, grouped in pairs as a way to simplify discussion.

Table 2

| | degree of voluntariness | |
	compulsory	consensual
universal	1	2
selective	3	4

extent of disclosure

Option 1: Universal-compulsory notification: "Make HIV status public knowledge even in the absence of patient consent," and

Option 3: Selective-compulsory notification: "Make HIV status known to select persons, even in the absence of patient consent."

Most arguments in favour of Option 1 or Option 3 justify their position in terms of the need for the general public (or, in the case of Option 3, certain individuals in the society or in special relationships with the person being tested) to know a person's HIV status as a means of guaranteeing personal or public safety. Persons supporting Options 1 or 3 often support universal or selective compulsory testing (Bennett, 1987). Others support Options 1 or 3 in conjunction with universal or selective consensual testing (King, 1991). Arguments for compulsory notification are most often framed in the language of beneficence, public health, and social utility; but also in the language of the right of the public or identified persons to know certain facts about specific individuals and/or associated risks from specific behaviour in which they are engaged. Such notification and disclosure might benefit not only the patient but other individuals who are at risk of contracting HIV and/or are ignorant of their own risk from the person tested (Landis, 1992, p. 101).

But pursuing either Option 1 or Option 3 raises a number of questions and concerns. The first problem is one of consistency with testing policy. It is not clear whether a selective-consensual testing policy could be maintained in the face of accepting either Option 1 or 3. Practically speaking, persons who suspect they are seropositive or in danger of being infected by HIV would be less likely to be tested voluntarily if they believed that desired confidentiality would not be respected (even if only selectively, as is the case with Option 3). Several studies suggest that the number of persons tested for HIV declines precipitously as the actual or the perceived level of confidentiality over test results declines.

A second argument particularly against Option 1 (but Option 3 as well) is

218

grounded in the moral principles of beneficence, public health, and utility. It is not clear that disclosing a person's HIV status significantly advances the public interest in terms of encouraging testing, improving the overall public health, or benefiting individual patients (Landis, 1992). Significant evidence suggests that even selective mandatory notification or disclosure policies (Option 3) reduce the incidence of the most effective and beneficial type of testing (voluntary testing). A selective mandatory testing policy might also reduce the general health of individuals who do not want to be tested and therefore forgo entry into specific institutions or take advantage of therapies that might benefit them. Studies suggest that those activities which are most effective in reducing the spread of HIV (education and personal counselling) are more effectively accomplished by pursuing various types of voluntary notification policies (Werdel, 1990; Howe, 1988).

A third argument against mandatory notification (whether universal or selective) concerns how breaches of confidentiality might undermine respect for autonomy, confidentiality, privacy, and the particular character of fiduciary relationships, particularly between physician and patient. As I have suggested, the only way to justify an infringement of individual rights to privacy and confidentiality would be to show that it is an essential guarantee to the wider public interest. While some marginal gains might be made over the short run in public health through a mandatory notification policy, evidence from similar programmes involving other sexually transmitted diseases suggests that long-term public health gains are rarely achieved by such mandatory notification programmes. At the same time, the cost in lost trust and respect for important liberal values from such policies is great.

Finally, mandatory notification policies can be criticised from the perspective of the principles of distributive justice and fairness. Pursuing a policy embracing either Option 1 or 3 may unfairly abridge the civil rights (including freedom and equal protection under the law) of some or all of a nation's citizens. At the same time, it reinforces the stigmatisation, ostracism, isolation, discrimination, ridicule, and even safety of many citizens (Werdel, 1990). Part of the problem with a mandatory testing and notification policy is that it gains its strength and power in part from the assumption that seropositive individuals are, as a class, not only the victims but more importantly the perpetrators and perpetuators of HIV. As a result, those who have been infected, at times through casual indiscretions, dangerous behaviour, or (increasingly) through the activities of others, but who nonetheless have exhibited the courage to be tested, are now forced to bear a disproportionate social burden for their seropositivity.

If these arguments justify the abandonment of Option 1, there remains a sizeable number of persons who support Option 3 – selective but mandatory notification of seropositive status to certain classes of persons. Here, I focus my analysis on the health-care setting, since this is the arena in which most debates over this option are developing in Hong Kong. The groups most often targeted to have their HIV status disclosed include (1) seropositive patients; (2) seropositive physicians or other HCWs who directly care for and treat patients; and (3) seropositive individuals who have close relationships with and/or are sexually intimate with others. In such situations, five questions need to be asked as a first step toward assessing the warrant and justification of such selective but mandatory disclosure or notification of HIV status.

First, does knowledge of a person's HIV status by a HCW or a patient increase the safety of that seronegative individual and/or the general public health? Most extant studies suggest that patient or HCW knowledge of each other's HIV status does not increase public health significantly. There are two reasons for this. HCWs, who increasingly employ strict infection control and treat all patients as potentially seropositive, already employ significant precautions that protect against the transmission of HIV. At the same time, HCWs do not put patients at risk of HIV in any statistically significant way because the prevalence of HIV among HCW is low to begin with, and infection-control policies also work effectively to prevent transmission of HIV from HCW to patient. There are, for example, no known cases of HIV transmission from HCW to patient in Hong Kong, and only two or three known *possible* incidents involving about eight persons in the United States (Stine, 1993, pp. 168–71; Ciesielski, 1992). Certainly actual risk does exist for HIV transmission in the health-care setting. And it may also be true that both patients and HCWs have a right, grounded in the moral principle of respect for persons, to know information that places them at even marginally increased risk in their encounters with each other. But given the statistics concerning HIV transmission in the health-care setting, it is difficult to advocate a compulsory-selective notification policy based on any sound public heath arguments (Pauker, 1990).

Second, we need to explore whether a policy of compulsory-selective notification is compatible with the other values to which we are committed, such as providing quality health care to patients, not making them the objects of discrimination, and respecting their autonomy and wellbeing. Ambiguity in response to these questions raises troubling issues for policy-makers.

Third, for what reasons should information concerning HIV status be provided to individuals? One way to answer this question would be to establish a functional and statutory standard that would determine where and how the disclosure of such information would be required to provide safe and efficacious health-care services, and then release information regarding seropositivity only for those reasons. Such policies are now appearing in some regions of the United States where the thorny issue of notification has been confronted (Health and Safety Code, 1985).

Fourth, which individuals ought to have access to knowledge of seropositivity? Even if we concede, for example, that some HCWs ought to have knowledge about a patient's HIV status (for reasons other than or in addition to diagnosing or effectively treating a patient), there is much debate about which HCWs should have access to that knowledge, and about how to limit access to specific individuals, institutions, agencies, or corporations.

Fifth, are there mechanisms and policies that might be instituted that would protect the broader confidentiality of a person's HIV status once it has been disclosed to select individuals? If this is possible, then that may strengthen the claims of some advocates of Option 3. But if this is not the case – if we know that confidentiality cannot be adequately controlled once such information is selectively revealed – then there may exist a strong argument against Option 3, perhaps even against some consensual testing and screening.

The problem of mandatory selective notification of sex partners or individuals with whom seropositive drug addicts share needles is more difficult to assess. Providing such knowledge clearly benefits at-risk individuals, many of whom have no idea of their risk (Landis, 1992). Further, affirming a policy of notification in such situations witnesses to important moral values such as respect for persons, non-maleficence, beneficence, and compassion.

Any mandatory notification policy has problems. It can be complicated by the fact that often the proper individuals to be notified cannot be adequately identified without the implicit consent of the person tested. Additionally, there may be no way to adequately guarantee the confidentiality of the person tested. Most important, the knowledge that such mandatory selective notification will take place (even if narrowly targeted and with confidentiality protections in place) will reduce the number of individuals who will submit to voluntary testing in the first place.

Option 2: Universal-consensual notification: "Make HIV status public knowledge with patient's permission;" and

Option 4: Selective-consensual notification: "Make HIV status known only in situations and to persons to which the patient consents."

Under Options 2 and 4, desired privacy and confidentiality would be protected at the same time that public health officials or HCWs would be asking patients to consider the wellbeing of others by communicating their seropositive status. Nonetheless, there is little reason, based on recent studies, to hope that patients will communicate their HIV status to intimates who might benefit from that information. One recent study has shown that when individuals were given the choice of personally notifying sexual partners of their HIV status, only 7 per cent did. However, provider referral with assistance in reporting (where public HCWs take on the burden of contact tracing and reporting) increased this rate more than seven-fold, but still only to 50 per cent (Landis, 1992).

These statistics suggest two conclusions. First, adopting Option 2 appears to be unjustified from a public health perspective. A simple public announcement of a person's HIV status will most likely fail to warn those individuals most at risk from an individual's infection. Indeed, those least at risk from contracting HIV from a person are the general public – the group targeted for notification in Option 2. Those most at risk from HIV infection are family and intimates – those who would be the targets of notification under Option 4. Hong Kong's dilemma about what to do in terms of notification is that, as liberal or emerging liberal societies, we are structured to limit and constrain public life, not private life. Yet it is most often in the context and settings of private life that HIV is transmitted (Harris, 1993, p. 11).

Second, these statistics suggest that, while Option 4 may be the most justifiable option for notification explored so far, its public health efficacy will require that extensive support, counselling and education be provided by the public health and medical establishment (Giesecke, 1991).

In the clinical setting, Option 4 suggests that physicians and public health workers encourage the disclosure of information to relevant individuals. But does such a policy imply that seropositive HCWs ought to notify their patients of their status? Various recommendations have been made in different settings and at different times that HCWs who are aware of their seropositivity ought to notify their fellow HCWs, representatives of the relevant professional monitoring boards, their employers, all of their patients, or only those patients with whom they engage in medical procedures.[9]

2. Present Notification/Disclosure Policies in Hong Kong and Recommendations

There is no policy of mandatory notification of HIV or AIDS in Hong Kong. The only exceptions to this policy are (1) a voluntary reporting system of statistical data that has been established by the Department of Health; and (2) a policy that requires HIV-infected HCWs to report their status to their medical society (Lee, 1994c). The efficacy of this programme has not yet been established, but it does allow monitoring and surveillance of infection among HCWs, provides HCWs with expert advice on how best to continue successfully and safely practising their profession in the face of the disease, and allows for independent review of HCW practices as a means to determining if seropositive professionals ought to continue in their professions (Lee, 1994c). It remains unclear whether such a policy is essential to assuring the public health, though it is clear that part of the justification for implementing this policy was to quell fears among the public. As Hong Kong considers further refinements of its policy, I would make the following recommendations.

1. Encourage the strengthening of confidentiality of test subjects and the results of their tests. It is not enough simply to state that there is an expectation for and obligation to request confidentiality. Policies, legislation and support for the implementation and enforcement of such policies needs to be established. Establish statutes that specify the particulars of consent to and the disclosure of results from HIV tests. Clarify penalties for breaches of confidentiality concerning HIV status. Particular attention needs to be given to developing policies that mandate how information regarding HIV status is handled after it is received, how it is stored and retrieved, how to limit access to that information, and setting standards for determining who has legitimate access to that information.

2. With regard to patients and the general public, pursue a policy of voluntary-selective confidential notification. I would require pathology and clinical medical laboratories to report the prevalence of HIV in tested samples as a means of strengthening surveillance of the population. Confidentiality can be assured if testing is done anonymously under a single-blind system.

I would support a policy that encourages patients who are tested to give permission to notify those HCWs who care for them and significant others with whom they have intimate contact concerning their HIV status. Provide volunteers to take on the burden of notification and follow-up counselling.

For reasons discussed earlier, I would not encourage any HCWs (including physicians, nurses or dentists) to notify patients or colleagues of their seropositivity. In a slight policy dissent from the direction that Hong Kong is taking, I might encourage (but not mandate) that HCWs notify local health-care authorities of their status. Given the large number of known and estimated seropositive HCWs and the low number of cases of HIV transmission to patients (one or two possible cases globally in a decade), such notification seems unnecessary (cf. Special Working Group, 1994).

Even where non-consensual testing is justified (e.g., cases concerning recalcitrant prostitutes, prisoners charged with rape, institutional patients or workers who have sexually assaulted another person, and in situations where health-care workers have been endangered with possible contamination in the exercise of their duties), strict regulations regarding the protection of confidentiality and of the notification of test results should be observed.

V. Conclusion

This paper has focused on HIV testing and notification. But it would be a mistake, in the public health and policy setting, to emphasise such programmes at the expense of education. It will be in the context of public education that the battle against HIV will be won or lost in Asia in the coming two decades. Education is expensive; but screening is more expensive, both per person contacted and per reduction in HIV case. When education programmes are targeted at high-risk populations, they presently remain the most effective way of reducing the rate of infection.

A good education programme will have several components. It will be multilingual and cognisant of the cultural differences of its target audience. It will need to be communicated through different media. And it will need to be packaged and targeted at individuals with wide variations in literacy competence. It will need to give attention to explaining several aspects of the disease: history and cause, epidemiology, clinical manifestations (or lack of manifestations), treatment (or lack of treatment options), and prevention and control. Finally, as Hong Kong has shown, the battle against HIV will need to involve government, NGOs and private citizens.

Hong Kong needs to vigorously pursue its commitment to establishing a humane, clear, comprehensive, and legally binding HIV policy for four reasons. First, such an approach is expedient. The sooner debate on these issues is initiated and a policy implemented, the less opportunity for dissension, confusion and disruption when a crisis strikes. A serious HIV epidemic may be on Hong Kong's doorstep, but it is not yet in the house. Viewing the establishment of health-care policy as both preparation for and prevention of such a crisis will do much to reduce the pain of the crisis once it hits.

Second, in light of the political unknowns of the coming decade, establishing a clear policy on HIV testing and notification that affirms the society's commitment both to public health and civil rights may provide Hong Kong with a powerful tool to combat the cultural and political influence of the incoming government of the PRC. The Letters Patent will cease to have any binding force on Hong Kong after 30 June 1997. The Sino-British Joint Declaration (1984) and the Basic Law (1990) may (but need not) be interpreted to bind the PRC to the stipulations of the International Covenant on Civil and Political Rights (ICCPR) for the post-1997 Hong Kong Special Administrative Region (SAR). Still, confusion about general issues of human rights and nondiscrimination remain, reflected in the PRC's opposition to the Hong Kong Bill of Rights, the failure of the PRC to endorse the ICCPR, the unwillingness of various parties in Hong Kong to support the establishment of a human rights commission, and the possibility that the PRC might reject the Bill of Rights in 1997 if it is construed as inconsistent with the Basic Law. Most worrisome is that, while there is substantive overlap between the Bill of Rights and Chapter 3 of the Basic Law, this says little about the inevitability of PRC respect for the Basic Law after 1997.

By affirming the testing and notification policy that I have advocated, the people of Hong Kong may be able to establish a substantive beachhead against some policies of the PRC in the areas of civil rights and health care to which the Hong Kong people most object. And since relatively "non-political" health-care policy is more likely to remain in place after 1997 than more "political" policies regarding the Legislative Council and local council representation and democratic elections, improvements in HIV/AIDS policy have a good chance of surviving the 1997 transition.

Third, a rational and efficacious HIV testing and notification policy might provide tested resources that could be commended to public health leaders in the PRC, particularly its southern and coastal provinces. Currently, the PRC does not possess a coherent HIV public health policy. There are several reasons for this. The crisis is nascent and localised in the southern and southeastern provinces. Political infighting and a lack of resources, particularly in light of the public health and public works demands of far-reaching infrastructure development and disaster relief (following the southern flooding of 1994), mean that prevention against a "hidden" disease like HIV is not being adequately addressed in the face of the visible problems of cholera, typhus, and local, short-term infrastructure redevelopment. Further, to admit a crisis might force the PRC to admit a number of other uncomfortable facts (AIDS is not just a foreigner's disease; the borders of the PRC are more permeable than the government wishes to admit; HIV infection might be interpreted as a comment on the defective character of the Chinese people).

By adopting the Hong Kong policy, the PRC might accomplish several proximate goals simultaneously. The policy I have advocated does not assume universal screening – thus it is a relatively less costly option than some others. It affirms communal values along with more Western, liberal values, thus allowing the Chinese to strategically justify their policy in terms of some traditional values. In any event, if Gerald Segal is correct in his broad assessment of politics in China, the decision to establish an HIV testing policy for China will not lie with the central government in Beijing or the ruling *nomenklatura*. It will fall instead to provincial leaders or even mayors to implement policies that are most efficacious for their populations (Segal, 1994, pp. 53–4, 58–9). One could thus hope for different – perhaps more effective – policies in the southern and northern coastal regions where the greater and more immediate threat of HIV exists. Given present trends in other areas (environmental law and policy, sewage treatment, infrastructure programmes; general models of modernisation) there are strong reasons to assume that those population centres outside the post-1997 Hong Kong SAR would at least examine, if not appropriate outright, a functioning and proven HIV public health programme if such exists in Hong Kong.

Fourth, the most far-reaching implications of the recommended HIV policy for Hong Kong will be at the level of ethos and values. Affirming the recommendations outlined in this paper would communicate in profound ways the moral values the people of Hong Kong affirm. Dostoevski observed that one could tell much about the level of civility in a culture by the condition of its prisons. That observation might be recast in the 1990s to suggest that one can tell much about the fundamental values and commitments of a society by the shape of its HIV and AIDS policy. This is not an attempt to sentimentalise the suffering of those with HIV and AIDS as a means of establishing a liberal social policy toward its victims. Rather, I am suggesting simply that confronting HIV testing and notification policy provides an opportunity for Hong Kong people to affirm its most cherished values and to witness to what this community takes to be decisive to its future flourishing.

(My sincere thanks go to Mr S.S. Lee, Special Consultant to Special Preventative Programme of the Hong Kong Department of Health, and Legislative Council representative Mr C.H. Leong for their observations, technical information and counsel. Without their encouragement and support this project would never have been completed.)

Notes

1. In Hong Kong HIV cases are increasing fastest in the heterosexual population (though the incidence of the disease is still greatest in the homosexual population). However, this statistic fails to provide information about rates of increase and per capita HIV rates in specific sub-groups. These statistics also fail to indicate the degree to which more widespread testing has influenced these statistics.

2. This has not been true of Africa or Asia, but for various reasons the demographics of HIV/AIDS in these regions has not been the focus of Western media coverage or a significant concern by Asian society.

3. The International Covenant on Civil and Political Rights (ICCPR) has functioned in Hong Kong since 1976 through common law, some limited legislation, and administrative measures. It was codified in 1991 in the Hong Kong Bill of Rights Ordinance and recognised by the British Crown through an amendment to the British Letters Patent (the effective Constitution of Hong Kong). Still, debate with the PRC over this development in light of divergent interpretations of the Basic Law, and the refusal of the Hong Kong Government to openly support the establishment of a human rights commission in the territory, raise serious questions about the ability of this legislation to stand after 1997 (Hong Kong Bill of Right Ordinance No. 59, 1991; Wacks, 1990; Chan, 1992; Witt, 1993, p. 30; Chan and Ghai, 1993; Beck, 1994; Chan and Beck, 1994a; Choy, 1994; Chan and Beck, 1994b).

4. There are two reasons why testing of these classes of persons is uncontroversial. First, the public health benefits gained by guaranteeing a low rate of transmission, and the right of recipients to know, and demand, a low probability of infection, takes priority over a person's right to donate. Second, rejecting a person's right to donate does not abrogate any autonomy-based negative rights or any important civil rights.

5. Here, the best argument for testing is not that children might be susceptible to HIV infection from their new parents. Rather, it is that society may wish to avoid placing children in homes where they might have to deal with the trauma of losing a parent for a second time.

6. This is a fairly popular but weak argument. HCWs have many different types of obligations to many people (including families, other patients, employers, the public at large, and themselves), not just to their patients. In light of this fact, it may not be reasonable to ask them to take such risks. HCWs are not saints and heroes, and it may be unfair to demand of them such supererogatory actions. It may also be unwise. As the risk of HIV infection among HCWs increases and they leave their professions in greater numbers (this will be particularly the case with nurses and ancillary professionals who do not have access to compensation levels that will encourage them to stay) the health-care system will come under an increasing strain that need not be exacerbated by additional arguments for HCWs to abandon their profession.

7. Guidelines proposed by the United States' Centers for Disease Control in July 1991 suggested such "voluntary" testing for professionals who might be involved with "exposure prone" procedures and as a result might infect their patients. But no cases exist where any patients have been infected in such procedures where infection control guidelines were even minimally followed, and there is serious debate over which classes of HCWs who should be tested.

8. There are two possible exceptions to this statement. One or two companies may still screen prospective or current employees for HIV, but that practice appears to have all but disappeared (McSherry, 1993). Some anonymous and statistical reporting of HIV testing undertaken at government-sponsored clinics is in place in the territory, but

the significance of this practice is generally acknowledged to provide less than fully accurate information on the prevalence of the disease in the population.

9. In the United States, legislation and recommendations, though very controversial and not at all coordinated or consistent with each other, are appearing that mandate the disclosure of HCWs' seropositive status to patients, co-workers, employers in certain cases, and professional review boards. Still, there are no requirements that healthy HCWs be tested.

Bibliography

Bayer, Ronald, Carol Levine and Susan M. Wolf, 1989, "HIV Antibody Screening: An Ethical Framework for Evaluating Proposed Programs", pp. 634–40 in Tom Beauchamp and LeRoy Walters (eds.), *Contemporary Issues in Bioethics*, 3rd edition, Belmont, CA, Wadsworth Publishing Company

Beck, Simon, 1994, "Move to Widen Human Rights", *South China Morning Post* 13 February, p. 11

Bennett, William J., 1987, "We Need Routine Testing for AIDS", *Wall Street Journal*, 26 May, p. 32

Bird, A.G., S.M. Gore, A.J. Leigh-Brown, *et al.*, 1991, "Escape from Collective Denial: HIV Transmission During Surgery", *British Medical Journal* 303 (6798), 10 August, pp. 351–2

Chan, Johannes M.M., 1992, "The Legal System", pp. 15–38 in Joseph Y.S. Cheng and Paul C.K. Kwong (eds.), *The Other Hong Kong Report 1992*, Hong Kong, Chinese University Press

— and Yash Ghai (eds.), 1993, *The Hong Kong Bill of Rights: A Comparative Approach*, Hong Kong, Butterworths Asia

Chan, Quinton, and Simon Beck, 1994a, "Move to Widen Human Rights", *South China Morning Post*, 13 February, 11

— and Simon Beck, 1994b, "Row Looms Over Rights Watchdog", *South China Morning Post*, 8 May, p. 1, 6

Childress, James F., 1987, "An Ethical Framework for Assessing Policies to Screen for Antibodies to HIV", *AIDS & Public Policy Journal*, Winter (2/1), pp. 28–31

— 1991, "Mandatory HIV Screening and Testing", pp. 50–76 in Frederic G. Reamer (ed.), *AIDS and Ethics*, New York, Columbia University Press

Choy, Linda, 1994, "Human Rights Body Rejected", *South China Morning Post*, 7 May, p. 4

Ciesielski, Carol, *et al.*, 1992, "Transmission of Human Immunodeficiency Virus in a

Dental Practice", *Annals of Internal Medicine* 116 (10), May 15, pp. 798–805

Committee on Education and Publicity on AIDS, 1992, *AIDS and the Workplace – Sharing the Challenge: A Seminar Proceedings*, Hong Kong, Committee on Education and Publicity on AIDS

Daniels, Norman, 1991, "Duty to Treat or Right to Refuse?", *Hastings Center Report* 21 (2), March-April, pp. 36–46

— 1992, "HIV-Infected Professionals, Patient Rights, and the 'Switching Dilemma'", *Journal of the American Medical Association* 267 (10), March 11, pp. 1368–71

Danila, Richard N., *et al.*, 1991, "A Look-back Investigation of Patients of an HIV-infected Physician: Public Health Implications", *New England Journal of Medicine* 325 (20), Nov 14, pp. 1406–11

Department of Health, Hong Kong, 1992, *Information on AIDS for Doctors and Dentists*, 2nd edition

— 1993, *Information on AIDS for Nurses*, 2nd edition, Hong Kong: Department of Health

Elder, Harvey A., 1991, "Risk Transmission from Infected Clinician to Susceptible Patients", *Update*, Loma Linda University 7 (1), May, pp. 3–4

Fineberg, Harvey V., 1990, "Screening for HIV Infection and Public Health Policy", *Law, Medicine, and Health Care* 18 (1–2), Spring-Summer, pp. 29–32

Fleck, Leonard, 1991, "'Please Don't Tell': Commentary", *Hastings Center Report* 21 (6), Nov-Dec, pp. 39–40

Furrow, Barry R., 1989, "AIDS and the Health Care Provider: The Argument for Voluntary HIV Testing", *Villanova Law Review* 34 (5), September, pp. 823–70

Giesecke, Johann, Kristina Ramstedt, Fredrik Granath, *et al.*, 1991, "Efficacy of Partner Notification for HIV Infection", *Lancet* 338 (8775), pp. 1096-1100

Gostin, Larry, 1990, "The HIV-infected Health Care Professional: Public Policy, Discrimination, and Patient Safety", *Law, Medicine, and Health Care* 18 (4), Winter, pp. 303–10

Harris, John, and Soren Holm, 1993, "If Only AIDS Were Different", *Hastings Center Report* 23 (6), November-December, pp. 6–12

Health and Safety Code, State of California, 1985, *Mandated Blood Testing and Confidentiality to Protect Public Health*, Section 199.19–199.27

Hilts, Philip J., 1991a, "Experts Oppose AIDS Test for Doctors", *New York Times*, 20 September, p. A11

— 1991b, "Congress Urges AIDS Tests for Doctors", *New York Times,* National Edition, 4 October, p. A9

Hoffman, Wendell W., and Stanley J. Grenz, 1990, *AIDS: Ministry in the Midst of An Epidemic*, Grand Rapids, MI, Baker Book House Company

Hong Kong Bill of Rights Ordinance No. 59 of 1991, *The Laws of Hong Kong*

Howe, Kenneth, 1988, "Why Mandatory Screening for AIDS is a Very Bad Idea", pp. 140–9 in Christine Pierce and Donald VanDeVeer (eds.), *AIDS: Ethics and Public Policy*, Belmont, California, Wadsworth Publishing Company

Janssen, Robert, Michael St. Louis and Glen Satten, 1992, "HIV Infection Among Patients in US Acute Care Hospitals: Strategies for the Counselling and Testing of

Hospital Patients", *New England Journal of Medicine* 327 (7), 13 August, pp. 445–52

King, Wayne, 1991, "New Jersey Moves to Report Names of People Found to Have AIDS Virus", *New York Times*, 4 December, p. A14

Landis, Suzanne E., *et al.*, 1992, "Results of a Randomized Trial of Partner Notification in Cases of HIV Infection in North Carolina", *New England Journal of Medicine* 326 (2), 9 January, pp. 101–6

Langone, John, 1991, *AIDS: The Facts*, Boston, Little, Brown, and Company

Lee, Ella, 1994a, "AIDS Study Planned", *Eastern Express*, 10 May, p. 8

Lee, S.S., 1994b, Personal Correspondence, 22 March

Lee, Stella, 1994c, "Health Workers Face HIV Rules", *South China Morning Post*, 20 April, p. 3

Lo, Bernard, and Robert Steinbrook, 1992, "Health Care Workers Infected with the Human Immunodeficiency Virus: The Next Steps", *Journal of the American Medical Association* 267 (8), February 26, pp. 1100–05

McNeill, Donald J., and Laurie A. Spieler, 1990, "Mandatory Testing of Hospital Employees Exposed to the AIDS Virus: Need to Know or Unwarranted Invasion of Privacy", *Loyola University of Chicago Law Journal* 21 (4), Summer, pp. 1039–74

McSherry, Mark, and Elaine Chan, 1993, "Secret AIDS Test for Job Seekers", *South China Morning Post*, 8 August 1993

Munson, Ronald, 1992, *Intervention and Reflection: Basic Issues in Medical Ethics*, 4th edition, Belmont, California, Wadsworth Publishing Company

Pauker, Stephen G., 1990, "HIV Screening: Nosocomial Epidemiologic Risks and Decision Analysis", *Law, Medicine, and Health Care* 18 (1–2), Spring-Summer, pp. 33–40

Rhame, Frank S., and Dennis Maki, 1989, "The Case for Wider Use of Testing for HIV Infection", *New England Journal of Medicine* 320 (19), 11 May, pp. 1248–54

Segal, Gerald, 1994, *China Changes Shape: Regionalism and Foreign Policy*, Adelphi Paper 287, London, International Institute for Strategic Studies

Special Working Group, Advisory Council on AIDS, Department of Health, Hong Kong Government, 1994, *HIV Infection and the Health Care Worker*, Hong Kong, Department of Health

Stine, Gerald J., 1993, *Acquired Immune Deficiency Syndrome: Biological, Medical, Social, and Legal Issues*, Englewood Cliffs, NJ, USA, Prentice-Hall

U.S. Bureau of the Census, 1994, *The Impact of HIV/AIDS on World Population*, Washington, DC, U.S. Government Printing Office

Wacks, Raymond (ed.), 1990, *Hong Kong's Bill of Rights: Problems and Prospects*, Hong Kong, Faculty of Law, University of Hong Kong

Wennberg, Robert, 1989, *Terminal Choices: Euthanasia, Suicide, and the Right to Die*, Grand Rapids, MI, USA, Wm. B. Eerdman's

Werdel, A., 1990, "Mandatory AIDS Testing: The Legal, Ethical, and Practical Issues", *Notre Dame Journal of Law, Ethics, and Public Policy* 5 (1), pp. 155–221

Wiseman, Alison, 1994a, "Women Face Bigger AIDS Risk", *South China Morning Post*, 15 January, p. A3

— 1994b, "AIDS Gap Closing: Doctor", *South China Morning Post*, 25 February, p. 3
— 1994c, "Maids to be Focus of AIDS Campaign", *South China Morning Post*, 25 April, p. 4
— 1994d, "Heterosexuals Hit by HIV", *South China Morning Post*, 27 April, p. 6
Witt, Hugh (ed.), 1993, *Hong Kong 1993*, Hong Kong, Government Information Services
World Health Organisation, Global Programme on AIDS, 1993, *The Current Global Situation of the HIV/AIDS Pandemic*, WHO/GPA/CNP/EVA/93.1, January 4

List of Authors

GERHOLD K. BECKER, Chair Professor of Philosophy and Religion; Director, Centre for Applied Ethics, Hong Kong Baptist University

LAURENCE GOLDSTEIN, Professor of Philosophy, Department of Philosophy, The University of Hong Kong

CHAD HANSEN, Reader, Department of Philosophy, The University of Hong Kong

IP PO-KEUNG, Dean, School of Arts & Social Sciences, Open Learning Institute, Hong Kong

RANCE P.L. LEE, Professor of Sociology, and Dean of Social Science; Head of Chung Chi College, The Chinese University of Hong Kong

LI HON-LAM, Lecturer, and Barrister at Law, Department of Philosophy, The Chinese University of Hong Kong

LO PING-CHEUNG, Associate Professor, Department of Religion and Philosophy, Hong Kong Baptist University

TERRY T. LUI, Honorary Lecturer, Department of Politics and Public Administration, The University of Hong Kong

MA HING-KEUNG, Associate Professor, and Head of Department of Education Studies, Hong Kong Baptist University

GAEL M. McDONALD, Associate Professor, School of Management, Asia Pacific International University, Hong Kong/Macau

PAK CHO-KAN, Lecturer, Department of Management, The Hong Kong Polytechnic University

JULIA TAO, Dean, Faculty of Humanities and Social Sciences; Associate Professor, Department of Public and Social Administration, City University of Hong Kong

FRANCES K.Y. WONG, Associate Professor, Department of Health Sciences, The Hong Kong Polytechnic University

RAYMOND ZEPP, Teaching Fellow, Asia Pacific International University, Hong Kong/Macau

JOEL ZIMBELMAN, Senior Fulbright Scholar 1993-94, Centre for Applied Ethics, Hong Kong Baptist University